COPY

Leadership for Lawyers

Essential Leadership Strategies for Law Firm Success

Consulting Editor **Rebecca Normand-Hochman**
Advisory Editor **Heidi K Gardner**

Consulting editor
Rebecca Normand-Hochman

Advisory editor
Heidi K Gardner

On behalf of the International Bar Association

Managing director
Sian O'Neill

Leadership for Lawyers: Essential Leadership Strategies for Law Firm Success
is published by
Globe Law and Business Limited
3 Mylor Close
Horsell
Woking
Surrey GU21 4DD
Tel: +44 20 3745 4770
www.globelawandbusiness.com

Print and bound by Gomer Press

Leadership for Lawyers: Essential Leadership Strategies for Law Firm Success
ISBN 9781909416789

© 2015 Globe Law and Business Limited

Table of contents

Introduction: the changing nature of leadership in law firms

Heidi K Gardner
Harvard Law School's Center on the Legal Profession
Rebecca Normand-Hochman
Venturis Consulting Group, Institute of Mentoring

Until recently, the concept of leadership did not resonate with most lawyers, apart from those elected or appointed to the highest management level of their firm.

Today, the most progressive organisations throughout the world are cascading their leadership functions to nearly all roles and levels of responsibility. Although their structure, governance and culture set them apart from many other kinds of organisation, law firms are about to embark on a similar journey. Whether leading a firm, practice, team, client project or oneself, leadership skills and abilities are becoming an essential part of the practice of law for all lawyers.

In fact, today's complex, hyper-competitive and fast-changing legal world demands that from an early stage lawyers develop leadership capabilities as part of their core skills. Whereas lawyers could once succeed primarily on their technical abilities, now they must develop capabilities to create a shared vision, lead change, develop strategic plans, encourage constructive dialogue, build partnerships and develop people.

This book has been designed as a practical guide to some of the most important leadership challenges facing the legal profession. The chapters in the first part of the book focus more on issues that lawyers will face in their day-to-day practice, such as leading partners towards collaborative client service, hiring outstanding client leaders (ie, rainmakers), leading virtual teams and leading the millennial generation. Topics also include an exploration of the links between mentoring and leadership, and ways that lawyers can learn critical leadership skills.

With somewhat more focus on issues related to leading a high-performance firm, the remaining chapters address power and politics in the top echelons of a partnership and shaping a firm's culture. Leading the firm through specific challenges is covered by chapters on leadership succession, leading post-merger integration efforts and leading in founder-led firms. The final chapter explores the use of Big Data and analytics to shape a firm's strategy.

When we developed a mentoring workshop for law firm leaders in Boston at the IBA Annual Conference in 2013, we agreed beforehand that we would link together mentoring, coaching and collaboration in the context of law firm leadership. Heidi had done extensive research on collaboration, and Rebecca had been focusing on the impact of mentoring in our profession. Coaching was increasingly accepted as a leadership tool in international law firms. When facilitating that workshop together, we were gratified to learn that senior members of the legal profession from over 50 jurisdictions fully appreciated the growing role that mentoring, coaching and collaboration play in leading successful law firms.

We followed that workshop by carrying out research on partner-to-partner mentoring in international law firms and embarked with tremendous enthusiasm on this book on leadership. Our aim in this collaboration is to meld the experience of practising law with academic insights to provide a unique perspective on leadership for lawyers.

We hope that the evidence, stories and wisdom shared by the authors of this book will inspire many lawyers around the world to develop their leadership talent and to lead their firm, practice, team or career with the vision, courage, self-awareness and mastery that are so important to their role.

Rebecca Normand-Hochman and Heidi K Gardner

Leading the campaign for greater collaboration within law firms

Heidi K Gardner
Harvard Law School's Center on the Legal Profession

## 1.	Introduction

Leaders of today's law firms are increasingly fighting a war on two fronts. First, they face the war for clients. The entrance of competitors from other jurisdictions is one battle in that war. International firms have entered previously homegrown markets in Latin America, for example, and regional firms in Asia face a surge of competitors into their jurisdiction. Regional tie-ups are another source of increased competition. Law firm leaders must also confront a range of new entrants into the legal market that have been propelled by regulatory changes such as the UK's 2007 Legal Services Act. Because such new providers are unburdened by traditional law firms' constraints they can provide nimble, cost-effective responses to shifting client demands. Along this vein, ever more sophisticated clients are pursuing outsourcing options and unbundling legal services so that they can send work – in whole or in part – to the lowest cost providers. Technological advances are further driving law firm leaders to rethink traditional ways of serving clients. Heightened pressure on fees and billing models, with rising influence from procurement departments and pricing specialists, are driving down both rates and realisation. Leaders fighting the war for clients could surely continue this list.

The war for talent is the second front on which law firm leaders must fight. Increased partner mobility has created a growing free agent mentality in some jurisdictions; aided by a growing fleet of legal recruiters (ie, headhunters), lawyers have a keen sense of their value in the marketplace and face far fewer cultural taboos about jumping ship for a more lucrative offer. In some of the hot markets, it is not unusual for lawyers with an in-demand specialty to receive three or more calls every week from headhunters or competitors. The entrance of international firms to previously domestic legal markets has fuelled competition for top-end lawyers. For example, when the US firms began their push into London, stories abounded of City lawyers doubling or even tripling their income by moving in the first wave of partners to join those newcomer firms. Markets that are not yet facing this international incursion may confront another kind of pressure: that is, leaders must be constantly vigilant about the health of their firm – both the finances and morale – or else risk that their hot talent may create spin-off practices or groups. Figuring out how to motivate and retain the firm's future partner cohort, the generation known as 'millennials', is another pressing challenge for law firm leaders. The war for talent is one that is facing law firm leaders across the globe.

This chapter lays out an approach for embattled leaders who need both a strategy and tactics to cope with this two-fronted war on their firms. Supported by our multi-year empirical research at Harvard University, it makes the case that by fostering increased collaboration among partners, leaders can make important strides in their dual campaign both to win clients and to secure their most valuable talent.

First, it lays out the evidence for how collaboration can help law firms to differentiate their offering by providing clients with a more sophisticated, tailored legal service that results over time in higher revenues, more profits and stickier clients. First at Harvard Business School and now at Harvard Law School's Center on the Legal Profession, our research for the last several years has examined collaboration among high-autonomy, powerful knowledge workers such as partners in professional service firms. Altogether, we have collected millions of data records across multiple firms, including a decade's worth of time-sheet, personnel and financial records. Statistical analyses on this vast database allow us to uncover patterns in the data that are difficult for the human mind to detect. We marry these quantitative findings with insights from hundreds of in-depth interviews with law firm partners, leaders and clients and even larger research surveys. Although many firm leaders intuitively recognise the power of collaboration for improving client service, our research substantiates those beliefs and provides them with the hard evidence they need to convince their powerful partners to change behaviours.

The next section focuses on those partners more specifically, showing how collaboration can help law firm leaders in their war for talent. We start by showing some of the effects of collaboration for individual partners. These benefits include improved performance and productivity for partners who are both originating legal work and who tend to focus more on the execution and delivery than on business development. This outcome represents a crucial way for law firm leaders to create sustainable competitive advantage. As one managing partner said:

> We can no longer squeeze additional productivity from individual lawyers – can't ask them to work harder or longer. Instead, we need to find ways to help them do higher value work more efficiently and effectively. Our clients tell us that if our partners truly collaborated across internal siloes, it would help to differentiate us from competitors.

Using data from our surveys of hundreds of partners in a wide variety of law firms across the globe, we reveal the kinds of benefits that lawyers themselves experience from collaboration; these findings can help law firm leaders understand where to leverage the positive effects for even greater change. Finally, to understand some of the interpersonal consequences of collaboration, the section draws on research from the fields of social psychology and behavioural decision making.

The chapter concludes with a set of recommendations for law firm leaders who are inspired to foster greater collaboration amongst their partners. Using science-based yet practical approaches can help law firm leaders find their own best strategy for winning both clients and talent.

2. Collaboration as a way to attract and retain valued clients

Why might collaboration – that is, getting your lawyers to work across organisational and disciplinary siloes to provide integrated legal services – be a crucial strategy in winning the war for clients? Answering this question requires us to take the client's perspective. As clients have globalised and confronted more sophisticated technological, regulatory, economic and environmental demands, they have sought help with increasingly complex problems.

Addressing these sophisticated client issues typically requires more than a single expert. Lawyers, like other high-end knowledge workers such as medical doctors or scientists, have become increasingly specialised in their expertise. Their narrowed focus is crucial to allow them to stay at the cutting edge of knowledge in their domain, but it means that they often need to rely on colleagues with complementary expertise in order to tackle their clients' most important issues. This opportunity is the heart of the rationale for why collaboration is an essential strategy. If it is done right, collaboration allows a firm to deploy an integrated team of experts who seamlessly provide the best possible solution.

But before we move on, it is necessary to clear up some confusion between 'collaboration' and 'cross-selling'. Firm leaders are often pushing partners to cross-sell, but lawyers have surely heard what general counsels uniformly report to us in our research: clients hate to be cross-sold. Specifically, they hate it when their lawyer who handles one domain offers introductions to other partners in the firm who can provide service in their own narrow domain (ie, the tax lawyer who proposes his real estate colleague to do strictly real estate work). It is the legal equivalent of "Do you want fries with that?" This sort of traditional cross-selling risks appearing more self-serving than added value for the client. If you give the clients the impression that you are more interested in generating incremental revenues for your firm than actually solving the problem that keeps them up at night, their suspicions about you will seep into other aspects of your relationship: how closely they think they need to monitor the bills, for example.

Instead, what clients want is for their lawyers to understand their issues deeply enough to offer sophisticated advice and to line up the right legal team to deliver it – no matter where in the firm the needed experts reside. This form of integrated client service that often crosses practice groups and other silos is what we mean by 'collaboration', and it is the kind of client service that leads to the benefits outlined in this chapter.

Our research shows that when firms can get their partners to collaborate across practices, offices or other internal boundaries, the financial benefits are unambiguous. One of the clearest findings in our research is the link between cross-practice collaboration and revenues. Simply put, the more practices that are involved in serving a client, the greater the annual average revenue the client generates, as the figure below shows (see figure 1).

Of course, the exact numbers depend on how narrowly your firm defines practice groups – for instance, is bankruptcy and restructuring its own practice or rolled in with a broader practice? In one firm we studied, moving from one to two practices serving a client tripled average client revenues, and the addition of each subsequent practice continued to grow fees. Clearly, if $1 + 1 = 3$, then the partners who are involved in cross-practice service are doing more than just referring their colleagues to provide their own siloed work.

Figure 1: the more practices involved, the higher the revenue

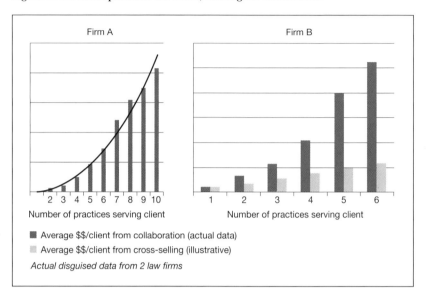

As more practice groups serve a client, each one of them earns more on average, suggesting that they are collaborating to create additional value, not merely cross-selling independent services. Figure 2 compares two scenarios: the solid bar shows the actual revenue increase, which is almost exponential with the additional practices. The greyed bar is just an illustration: it shows how much the firm would have earned if each practice had merely been contributing its own siloed work – that is, the classic outcome of cross-selling. To convince yourself and your partners, run the numbers in your own firm. Although the outcome may not surprise you, it is crucial for convincing partners whose objection to collaboration may be:

> *But if I introduce other practices into my client, it might jeopardize how much the client is willing to spend on my services. Isn't there a limit to how much they'll spend with any provider?*

In firms across the globe the reality is different: providing multi-practice client service increases the average revenue of each practice.

In international firms, we find a similar pattern for cross-jurisdiction work: client projects involving offices in several countries are significantly more lucrative than single-office engagements. Again, even if you are not surprised, having clear evidence is helpful to back up your assertion that clients demand seamless cross-border service, and that they are willing to pay for it.

So what is the rationale behind the findings? First, having more partners involved with a client gives you more information about that organisation's needs, priorities and preferences. Also, having more people involved with a client who are prospecting for work ought to drum up more business. Assuming that your account teams effectively communicate (see below), you can leverage these insights to spot opportunities that your less-involved competitors might overlook. The data bears out this reality: the more practices involved, the more projects per annum (see figure 2). As one law partner explained:

Getting more of our people in front of the client more often created a virtuous cycle because we became the top-of-mind advisor across their legal department. When a new matter came up, we were the go-to team. It simplified life for the client who didn't need to make a conscious decision or wonder if their colleagues were going to question their choice.

Figure 2: the more practices involved, the more projects per annum

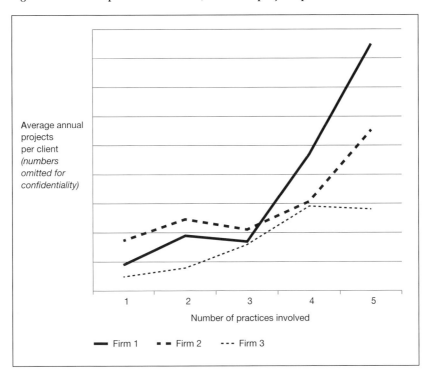

The insights that partners develop from cross-firm client service boost revenues by allowing them to do not just more work, but more sophisticated work. That is in part because cross-specialty work is likely to be less subject to price-based competition. Whereas clients view an engagement involving single-specialty expertise (eg, about a basic tax issue) as a commodity that can be awarded to the lowest bidder, they know that cross-specialty work is complex and harder to accomplish effectively. Similarly, cross-border work is often especially complex and demanding – think, for example, of issues that arise when multinational companies merge or the multiple jurisdictions that can be involved in litigation resulting from an oil spill – and so delivering seamless service across national boundaries can be an important differentiator for firms.

Furthermore, cross-firm collaboration allows professionals to gain access to more senior executives who have broader responsibilities, larger budgets and more sophisticated needs. For example, a tax partner might serve only the tax director as his client; once he teams up with colleagues who are experts in intellectual property, competition and regulatory law, then the team can address the most harrowing problems facing the general counsel – or even the chief executive officer or the board. In an economic downturn, in particular, the in-house legal department may have its budgets slashed but the board and the most senior executives retain the option of hiring external advisers to help with the projects they deem the company's most strategic ones.

In the long term, engaging these executives through multidisciplinary projects creates client stickiness by creating switching barriers. As the general counsel of a Fortune 100 company explained:

> *Despite what they think, most individual lawyers are actually quite replaceable. I mean, I could find a decent tax lawyer in most firms. But when that lawyer teamed up with colleagues from IP, regulatory, and ultimately litigation, I couldn't find a whole-team substitute in another firm.*

We are careful not to use the word 'loyal' to describe this outcome. Loyalty implies that clients are devoted to their provider based on their personal relationship or perhaps out of a sense of obligation. This sort of faithfulness might result from exceptional client service – surely, the chief executive will feel deeply grateful to his consulting team who helped him anticipate the competitor's moves so that he looked like a hero in front of the board. Earning this trusted adviser status means that you will not need to keep auditioning for each new project. But even if you cannot count on this form of loyalty, providing multipractice service creates stickiness that stems from a unique market position.

The ultimate question, then, is whether multipractice service increases profits and not just revenue. The fear, of course, is that once you get deeply embedded in a client with huge teams from across your firm, the client will start using his buying power to demand discounted rates and other freebies. Why bother doing more work for less money? Our research suggests that this possibility is real, but that – on average – clients served with multipractice engagements are more profitable in the long run. Although I cannot share detailed findings for confidentiality reasons, I am allowed to reveal that the data from some major international law firms shows that the profitability (in percentage terms) holds nearly steady as more practices are included in a client's service mix. Given that the law firms are earning about the same percentage on much higher revenues, it is clear that the overall profits stemming from cross-practice service are significant. I strongly encourage law firm leaders to undertake similar analyses with your own data; if you find a different pattern, then it should trigger deeper inspection about the mix of practices and the nature of your negotiations. Overall, more complex work should command higher (or at least steady) margins, as one partner said:

> *The clients are much more generous on fees because if it's so big, the deal's got to get done, and they cannot waste time negotiating or nit-picking.*

As a leader, you need to be vigilant in determining – through hard data and rigorous analytics – which clients are profitable for your firm to invest in. Overall, I expect you will find a pattern that illustrates what one Fortune 100 chief finance officer recently told me about the link he has observed between his company's external advisers' services and their profits: "Margins rise with complexity."

3.   Collaboration as a way to motivate and retain valued talent

Professional services guru, David Maister, asserted some time ago that "there is a close connection between morale, commitment, and productivity in professional service firms", and research since then has continued to back his finding by showing the psychological principles at play.[1] We can now understand a clear relationship between collaboration, partners' motivation and attitudes towards their firm, and ultimately their effort levels on behalf of the collective good. These general research findings are supported in our research surveys across a wide range of law firms throughout the world.

3.1   Commitment and belonging

In research across a range of organisations, findings show that the higher the number of formal or informal connections between a person and their colleagues, the more they are committed to both their job and their organisation. Employees who work more in teams develop a stronger psychological attachment to the organisation, such that they tend to see the firm as an important part of themselves. Have you noticed how some of your partners tend to say things like: "We are looking to grow in the X market" or "We take it seriously when a partner says Y"? In organisational behaviour research, those sorts of 'we' statements are a strong predictor of not only a person's desire to stay in an organisation but also his willingness to engage in critical firm-building activities like mentoring, recruiting and management tasks.

Likewise, our survey research confirms that many lawyers' motivation and sense of belonging increases as a result of their collaborative experiences (provided the teams are well executed, which is not always the case – more on that below). Many partners who had participated in collaborative client service reported that the most important benefit for them was the opportunity to meet new colleagues or deepen existing relationships. For example, respondents wrote about "the camaraderie that comes with working as a group", and another suggested that collaboration was welcome because otherwise "being a partner can feel quite lonely sometimes". Partners also mentioned how collaboration helped them feel supported in their work. For example, one wrote: "A problem shared is a problem halved – it is reassuring to have the right expertise on hand. I feel more supported and less anxious about the responsibility I carry." As discussed below, leaders have a role to play in helping to ensure that collaboration leads to these positive interpersonal outcomes.

3.2   Meaning and mastery.

Another way that collaboration amongst partners can increase motivation is by giving people a broader perspective on clients' problems and knowledge of how their particular expertise contributes to a bigger solution. Psychology research has long suggested that when a person feels like their work has meaning and is important to their organisation (or perhaps for lawyers, to their client), then they will exert more

---

1   David Maister, *Managing the Professional Service Firm* (Free Press, 1993), p 18.

effort and become more committed, both to their colleagues and to their organisation.

In our surveys of law firm partners, one frequently mentioned benefit of collaboration related to participants' ability to learn from their peers during collaborative work. Respondents talked of:

- gaining knowledge about what other parts of the firm are up to, as well as market opportunities;
- a broader understanding of what the client's business is, and which individuals to target for a particular business proposition; and
- learning more about nuances of other colleagues' business lines.

Beyond knowledge, partners also mentioned developing their professional capabilities through collaboration, such as enhanced skills in:

- problem solving;
- preparing for client pitches; and
- communication.

Achieving mastery over one's work is a strong predictor of motivation, and this outcome of collaboration will become increasingly important for leaders to pay attention to as more millennials (ie, people born roughly between the early 1980s and mid-1990s) take on more client-facing responsibilities.

For more on this topic, see Bresman *et al*'s chapter on leading millennials in this book.

3.3 Goal alignment

Research also shows that the more contact a member has within an organisation, such as the kinds of work experiences that happen on deal teams or joint pitches, the stronger their belief in and acceptance of the organisation's values and goals. Law firm leaders often bemoan their lawyers' referring to 'my clients' instead of talking about 'our clients'. These research findings show that more collaborative experiences will motivate people to move beyond seeing themselves as a franchise and instead view themselves as part of an interdependent team. In our research surveys, law firm partners often back up this point of view when answering about their personal experiences of collaboration. One wrote, for example, that he valued teamwork with fellow partners because it produced "the feeling that colleagues and I are working towards a common goal, namely the success and prosperity of the firm as a whole".

Leaders must understand that collaboration does not just make people feel as if their outcomes are more closely aligned with the firm; our empirical research shows that collaboration actually does provide a win-win opportunity for both the partners and their firms to improve performance. These results have been detailed at length elsewhere,[2] but we can summarise here three crucial outcomes for partners who

---

2   HK Gardner, "When Senior Managers Won't Collaborate", *Harvard Business Review*, March 2015; HK Gardner, "Why It Pays to Collaborate", *American Lawyer*, March 2015; HK Gardner and MA Valentine, "Collaboration among Highly Autonomous Professionals: Costs, Benefits, and Future Research Directions", in S Thye and E Lawler, *Advances in Group Process* (Emerald Publishing, 2015).

engage in collaboration. First, we find that rainmakers who systematically involve other partners in their work benefit by significantly growing their books of business in coming years, even controlling for the size of the rainmaker's book in the starting year. In other words, no matter how much work the partner generates this year, if they refer that work to other partners rather than hoarding it, then their origination amount will increase significantly the following year. Second, partners on the receiving end of such work referrals also benefit. Referrals not only make it easier to reach individual revenue targets that same year, but the experience of working with others helps the partner to build his reputation amongst colleagues, which results in increasing referrals – and hence revenue – in subsequent years. Third, collaboration raises a partner's profile not only with colleagues but also with clients. Across the law firms studied, we found that the more cross-discipline projects partners worked on, and the more complex each one was, the more their hourly rates increased in following years. Again, these analyses were all statistically controlled for alternative predictors of work volumes and rates. After accounting for the effects of a partner's practice, office, tenure, gender and other variables, we still find that collaboration patterns are very robust determinants of individual partner performance. Equipped with these findings, it should be easier for leaders to help convince partners to make the investment in collaboration.

3.4 Retention and alumni loyalty

When partners are better at collaboration, they are more likely to involve more junior partners and senior associates in their client work because they see the value of engaging other smart minds, and they need the leverage to be able to service their growing client base. Pulling juniors onto their teams not only gives those teammates increased opportunity to learn and demonstrate new legal capabilities (ie, the mastery element mentioned above), but also provides an opportunity for greater mentoring. Both these aspects in turn enhance the desirable retention of high-performing associates and young partners.

Even for the lawyers your firm does not manage to retain, a collaborative approach is likely to be important for their ongoing loyalty after they have moved on. How important is this factor? Some firms have managed to turn their loyal alumni base into a loyal client base, which is a very hard factor for others to replicate.

4. Action plan for leaders to enhance collaboration

Typically, when we start talking to lawyers and law firm leaders about collaboration, their first instinct about how to foster it revolves around remuneration. Surely, they suggest, there must be a straight link between collaboration and a firm's compensation system, right? Not quite, we find.

Granted, a firm's compensation system plays a large part in shaping partners' behaviour, and probably explains why some firms are, on average, more collaborative than others. In general, firms that operate with a single firm-wide profit pool and then measure and reward their partners based on their contribution to the firm's overall financial health tend to promote cross-firm collaboration rather than provincial competition between partners vying for a better local profit and loss.

Maister asserted the collaborative benefits of the 'one-firm firm' decades ago,[3] and the consensus among general counsel that I interview is that they can still see that lawyers from firms with lockstep compensation are more collaborative than those from more eat-what-you-kill systems.

However, differences in compensation structures cannot explain differences between partners in the same firm, where they are all (presumably) subject to the same remuneration system. In our research, we find that each firm has a wide spread of collaboration. While some partners already collaborate extensively by actively seeking opportunities to engage colleagues in cross-disciplinary matters, others spend most of their time working in silos (eg, executing by themselves nearly all the work they originate or handing it off to subordinates rather than peers). For example, in one typical firm we studied, about a quarter of the partners referred work to other partners fewer than 10 times during the eight years covered by our study, whereas an equal number of their peers referred more than 80 matters to their colleagues in that same timeframe. The rest were spread out in between. If compensation were the sole, or even primary, driver of behaviour, would we not see more homogeneous behaviour from partners who are all facing the same incentives within the firm?

Besides, completely overhauling your compensation systems is risky, complicated and massively time consuming and is not a reasonable option for most law firm leaders – at least not in the short term. For now, we suggest that you focus on actions that move your partners along the collaboration continuum. Imagine how much value your firm – and partners and clients – would get if you could help some average collaborators or even more siloed lawyers to start serving more clients with more multipractice, sophisticated service. Some partners might not be cut out for collaboration, and you need to think hard about whether they are so toxic to the collaborative culture that you are trying to build that you need to find other ways to deal with them. But the action plan below lays out clear steps that law firm leaders can take to increase collaboration in their firms.

In general, the reason that partners are not collaborating more is that they do not believe that the approach will benefit them. They see the foray into collaboration (eg, finding a partner with the right expertise who can serve their client with the utmost competence and professionalism) as too costly and risky, while the benefits seem long term and uncertain. Leaders therefore must take two broad approaches to help professionals get over the initial hurdles to effective collaboration. They act as coaches in order to lower cultural barriers, and they act as architects in order to lower structural barriers.[4]

4.1 The leader as coach

(a) Share the work and the credit
Leaders who want to build a culture of collaboration should begin with themselves,

---

3   David Maister, *Managing the Professional Service Firm*, (New York: Free Press, 1993), chapter 2
4   For more about actions that leaders can take to foster collaboration, see HK Gardner, "When Senior Managers Won't Collaborate", *Harvard Business Review*, March 2015.

modelling collaborative behaviour and then holding partners accountable for similar actions. Remember, we are not talking about pure collegiality – being civil is crucial, but true cross-firm collaboration requires specific actions that go far beyond being collegial.

First, be sure that you are a visible collaborator. Make a point of handing off work and supporting others' pitches without expecting personal gain. When someone approaches you with a client opportunity, think about whether there is a credible alternative such as a newly elevated partner or lateral hire who really needs the work to build his reputation.

When you work with others, you must look to give credit and recognition. After a client meeting, take a minute to send a short email thanking a colleague or associate for their participation. The more specific you can be, the more sincere the note will be. Rather than, "Thanks for a great job", write, "Nice job prepping the cost analyses for our meeting with the VP. Did you see how those numbers helped change his mind about whether to proceed?" If you commit to send only one note to one colleague after each key meeting, you are much more likely to do so than if you promise yourself to be 'much better' at sharing credit. Also, never think that someone is above praise – even a highly successful, senior lawyer is likely to appreciate being recognised and given credit for his work.

Verbal recognition is also powerful, especially praise in public. But do not underestimate how much people might hang on your words. People are keenly aware of how they stack up not only against your expectations, but also against each other. So make sure your efforts are broad-based and will not be perceived as favouritism based on anything except pure merit. This can be achieved by being specific in your remarks and keeping them focused on the behaviours the lawyer displayed that you want others to replicate.

Another way that you can build a culture where people share credit and recognition is to hold your partners accountable for doing it well. If you are in a formal leadership role, tell the partners that you expect to hear about others' success; ask them to write directly to the person who contributed and copy you in on the message. If you know a partner has just had a major win, ask him who else played a role and encourage them to reach out. Remember, even if you are not the official leader of a project, you can still share credit with teammates. Make sure to copy in the team leader as a way to prod him to take similar action next time.

(b)   *Develop a pipeline of capable contributors*

From our surveys of hundreds of professionals across many firms and countries, we know that one of the biggest barriers to collaboration is distrust of others' competence. Partners have concerns that colleagues will not uphold high enough levels of quality and responsiveness. These possible dangers understandably make partners risk averse in choosing whom to work with. Typically, when they have an opening on their team they turn to the most senior partner, the 'grey-haired guru' with a sterling reputation.

So what is the problem? First, the gurus are almost always overloaded. They may devote just enough time to address the specific issue with their expertise, but they

are unlikely to go much further, say in coaching the lead partner on:
- how to contextualise the advice to convince clients; or
- brainstorming competitor reactions; or
- pitching in on follow-up work.

Secondly, the more junior professionals – the ones who are hungry for work and client opportunities – rarely get the chance to contribute. Economists might be puzzled at a market with both excess demand (for expert input) and excess supply (for chances to contribute) that seemingly will not clear. Certainly, it is inefficient to have overloaded professionals and, at the same time, underutilised high-potentials.

What can the coach do? You need to help develop a pipeline of capable contributors. Start to take some calculated risks by involving less obvious players on your team. This move is smart because ambitious junior partners are more likely to commit time and energy to your broader client effort. One law firm partner struggled to build a committed team to provide the expanding set of services her client's general counsel was willing to buy from her – even though the client had been deemed a global priority account. Even asking the practice heads and office managing partners did not turn up partners who were keen to invest their precious time in developing a demanding client. Ultimately, she used her own network to uncover a recently promoted partner who was keen to get involved. After just one year, this junior partner has made huge strides in the account, earning trust and further expanding the set of services.

Involving a less-tested colleague on your team may initially feel risky and you will need to make sure they are thoroughly briefed and ready to contribute. For your own comfort, you will want to take the time to check in more frequently than you might with a more experienced pair of hands. By these leader-as-coach actions you will help to develop a channel of talented professionals who others will come to see as trustworthy. But this sort of forward thinking is more than just altruism. Chances are that you will learn a lot from more junior colleagues who can bring unique perspectives from their interactions at different levels within the client.

(c)   *Send the right signals*

When hiring, leaders need to resist the temptation to bring in "high-performing jerks" who might be a toxic influence on a collaborative culture, and instead seek candidates who have a track record of working across boundaries to build expansive client portfolios. This strategy takes longer because the newly hired partner will not be able to wield a huge book of business immediately. But how often does that actually happen, even for lone wolf hires who claim they can transport their clients? Surely, if you want true multipractice collaboration, you must avoid poisoning your culture and demotivating collaborative partners whose compensation you might need to raid to fund the hiring of superstar rainmakers. Hiring high-quality partners with a history of collaborative client service not only sends the right signals, but pays off in the long term – provided you integrated them properly into your firm (more on that below).

Leaders also need to be careful about the signals they send when commending players for great outcomes. If a partner made a big sale but did so as a lone wolf, the leader should not only refrain from celebrating the win but talk with the partner about better ways to achieve the same outcome. You also need to celebrate those who contribute primarily by delivering work on others' projects so that you avoid a culture that disparages "service partners". One chief operating officer described this problem as partners believing that "some people are rainmakers but others just get wet".

4.2   The leader as architect

(a)   Build a fair and constructive performance management process

Leaders need to strike the right balance in their evaluation system such that collaboration is expected and rewarded, but measured holistically rather than formulaically. Remember, including very specific metrics, such as the number of referrals or multipractice pitches, can be gamed, and so rewarding them in a mechanical way is counterproductive. Firms need to take a two-pronged approach. First, be sure to reward the outcomes of effective collaboration, including:

- rising levels of client satisfaction and client retention;
- growth in the revenue and profits from existing accounts; or
- the acquisition of new clients in target areas.

Many law firms' existing software enables them to calculate these metrics efficiently. Even better, approaches to measure client satisfaction such as the Net Promoter Score would be optimal because they can capture data about how the outcomes were achieved. For more on this topic, see Zeughauser's chapter on data and analytics in this book.

Secondly, to help ensure that results are achieved in ways consistent with building a collaborative culture, you will need to include measures that capture partners' contributions to non-billable collaborative efforts such as mentoring, sharing knowledge or giving advice. One law firm, for example, has made 'Collaboration and teamwork' the first of seven criteria in their Balanced Scorecard used to assess partner performance. Every partner has his performance on that criteria rated annually. Inputs include, for example, how many times a partner has shared knowledge to enable cross-practice pitches. This firm also has a credit system where partners allocate credits to partners who have helped them be more successful, and this soft metric feeds into partner performance assessment and remuneration. Together, these approaches help by creating a common language and clear reference points for performance discussions, bonus awards and goal setting. They also allow the firm's leadership to reinforce the importance of collaboration and knowledge sharing in various communications throughout the year, not just during compensation season.

(b)   Engineer ways to increase trust and familiarity

Trust can be especially hard to build in firms that grow rapidly, either through mergers or extensive lateral hiring. But trust can be stretched thin in all firms when

19

lawyers need to work with others who are located in distant offices. For more on this topic, see Mortensen's chapter on virtual teams in this book.

The most successful firms pair lateral hires with a successful homegrown partner who is responsible for introducing the newcomer to both peers and clients, thus spreading the role of coach beyond just the top executives. Beyond this, some firms have introduced a secondment programme in which senior associates or recently promoted partners spend six or 12 months in an overseas office. When they return home, they continue to serve as important links between offices. One firm could typically trace at least three, and sometimes 10 or more, new international referrals between a secondee's home and host offices in the year following their return. Some of these referrals went directly to the secondee, but many went to colleagues, with the secondee playing a brokering role. Partners said that they would not have known or felt comfortable to contact a partner in the overseas office without that recommendation.

(c)   *Build systems to spread knowledge*
In order to offer clients a sophisticated service, professionals need to know:
- what expertise exists across their own firm,
- how it maps onto their clients' needs, and
- when it is better to refer work to an outsider.

As firms grow, keeping up to date with credible inside offerings becomes increasingly difficult. In our surveys across many professional firms, this lack of knowledge was one of the most frequently cited barriers to collaborating. To increase collaboration, leaders can help professionals to learn about others' expertise, identify cross-practice opportunities and find competent partners to collaborate with. The following list includes some possible approaches:
- Monthly workshops at practice group meetings that include short presentations from experts in high-potential areas. They are most effective when they use an actual client case by way of illustration. One firm records the presentations and archives them on their intranet for future firm-wide access. It is an effective way to help to integrate lateral hires and for getting new partners up to speed on the firm's experts across practices.
- Rigorous onboarding of lateral hires, including having them do roadshows to highlight their expertise and pairing them with partners who are responsible for introducing them to others.
- Regular 'speed-dating' events in which a topic expert has five minutes on a one-to-one basis with other partners to explain why their clients should be interested in this particular topic. Simple but effective.
- A practice manager or other 'honest broker' who can connect professionals with credible experts and give a balanced view of how and why many of those services might benefit other clients.
- Internal newsletters featuring recent collaborative success stories so that professionals understand how others in the firm have combined expertise to solve client issues.

- Intranet-based tools for professionals to announce client opportunities, find experts and ask or answer questions ought to help, but most firms find that they fall flat if the work required from partners is burdensome. A successful knowledge system needs to have an initial push to ensure critical mass is achieved within the first couple of months, and then make upkeep simple. For example, when one firm launched a new system, leaders asked support staff to populate the tool with the administrative details of client contacts. Then they set aside an hour at the firm's annual conference and mandated that partners spend the time inputting details about their most critical contacts – the sort of information that support staff may not have known. These joint efforts guaranteed that the tool had enough usable information to make it functional within its first month of operating. Partners reported that it was highly useful to check an app on their smartphone while in the taxi on their way to a client and double-check their colleagues' latest initiatives with that client. (Granted, you would ideally want partners to do this long in advance of their taxi journey, but this is a step in the right direction!)

5.   Conclusion

Playing the roles of both coach and architect, leaders of today's law firms have the opportunity to foster collaboration amongst their partners – a crucial source of competitive advantage to win the most valued clients and the best legal talent. Most law firm leaders have committed to a strategy of serving their clients' most complex, pressing problems. Their best partners buy into this strategy because they aspire not to be seen as a mere legal technician but to become a trusted adviser who helps clients on their thorniest, biggest-risk issues – regardless of whether they fall under the lawyer's own specialist domain. Doing so requires them to collaborate with multiple fellow partners whose expertise must be integrated, often in novel ways. As partners gain experience with this sort of collaborative client service, they come to understand the benefits in terms of stickier clients, higher personal productivity, stronger working relationships with their peers and a greater sense of personal fulfilment. Law firm leaders who act now to foster collaboration across their firms thus stand a much greater chance of winning their market's most-prized clients and most-treasured talent.

Hiring rainmakers as client leaders

Stuart Sadick
Heidrick & Struggles

1. Introduction

Law firm leaders have long sought the holy grail of control over revenue flow. Talk of evergreen services and evergreen clients reflects a longing for a reliable revenue stream. But for several decades, it has been getting more and more risky to assume that any service offering or client relationship will be long term. Even long-term clients are now more likely to put new business out for bid. A law firm's growth therefore depends increasingly on its ability to keep attracting new clients and to keep winning work from them. In short, it depends on rainmakers and therefore on the crucial role of firm leaders in figuring out how to hire, develop and retain them.

For many decades, we have known that buyers of professional services want to deal with a professional who sells, not a professional salesperson.[1] This is the case more than ever for legal services. The higher up the buyer's position in the client organisation, the more important the client's issue and the more costly the legal service. A law firm with many partners capable of accessing senior executives, generating leads, identifying market trends, modifying services to address new demand and converting specific leads into new business – in other words, a firm with many rainmakers – has a competitive advantage and can justly feel some confidence in its revenue flows. That, in turn, means that a law firm's ability to deploy rainmakers is a strategic competence. Many law firm leaders, however, fail to treat it as one and instead act opportunistically.

A recent paper[2] examined this topic among various professional services firms. This chapter, focusing on law firms, will offer a systematic approach for law firm leaders to improve the hiring, development and retention of their firm's most valuable client leaders. This approach is the result of research conducted by myself and through dialogue with numerous individuals responsible for hiring rainmakers within law firms, as well as with rainmakers themselves.

2. Make-or-buy decision for sourcing rainmaker talent

Obtaining a new rainmaker is essentially a make-or-buy decision. You can promote your own people or you can hire rainmakers away from another firm. In either case,

---

1   Warren J Wittreich, "How to Buy/Sell Professional Services", *Harvard Business Review*, March–April 1966, p. 129; David Maister, *Managing the Professional Service Firm* (New York: Free Press, 1993).
2   "Make or Buy Rainmakers?" by Stuart Sadick (partner, Heidrick & Struggles) and Ford Harding (founder, Harding & Co).

planning and investment will increase your chances of success. Promoting from within calls for an investment in education and skill-building; hiring from the outside calls for an investment in integration coaching, or onboarding. In my experience, firms do not always understand the full significance of these make-or-buy decisions.

Figure 1 represents four basic alternatives as a matrix. From left to right, firms can either promote from within or hire from outside. From top to bottom, they can either help increase the success rate by investing in significant mentoring, coaching and training or not. As this chapter will show, the two lower quadrants represent cases where filling rainmaking positions is divorced from significant mentoring, coaching or training and should be avoided. However, they remain commonplace.

Figure 1: Firms can either promote from within or hire from outside. They can help increase the success rate of either approach through mentoring, training and coaching.

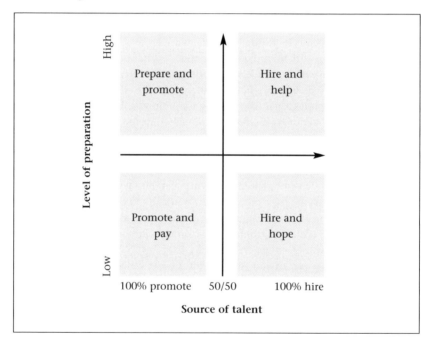

2.1 Low preparation and internal sourcing: 'promote and pray'
The lower left quadrant of figure 1 represents what we call the 'promote and pray' approach. Firms promote their own people into partner positions that require them to generate business, then pray that enough of them will succeed as rainmakers to sustain and grow revenue. But firms with this approach do little to actually train them for their rainmaking responsibilities. Instead, they rely on the name and prestige of the firm to open doors. This approach can work adequately in an up market when the opportunity cost of devoting staff time to training seems high and

a wealth of opportunities gives new partners a chance to learn business development on the job. It is less than adequate in downturns, just when training dollars become scarce. As one member of a large accounting and consulting firm put it:

We hire and promote our people [to partner] on the basis of their technical ability and then it's sink or swim on whether or not they can bring in business. It causes a lot of turnover.

2.2 High preparation and internal sourcing: 'prepare and promote'

The obvious alternative, represented by the upper left quadrant, is to train newly promoted partners to be the rainmakers you expect them to be. The 'prepare and promote' approach offers several advantages:

- The firm has more control over a key resource – its own people – which lowers your exposure to the risk of bringing in senior people from outside.
- Non-partners have a greater chance of making partner, a strong signal which allows you to retain talent you might otherwise lose.
- The new rainmaker is well acquainted with the firm's services and culture.
- The firm develops a robust rainmaking culture.

Despite these advantages, many law firms have no formal process for helping their attorneys become rainmakers. They lack either the foresight or the resolve to:

- screen entry-level hires for their interest in and aptitude for business development in addition to their ability to commence client work immediately; and
- spend time and money preparing people to be rainmakers, preferring to apply their best people's time fully to billable work, especially during a business boom.

2.3 Low preparation and external sourcing: 'hire and hope'

Firms need to hire outside rainmaking talent when it is not practical to fill a position from within; for example, when they enter a new practice area or a geographic market that requires specialised or local talent. But, again, there are better and worse ways to do this. The lower right quadrant represents the 'hire and hope' approach (ie, a firm recruits a rainmaker from outside but then invests little time or effort to help him learn about the firm's people, services, clientele and culture). This is not likely to work well. Success in one firm does not necessarily foretell success in another. For example, the ability to build strong networks in the new firm is key to understanding the firm's resources and market position and how best to position oneself as a new player within the firm. The newly hired rainmaker, recognising that he is in a sink-or-swim position and eager to prove himself, typically rushes into the market and starts selling before becoming adequately prepared and thus ends up trying to sell his new firm as if it were his old one.

2.4 High preparation and external sourcing: 'hire and help'

It should be clear by now that providing recruited rainmakers with coaching and training to integrate them into the firm greatly increases their success rate. This is the 'hire and help' approach represented by the upper right quadrant.

Note that 'prepare and promote' and 'hire and help' are not mutually exclusive. My colleagues and I observed many firms that pay substantial recruiting fees to hire rainmakers and integrate them into the firm (hire and help) while spending nothing to prepare those promoted from within the firm to partner for revenue-generation responsibilities (promote and pray). It is no wonder that these firms need to recruit from the outside so often. Internally, they get what they pay for, which is a record of promotions that do not work out.

3. Distorted views about sourcing rainmakers

Make-or-buy decisions about rainmakers are hampered by distorted views about their development and recruitment. These misunderstandings are outlined below.

3.1 Rainmakers are born, not made

In my experience, this common belief is simply untrue. Human capabilities are seldom distributed in a dichotomy. While there are people who will succeed at business development without much help and people who will never master it, many more can make rain if they develop call and meeting discipline through learning how to build referral networks and how to sell face-to-face. These are trainable habits and skills; many attorneys who lack a natural sales ability have learned them. Attorneys who learn ethical ways to bring in business and who experience the satisfaction of doing so often transform themselves into rainmakers. For example, one attorney at a well-known firm had been written off as a rainmaker but, after two years of systematic development, became the firm's top originator of new business. We have seen professionals, who have been passed over for partnership, learn to develop new business with a passion.

3.2 Our rainmakers will train their successors

This is generally wishful thinking. Many partners are not good mentors; they have forgotten what it is like to start building business from a base of zero and only a few contacts. My colleagues and I found that perhaps 20% of all rainmakers make good mentors and they are not evenly spread across firms. Rather, they tend to concentrate in firms with development cultures, where rainmakers are retained and rewarded not only for the money they bring in but also for their mentoring abilities. Lacking such a company culture, rainmakers often find responding to clients and prospects more urgent than mentoring. They do a lot of their rainmaking by phone, which makes it hard to demonstrate to junior colleagues how the job is done. Some rainmakers are afraid that a junior colleague shadowing them at a pitch meeting will say one wrong thing and undo months or even years of work. Some are wary of creating competitors. If your firm's rainmakers are not mentoring successors now, why do you think they will do so in the future?

3.3 Our great delivery will attract rainmakers

There are several misunderstandings at work here. First, the rainmaker's own firm probably has good delivery too. Secondly, good delivery is not necessarily the dominant criterion by which established rainmakers select a firm. They look at a variety of factors, including risk. Thirdly, they may suspect that your superior delivery results from a service and utilisation culture in which sales ability is not fully respected. Fourthly, they may question whether the support staff behind such excellent delivery knows how to support a rainmaker's sales efforts.

3.4   Associates should focus only on delivery

Some people believe that anyone below the partner level should not waste time on phone calls and emails to former clients and other market contacts. This opinion is usually advanced by someone who cannot develop business himself or by a young rainmaker concerned about delivery and lacking the foresight to start developing new rainmaking talent in the firm. No one can be turned into a rainmaker overnight; the sooner your people starting learning how to develop business, the more likely they will be to succeed once they are partners. In addition, the strength of the relationships they build early in their careers increases their odds of making sales later.

3.5   We can recruit a rainmaker because we are special

Rainmakers usually have plenty of job opportunities to choose from, so even if your firm does have a great concept and intellectual property to support it, this may not be as compelling as you expect. A rainmaker is likely to see a small firm, a new firm, a firm with an unconventional offering or one that does not seem as well differentiated to him as it does to you as a risk he does not need to take.

3.6   We have a collegial firm that will welcome lateral hires

Are you sure that your firm's collegiality will be extended to a newcomer who is probably being paid more than most of the firm's proven rainmakers? Are you sure the new rainmaker will fit in with your firm's culture, including its style of collegiality?

4.   Recruiting rainmakers

Most law firms are focusing at least to some degree on recruiting rainmakers. A recent American Lawyer survey showed 2,736 lateral moves at AmLaw 200 firms in the year from October 2013. This was a 7% increase over the 2013 survey and came close to the record high of 2,775 lateral moves in the 12 months ending September 30 2009. Law firms are consolidating and, as they do, it is the rainmakers who are in highest demand. For that very reason, firms are often sloppy in their hiring process when it comes to a rainmaker, relaxing the rules in order to make the hire before some other firm does. Yet such victories are self-defeating. Plenty of evidence shows that law firms have real problems recruiting rainmakers who succeed in the long run. The rest of this chapter focuses on the steps a law firm's management can take to get this strategically crucial process right.

4.1   Identify the need

While choosing a hire may seem as simple as choosing the candidate with the most available revenues, the best rainmaker hires occur when the firm has defined a specific need that offers an opportunity for both the firm and the candidate. One way to be specific is to use a position justification template, which might include:

- an overview of the role;
- general duties;
- the business case for the role, including both the strategic intent (eg, we need to build this practice group because our clients expect it or our competitors are leaving us behind) and the economic justification (eg, if it is a client-facing role, the amount of revenue the individual is expected to generate and the total cash compensation);
- reporting relationships (if any);
- the education, skill and experience required or desired;
- personal characteristics;
- expected performance metrics.

This approach forces firms to be clear about what they require and to use that clarity to gain alignment – or identify misalignment – early in the process. As they create their own list, firms should be encouraged to identify the variations that work best for them. Such a list also assures candidates that the firm has given this role serious thought and their role would have the top leaders' support.

Specifying the desired personal traits is more important than it may sound. Every firm has a culture, whether people think about it or not. Candidates are generally hired for their skills, background and competencies, but when they stay it is because they are also a very good fit with the firm's culture. No matter what revenues a new hire brings in, they are probably not worth the disruption caused in a law firm by a bad cultural fit. Note also that if the firm is trying to change its own culture, each new hire is an opportunity either to further that goal or sabotage it.

4.2 Target the candidate population

While social media definitely offer increased access to potential recruits, the most senior talent – rainmakers in particular – are not necessarily looking for new jobs and thus can be hard to locate. It is, therefore, all the more important that the firm takes care to target the right candidates. Given the defined position of the firm, where and how is the firm most likely to find such a candidate? How can it be reasonably sure that it has been thorough in exploring that candidate population? What trade-offs might be involved in looking at a particular candidate population? For example, if the rainmaker has a key client relationship that cannot move to the new firm with him, do we feel that the rainmaker is skilled enough to develop another client in that same sector, hence avoiding the conflict?

Without such a disciplined approach, it is too easy to miss out on some of the best options, including some that may be considered non-traditional.

4.3 Engage the candidate population

Different means of engaging the target candidates are appropriate in different situations. Many law firms, for example, have created the role of director of recruiting, responsible for lateral hires (as differentiated from campus hires). Other law firms have developed an internal recruiting capability, often called director of professional recruiting. Some in this role have developed their recruiting expertise while working in a human resources department; most have had some experience in a professional recruiting firm, either legal recruiting or executive search. My colleagues and I observed that these individuals are less prone to call directly into the candidate marketplace: 'It feels odd to call directly into a competitor. Professional courtesy.' They are highly effective with potential candidates who contact the firm, but as I pointed out earlier, the rainmakers you seek are not necessarily looking for a new job.

There are search professionals who focus on senior-level recruitment. Some work in specialised legal recruiting firms, others pursue this specialisation within executive search firms. Others focus exclusively on hiring senior partners (such as practice leaders), some on senior staff roles and some on both. Whether we call them recruiters, headhunters or executive search consultants, they offer access to candidates who may not respond to a direct call from your firm and whom you may never happen to meet socially. But, more importantly, the best of these recruiters can serve as trusted advisers, helping you shape the role you seek to fill and create alignment concerning it and contributing a valuable marketplace perspective on matters such as motivation and competitive compensation.

Keep in mind that the best recruiter is not the one who claims to know every possible candidate, but rather the one who understands that there are always more possible candidates to identify, target and develop. Even the most extensive database will quickly become out of date. You need a recruiter who can keep finding the next generation of talent champing at the bit. They are often the most open to new opportunities and often have the most energy and new ideas.

With potential candidate inquiries, there is a fine line between selling the opportunity to the candidate and developing an initial perspective on whether that candidate is suited to the role. Developing that perspective takes more than one call or meeting. Even if you conclude that a particular candidate is not suitable, it will be worthwhile finding out how he feels about the role and the firm. As an example, you may decide to pass on a candidate because he does not meet the key criteria. But how you treat that candidate, including how you explain the decision to not move forward, will have ramifications far beyond this one interaction. The best process is one that recognises that the reputation of the firm is at stake with each candidate interaction. This is your chance to either build goodwill in the market or to leave potential candidates (and whomever they know) with a bad impression of the firm.

The initial contact will generally not allow for a deep evaluation, particularly with rainmakers, who are seldom willing to disclose much detail about their book of business and key clients so early in the process. A well-managed process will identify what key questions need to be asked at this early stage and carry that information forward as the process moves ahead and the candidate meets more people in the firm. We will discuss this in more detail below.

4.4 Conduct the interviews

This is where a well-orchestrated process will shine and a poorly orchestrated process will fail. A well-managed process starts with an aligned conversation among the interviewers and decision makers about what will be evaluated (criteria such as experience, competencies, style and motivation), how and by whom. Different interviewers will have different views of what 'good' means. Too often we hear, "Well, I couldn't put my finger on it, but I had a good gut feeling." Wherever possible, it is important to substantiate such feelings with observed detail and evidence (ie, what the candidate said and did).

Since candidates will interact with different members of the firm who have different styles, it is important to identify who will be involved and to try to build consistency into the interviews. This is a matter of coordination, including the logistics of setting up interviews, pre-interview preparation and post-interview debriefing. The devil is in the detail; this is where objective, actionable information is either kept or lost.

I advocate multiple interactions; for example, a first interview of approximately 60–90 minutes to gather data and build an initial assessment, then several more social interactions. Too often we fall in love with a candidate on the first date and then do not make the effort to see how good the fit really is. Ideally, the interview settings should be private and free from distraction.

Taking notes during an interview can be off-putting but serves the purpose of creating real data that can be evaluated and compared with other interviewers' notes. As mentioned earlier, everyone will have his or her own point of view, but evidence should take precedence in sorting through the different opinions.

The interview is a two-way process; the candidate is also trying to gather information about the role, the firm and its culture. Sometimes a candidate tries to gain control of the interview by asking questions without answering those of the interviewer. This is an easy trap to fall into but can be managed by:

- asking the candidate to hold off on a certain level of detail for now; and
- promising to provide more time for those questions later.

Here are some rules of thumb for interviewers:

- If you are doing all the talking, you are not learning nearly as much as you need to.
- If most of your questions can be answered with a 'yes' or 'no', you are not asking the right questions. The best questions are open-ended, enabling the candidate to tell about a situation, a success, a challenge, etc.
- If you are not starting to form a view about the candidate's suitability during this first interview, you are not doing what you need to do.
- If you are not identifying the next set of questions and who should ask them, then you are not moving your search forward.

Remember that even very personable attorneys may not be used to interviewing. The best interview process therefore includes training for the interviewers, including:

- how to set up an interview,
- what questions to ask,
- how to manage the time,

- how to develop a view, and
- how to decide on the next step.

Such training is also an opportunity to identify the interviewers' differences of opinion on the interview process and design the best possible process for the candidates as well as for the firm.

4.5   Qualify the candidate

While the purpose of an interview is to learn about a candidate, the goal of the interview process is to reach a decision about whether the candidate should be further considered and, ultimately, whether he or she should be hired to fulfil the need defined in the first step. I therefore draw a distinction between interviewing and qualifying. The purpose of interviewing is to get to know the candidate as well as possible, bringing to bear as many different points of view as possible. In the qualifying process, that data is gathered and aligned with the defined need.

It is not unusual for the defined need itself to evolve during the hiring process. Sometimes the interviews with different candidates help clarify what the role should be and what the right candidate would look like. The hiring team needs to be able to recognise and discuss such changes in the game plan. External factors may also change the defined need. For example:

- Given regulatory changes, does the firm still want to invest in a particular practice?
- Is a particular candidate's book of business still as relevant?
- Does the candidate's book of business perhaps provide a different opportunity than the one the firm had in mind to start with?

There are different ways to collect and share the information gathered through interviewing. I favour asking interviewers to:

- develop a view based on their interviews;
- document it (possibly using a structured written assessment form); and
- make sure that it is based on evidence (not only on gut impressions) and that it includes a balanced assessment of the candidate's positive and negative aspects.

There will always be trade-offs but what is important is to make them strategically rather than inadvertently.

It is also important for the interviewers to share their evaluations, although this should happen after they have documented their individual impressions, lest the loudest voices drown out those who feel less empowered to share their opinions. Of course, sharing evaluations and the evidence behind them takes time, but it helps align the hiring team on what 'good' means.

Since even the best candidate will not be perfect, this is also the opportunity to start drafting a development plan, including what exposure the candidate will need once joining the firm, what resources will be required and what key relationships will need to be built. For example, a candidate was hired who, while he had a great depth of sector experience and was able to build business in that sector, was relatively less experienced in a different area that was key to the hiring firm. Exposure to colleagues in that area, as well as clients, was an instrumental part of the candidate's development plan. It is too easy to fall in love with a candidate in the interview process, downplay the possible gaps when making the final choice and then forget about them altogether once the candidate has joined the firm.

4.6   Check references

However carefully the members of the hiring team form, support and document their impressions of the candidate, it is also important to make use of references to validate and/or challenge those impressions. Often these references are not 'go/no-go' references, but rather conversations that will shed additional light on what the team has learned for itself. Hearing critical comments about a candidate may help the hiring team improve its development plans. As an example, a reference pointed out that a candidate was exceptional, a very strong rainmaker, but needed to hone his management and communication skills further; could get ahead of himself in his enthusiasm and drive; and needed to do a better job of explaining where he was heading, especially to others on his team. This additional knowledge allowed the team to make the hire with their eyes open to the kind of support that the partner would need during his integration and beyond.

Timing is important. For example, I distinguish between early quiet references and final references. For legal and ethical reasons, any reference that will jeopardise a candidate's current employment should be avoided. An early quiet reference should therefore be based on the market's general point of view about the candidate or on the reputation he has gained by working with others. Do not ask direct questions about the candidate. A better approach is to ask, for example, "Who, in your opinion, are the top five people in this space?" If no one on the team knows someone who knows the candidate, LinkedIn will often turn up a connection.

Once the negotiation process – discussed in the next section – has begun and the candidate is on the way to receiving an offer, the time is right to ask him or her for detailed references. Make it clear that you do not want to jeopardise their current situation, but also that, before making a final offer, you will want to conduct a 360-degree reference, speaking with six to eight people, including subordinates, managers, peers and clients. The choice of references should be aligned to the defined need and should be based on specific evidence of how the candidate performed in different situations.

If a third-party recruiter is conducting the references, it is still a good idea for some members of the hiring team to speak with some of the references as well. Have the recruiter explain your wish to the reference and seek their approval. Such conversations can provide additional useful information and can also help the firm build connections to other businesses.

4.7   Negotiate the offer

The negotiation process is critical and often mismanaged. The candidate will have developed certain expectations of the role, the compensation and other matters that will need to be aligned with the firm's expectations. Think of it less as negotiating the best deal than as finding the best win-win solution. For example, letting a desirable candidate negotiate compensation well beyond that of his peers in the firm will land him in a difficult position with them once he comes on board.

If your firm is working with a recruiter and has developed a trusting relationship, this is a good time to use that recruiter as a middleman, sounding out the terms of the offer with the candidate. This can also be handled by an internal director of recruiting. Ultimately, though, the final negotiation should include the hiring manager, as it will lay the foundation for his relationship with the new partner.

4.8   Close the deal and hire the candidate

Even if the firm and the candidate feel that they have reached closure, it can still all go wrong. The candidate's current firm may come back with a counter-offer. The candidate – or his spouse – may start to question the move. It is important, therefore, to stay close to the candidate and to test his readiness to make the decision and to tell his current employer. The deal is not really done until the candidate shows up on the first day and is still there the following week.

4.9   Onboard/manage/develop

In fact, the hiring team's work is not finished even then. Research on the emotional state of new hires has found that an early sense of euphoria and excitement is typically followed by a dip when reality strikes. Finding a place in the new team and possibly in a new market, reconnecting with previous clients to explain the change and ramping up new business from a different platform can be a lonely process. The hiring team should stay close to their new hire. Certain relationships established during the hiring process should now be leveraged. The new hire should get plenty of direct, constructive feedback. It should never be assumed that all is well; that is most unlikely after such a significant change. The success of a great hire will depend significantly on how carefully and effectively he is brought into the firm (as opposed to being left to sink or swim). A well-managed process also helps to reinforce the culture of the firm by demonstrating what 'good' looks like, by modelling the expected behaviour and by making a safe space for conversations that will allow the new hire to ask uncomfortable questions.

5.   Hiring other senior leaders in law firms

While we have focused on hiring the rainmaker, the same disciplined process can apply to other senior hires in a law firm, such as chief operating officer, chief marketing officer, chief financial officer and chief human resources officer.

6.   Summary

This chapter has laid out a process for hiring a rainmaker in a law firm. The process is not theoretically complex, but there are a lot of details that need to be right. If the process is left to chance, as it often is, there are far too many ways for it to fail, as it often does. These failures are costly and demoralising enough to justify the time and effort it takes to prevent them.

Leading teams of lawyers in an increasingly global and virtual world

Mark Mortensen
INSEAD

1. Introduction

Success in today's economy requires collaboration. At its simplest, it is rare to find any meaningful work in today's professional service firms that can be completed by a single person. Indeed, teams have become a building block of almost all firms everywhere around the world – something which holds true across all industries and sectors. Beyond simply increasing the scope of our work, teams can foster the flexibility, innovation and adaptability demanded in our knowledge-driven economy. Teams increase intra- and inter-organisational knowledge flow, improving the skills of individual employees while diffusing culture, ideas, innovations and best practices.

Going a step further, global teams allow firms to provide integrated solutions to global clients who increasingly face global issues. Clients want counsel to address and solve their problems the same way they face them – globally. When a US-based multinational's trademark is being infringed upon in Germany, China and Australia they need to know that their discussions with counsel in New York are mobilising the necessary associates and partners in Frankfurt, Shanghai and Sydney. They want to know that their case is being handled by individuals who have deep knowledge of the distinct local contexts and the relationships needed to either settle or pursue litigation while at the same time feeling confident that any local solutions will be well integrated into a global solution that matches their brand strategy. In some cases, such global collaborations help firms to identify and capitalise on innovative solutions that may form the basis of new services and may attract new clients. It is for these reasons that many major firms have experienced substantial international growth in the past few years.

With those benefits, however, also come greater costs. Global collaborations incur significant coordination costs such as:

- projects delayed due to incompatible schedules;
- cross-cultural or linguistic misunderstandings creating non-billable rework;
- technology failures causing deadlines to be missed.

The stakes are higher as global projects tend to be some of the biggest and most important within a firm's portfolio. Because such projects are increasingly impossible to avoid, firms must learn how to reduce that overhead and improve their effectiveness. Those who are unable to master – or at least manage – these challenges will find themselves facing massively increased overhead without a corresponding increase in revenue.

This chapter explores the unique obstacles facing global collaborations within professional service firms and how best to overcome them. In the first half of this chapter, I outline the core effects of working at a distance – some expected and some unexpected. In the second half, I outline some tactics derived from observations of best practices in the field augmented by research findings.

2. The effects of working at a distance

At their core, global teams introduce distance. The most straightforward is physical distance, arising from members of your team being spread across different cities, countries or continents. Frequently, however, we introduce other types of distance at the same time.

Some teams also face cultural distance, bringing together team members holding different expectations and behavioural norms. Take, for example, a firm serving a Los Angeles based multinational that has a trademark being infringed upon by a competitor in Brazil, the United Kingdom, Japan, Singapore and Australia. To effectively implement a global response requires collaboration among parties based in all locations and all cultures. The directness that is highly valued by American and Australian counsels will be viewed as rude or insulting to their Japanese counterparts – even while the Japanese and Brazilian partners disagree significantly on how deadlines are interpreted and managed.

That same team faces linguistic distance as a result of bringing together individuals with different mother tongues. The simplest incarnation of this is a language barrier in which only part of the message gets through. To combat this firms introduce policies (eg, mandating English as the firm-wide language) and practices (eg, having each site recap key expectations and deliverables). The real barrier posed by language, however, is not about information flow, but power. Alex, an American associate, is able to rapidly craft complex, nuanced and subtle arguments in support of his points while Junichi, a senior partner in Tokyo, finds his arguments are slower, overly-simple and far more blunt than they would be if he were able to make them in his native Japanese. Alex, however, feels frustratingly confused when Mahesh and Jason, his counterparts in London and Sydney, compare aspects of the present case to the previous one while watching cricket at the weekend. On top of this, both Alex and Jason frequently fail to capture the real meaning of Junichi's points because they cannot read 'the words between the words' – a common problem when people from low context cultures and languages work with colleagues from high context languages.

Many cases also introduce temporal distance – collaborations that span time zones. When the lead partner in Los Angeles revises the litigation strategy during the morning, she must wait until the following morning before hearing the issues her changes raise for the senior partner in Singapore, who similarly must wait if he wants to get revised figures from the London office. When the team faces court-imposed deadlines or must counter opposing counsel's filing, delays like this can mean the difference between success and failure. Even absent external deadlines, spanning time zones reduces opportunities for the real-time conversations that all teams need in order to produce the coordinated legal strategy that their clients expect. While important deadlines may provide more than enough cause for associates and partners to work late and through weekends and holidays, the same cannot always be said for other parties like contractors or plaintiffs on whom a case may depend. This adds significant logistical coordination for the team to keep abreast of differing schedules for national holidays or even – as in the case of much of the Middle East – what days constitute the weekend.

Lastly, every team that interacts with, for example, co-counsel in another firm, an investment bank on a transaction or auditors on a restructuring, faces organisational distance. While large projects or cases have long required collaboration across divisions within a firm, increasingly teams must work across the boundaries of firms themselves. Many smaller firms in the international legal arena – or those which have chosen to use a network, rather than mergers – routinely work with their partner firms in other jurisdictions. One driver of this is increasingly sophisticated clients who are unbundling legal services and sending different pieces of work to different 'right cost' providers. In such cases, firms must work together to provide services integrated with those of other firms. Another driver is consolidation through non-organic growth such as mergers and acquisitions – frequently resulting in counsel collaborating across firm boundaries

While the effects of cultural, linguistic, temporal and organisational distance are bad enough independently, the effects are even greater when they line up, as they often do, in distributed teams. The effects of differences within teams multiply when so-called 'faultlines' – the lines that divide a group on the basis of some characteristics (eg, culture, language, timezones) – line up. Compare two versions of a litigation team involving partners from two firms, working in London and Sydney, and specialising in tax and real estate law. While any of those characteristics – firm, location or specialisation – might be a source of division and tension in the team, they can also be sources of similarity.

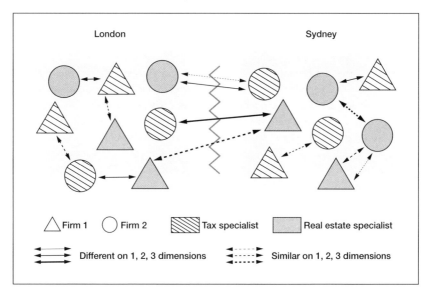

However, the situation becomes exponentially worse if all real estate specialists are working for one firm in London, while all the tax specialists are in the other firm and working in Sydney. In that situation the differences within the team lines up, with all the traits reinforcing one another. This strengthens the faultlines within the team which, like tectonic plates, is just waiting to fracture and draw attention to differences within the team.

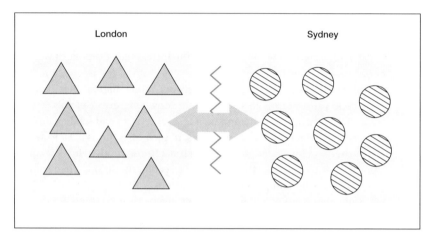

Obviously this is not always the case. Partners in New York working with colleagues in São Paulo have to deal with distance, language and culture, but not time zones; a team split between Washington DC and Sydney spans a larger distance and many time zones, but has the benefit of a common language. However, different types of distance are frequently correlated.

Across all of these types of distance it is important to keep in mind the difference between the problem and how it is experienced. The best illustration of this comes from a discussion I observed in an American–Japanese collaboration reviewing how the team handled the large number of hours separating their offices in San Francisco and Osaka. They had adopted the commonly espoused best practice of 'rotating the pain', that is alternating the timing of their meetings so that neither location had all of the late night calls. It was only during a face-to-face all-hands meeting that someone asked an eye-opening question: "where did everybody take a midnight call?". The results were striking – everyone in Osaka took calls in the office while everyone based in San Francisco took their calls at home. While motivations ranged across cultural norms, language proficiency and the lack of a home office, the end result was the same. The Americans had dinner with their families, had a conference call in the comfort of their home office and stumbled down the hallway to their beds. The Japanese stayed in the office and hoped the meeting ended before the last train stopped running – lest they sleep in a nearby hotel or at their desk. As in this case, we frequently focus on bridging these different types of distance without addressing how they are experienced.

The types of distance outlined here should come as no surprise – they are well-known issues and the bread and butter of a whole host of consultants ready to help you optimise your global teams. They are not, however, the most direct shapers of global team effectiveness, nor where you focus your efforts to get the most return on your investments. While you can spend substantial time and energy trying to tackle cultural differences, time zone issues and technology effects one at a time, a far more efficient strategy is to address them where they converge and impact team effectiveness. For this reason, your focus should be on two other types of distance with far more direct and far-reaching impact on team effectiveness: psychological distance and informational distance – both of which are triggered by each of the types of distance discussed above.

2.1 Psychological distance

The different types of distance identified pose problems in their own right, but also trigger psychological distance. To get a gut feel for this just ask yourself whether you feel closer to your local colleagues than those working in another office. The answer is undoubtedly 'yes'.

The problem is that psychological distance is at the root of a process which we use to help deal with the increasing complexity of our daily lives. We all know that the world is incredibly complex and the unfortunate truth is that it is beyond our cognitive ability to fully understand every person, process and social interaction we experience in a world that is itself increasingly complex and fast paced. To manage the complexity, our brain simplifies the world by grouping things together in cognitive buckets. Rather than thinking about all 23 people handling tax law as unique individuals, you find ways to group them together: associates versus partners, litigators versus arbitrators versus mediators, London-versus Hong Kong-versus Sydney-based. This process, which psychologists call 'social categorisation', helps us to cope.

The problem arises when we place ourselves into one of those categories. That placement fundamentally changes our view of those people we consider to be in the same group (our ingroup) and those who are not (our outgroup). We treat our ingroup more favorably and our outgroup more negatively and this distinction shapes many dynamics critical to effective team functioning. We are less cooperative with our outgroup, we communicate and share information less with them, we feel less attached and give them less support, and ultimately we evaluate them more poorly and are less satisfied with them. All this just by creating a distinction between 'us' and 'them'.

This categorisation process is extremely easy to trigger – psychologists have been able to trigger it by grouping people by irrelevant criteria (eg, eye colour) or even at random. When given a basis for categorising others, our brains do so automatically (it saves us cognitive energy) and subsequently we begin to treat each other differently. While this fundamental psychological process is at work in collocated and global teams alike, the types of distance noted earlier – physical, cultural, linguistic, temporal, organisational and technological – all trigger it. If you doubt you do it, ask yourself a simple question (and answer honestly): When working in a dispersed team, do you find yourself saying "WE do things this way, but THEY do it like that"? Just like a 'tell' in poker, this is evidence of the psychological process of categorisation you are engaging in below the surface and that process introduces tension, damages trust and reduces performance.

2.2   Informational distance

While psychological distance and the process of social categorisation affect how we feel about our distant colleagues, we face a second obstacle in what we know about them. The cornerstone of any effective communication and collaboration is common ground – information that all parties share, and know they share. This common body of information helps us to interpret situations and better understand one another – to calibrate our frames of reference and expectations, making us more efficient while at the same time reducing misunderstandings.

When working face to face, we pick up and use a tremendous amount of this ambient information in order to understand our colleagues. Most of our data collection is unconscious as is our subsequent use of that information. Think about the last time you walked into an important meeting; consciously or not, you noticed the dynamics of the people in the hallway, with one glance you gauged the mood of the individuals in the room, during discussions you picked up on subtle non-verbal cues to understand and predict the direction of the arguments, and all this against a backdrop of knowing everything from local news stories and recent office events to personal information about the relevant parties and even the weather. Every one of these pieces of information gets fed into the mental database we use to interpret, understand and react to daily events.

On its surface, the issue is simple – you do not (and in fact cannot) have the same amount of knowledge about your distant collaborators. Simple as the problem is to explain, it has far-reaching and complex effects that cause collaboration to break down. While millions of years of evolution have programmed us to pick up and use all of these as sources of the data, we are not that good at doing so over intermittent visits or, even worse, video links or phone calls. Think about your last phone or video conference:

- Did any of your distant colleagues' behaviours not make sense to you?
- Did you have differing expectations for the content or timing of deliverables?
- Did you get a sense that there were other issues behind the scenes that were affecting their decisions?

Laura, an associate based in San Francisco, shared this experience:

I had emailed João in our Lisbon office asking for an update on a pending motion. As he was usually very quick to respond, when I hadn't gotten a response in a couple of hours I resent my message. I immediately received a very angry reply telling me he was looking into it and that I was being unreasonable expecting such a fast response. What I didn't know was that João and his wife had just had a baby and he was terribly sleep deprived. Everyone in Lisbon knew it and were all pitching in and cutting him slack. Me, I had no clue.

Frequently, issues arise not due to lack of information but miscalibration of the information that has been shared; 'rain' during the Delhi monsoon season and 'snow' during a hard New England winter are non-trivial events – so when half of your team miss a meeting due to 'bad weather', you know when to cut them some slack.

The causes of this lack of information are both technological and behavioural.

On the one hand, despite recent advances in communication technology and counter to the promises of technology vendors, we have not yet arrived at a point where telepresence is 'just like being there'. While technology will continue to improve, the truth of the matter is that the members of a litigation team split between San Francisco, Frankfurt, London and Shanghai will never know as much about their colleagues and the context affecting their actions and attitudes as they will about the colleagues who work down the hall. Communicating through technology filters out certain cues, some of which would help us to create mutual knowledge.

At the same time, we behave differently in global teams. Our communications are measurably more task-focused. While this may seem appealing with respect to reducing billed hours, in reality it means that we share less of the contextual information required to efficiently collaborate. Ultimately this results in a net reduction in efficiency and productivity.

3.   What can we do?

Addressing the issues posed by psychological and informational distance takes effort. Below are a few tried and true methods for overcoming these issues and improving distant collaboration.

3.1   Fight psychology … with psychology

Now that we recognise that our brains put people into categories, the risk you face is that the members of your team see each other not as 'one of us' but 'one of them'. The bad news is that there is nothing you can do to stop yourself – or anyone else – from this subconscious process of forming categories and playing favourites. The good news, however, is that while we cannot stop grouping people, things, events and behaviours into categories, we can influence what those categories are. Your objective should not be to try to eliminate categories but to be more mindful and choose them.

One of the biggest challenges posed by the process of categorisation is that it is easily triggered. This is also one of our greatest tools. Since just about any noticeable difference within your team will form the basis of categories, your task is to make sure that the categories that come to mind are the ones that bring you together, not the ones that drive you apart.

As Penelope, the lead litigator in a global team, shared:

It was clear our team was not playing nicely. My associates' emails frequently placed blame on how 'they' in the other office weren't giving us what we needed, when we needed it, and the emails we got back made it clear that sentiment was the one thing both offices agreed on. I scheduled a video conference and reminded everyone on both sides that we all had the same objective and that if we weren't going to work together, we might as well just give up – because we certainly weren't going to win the case. Reminding everyone about our shared purpose and reliance on one another really snapped the team back together and turned things around – though I did have to remind them from time to time …

Penelope got the members of her team to shift their focus from their local offices to the team as a whole by using the most obvious and powerful thing everyone had in common – the purpose that brought them together in the first place. While her team still thought in terms of categories, the category was no longer the local office, but the team as a whole. Built on some of the same foundations as the trust falls, ropes courses and wall climbs found in many team-building exercises, and the branded mugs, pens and tee-shirts that litter our workspaces, there is an important difference. Such activities and trinkets are one-shot interventions at a single point in time – typically at the launch of a project, intended to distinguish and reinforce the identity of a team relative to the rest of the organisation. The problem is that on a day-to-day basis dispersed teams are faced with repeated and ongoing stimuli (eg, distance, time zones, culture, language, technology) that highlight the differences across sites. Therefore, what you need is an equally ongoing set of triggers that reinforce the similarities. The most powerful and strongest of these is your team's common purpose.

That common goal is the glue that binds teams together. Teams that work to remind their members both of their shared objective and their reliance on one another to achieve it, find that their differences are reduced in comparison to those that do not. This can be accomplished in very straightforward ways, including:

- revisiting your progress towards the team's stated objective at the start of meetings;
- celebrating milestones and intermediate successes;
- highlighting situations in which members provided crucial assistance across locations; and
- having shared experiences such as cross-site visits.

While these are overall good practices, engaging in them with an eye towards promoting a shared identity helps keep them on target and clearly illustrates and reinforces their value. This, of course, comes with an important caveat – if a team's members do not have interdependence across its locations, this strategy will not work. However, if that is the case, you should be asking yourself why you are labelling this as a team in the first place.

3.2   Create shared knowledge to increase understanding

Recognising that we lack much of the contextual information about our distant colleagues that we normally rely on to interpret and understand their attitudes, cognition and behaviours, we must find ways to recognise and share that information. What makes this task challenging is the sheer volume and scope of the information in question. No technology will ever be able to capture and transmit all the information that affects your cognition and spending your time trying to relay it is clearly unrealistic. There are, however, a few simple best practices that can start the ball rolling and better prepare your team.

(a)   Give (and take) a virtual tour to provide context

If you plan to work together frequently or for an extended period of time, the more you and your distant teammates know about each other's environment, the better you will be able to make sense of one another's behaviour. Ideally, your team would visit your distant colleagues for the opportunity to experience their environment and routine, as mentioned below. While such a trip is often too costly, a few alternative steps can help dramatically. At the start of a project, give each person just a few minutes to share a bit of their context. This does not mean name, rank and serial number or not so self-effacingly sharing their pedigree, but sharing what elements of your environment each of you thinks is most likely to affect your ability to collaborate effectively. Kai, a senior partner in the Copenhagen office, shared a helpful approach:

> I started to work on a matter with a partner in New York and knew he and I would be having a number of late night – or early morning – video conferences. So I took five minutes to give him a rundown of my workspaces. It didn't take long but I focused on things that were most likely to interrupt future calls: my co-counsel on a major tax litigation, my occasionally over-eager assistant, and – when working from my home office – my dog. The interruptions were much easier to deal with when they came up because he was expecting them.

Whether a quick pan of a webcam or a verbal walk through, the objective is to help your distant colleagues understand the environment in which you are working.

(b) Gain direct and reflected knowledge to create perspective

Taking the time to visit your distant colleagues provides critical and often irreplaceable information. Once you have returned home, that information will help you better understand and interpret your again distant collaborators' behaviour. As Marcus, a partner from Boston, noted:

> When I travelled to Delhi for a meeting during monsoon season, I discovered I had to recalibrate my understanding a bit. I suddenly understood that when my colleagues there cancelled a meeting because of rain, they weren't joking around. I had never seen rain and flooding like that, but they all took it in stride. I just hope I get a chance to return the favour and give them a chance to see New England snow…

When members of your team have the opportunity to visit and learn about their distant colleagues, they gain important direct knowledge about their colleagues' local environment. That information can fill gaps in their understanding or, as in the case of Marcus, help them to calibrate what they already know. Visits, however, can also provide reflected knowledge of how your office is viewed by your distant colleagues. As Bente, a partner from the Berlin office, noted:

> It's a totally different view: standing a bit aside and looking from outside of the system. Of course, I understand much better how Germany is seen by other offices of the firm worldwide. There is certainly a big difference between working in Germany, and dealing with Germany while working abroad.

In a recent field study[1] we found that when people are abroad, their interactions with their home office helped them learn how distant teammates understood the environment, people, dynamics and events that shaped their interactions. That

---

1   M Mortensen and TB Neeley, "Reflected Knowledge and Trust in Global Collaboration", *Management Science*, 2012, 58(12), pp 2207–2224.

knowledge significantly increased trust. While direct knowledge is the basis for the age-old wisdom of 'walk a mile in their shoes', reflected knowledge helps us to learn what contextual information our colleagues use to understand us. Importantly, this helps us to better understand and improve the information we share when we get back home and return to business as usual.

The benefits of direct and reflected knowledge are one of the reasons that secondments are so powerful in creating a uniform culture in a firm across the globe. By rotating associates, or even partners, on temporary assignments to other offices, firms gain a tremendous boost in their lawyers' ability to work efficiently and effectively on global, virtual teams.

(c)   ***Keep knowledge current to stay relevant***
Our world is not static, and neither is the mutual knowledge problem. Our work environments are constantly changing and, as a result, we need to continually update the knowledge that we hold and use to effectively collaborate with distant colleagues. This requires ongoing efforts to keep yourself and others up to date. The most efficient way to do this is with regular context updates – quick updates on major changes in each location.

This does not mean updating your colleagues on new details that you have discovered or conversations you have had relating to the case you are working on – that information will (or at least should) come out in status updates as you track your progress. This is about things outside the scope of the work at hand, but likely to affect it. As Michael, a partner in Silicon Valley, explained:

I was working on an IP matter with colleagues in New York, and we got in the habit of taking a few minutes each week to fill each other in on what was going on locally. It wasn't directly relevant to the case but that knowledge ended up being critical because it helped me know which other partners or senior associates in that office had related experience and how busy they were in general. Others might question the value of this time investment – especially when we're supposed to be billing by the six-minute increment! – but we found that it paid off enormously because we got quick turnaround from an expert when a couple of critical questions arose.

This information takes many forms, including: changes in personnel or office restructure that will affect the resources you might draw upon in the future; new office or local practices or protocols that constrain the way in which you work; or even non-work events (eg, local political change, strikes or other social movements, major news headlines) that are likely to affect people's thinking or their perspective.

Some might argue that it is a waste of time to exchange such non-work information – particularly in the face of partners and associates who are suffering from overload. However, it is important to remember that our brains and cognition do not obey work boundaries. Consciously or not, your teams' decisions are affected by their contexts so you should be aware of them and ensure that the teams are as well informed as possible.

3.3   Foster spontaneous interaction to boost shared identity and understanding
In addition to targeting the issues of unshared identity and unshared context

separately, a few techniques tackle both at the same time. One such two-bird-stone is spontaneous communication. As long as people have worked together we have recognised the importance of those unplanned, spontaneous interactions that occur during shared activities, such as:

- getting coffee, water or food;
- exercising; and
- commuting.

On the one hand, they serve as a bonding agent, a shared experience that brings people together and helps them to form relationships with one another. In doing so, these interactions help to foster a sense of shared identity. Just consider whether those coffee-pot chats help you better relate to your co-workers and you will realise that it is true. On the other hand, they are important conduits for the exchange of all types of information. We learn who and what others know, allowing us to better leverage their abilities or connections. We learn about successes and failures which we can apply to our own challenges. We learn what is happening and who is involved which we use to calibrate our observations.

The problem is an obvious one – when we are working at a distance we just do not have the natural opportunities for these types of interactions. While this is not surprising, our research has discovered an interesting twist. While spontaneous interactions occur less often and less readily in dispersed teams, when they do occur, they produce a marked improvement in shared identity and shared understanding – and those effects are much stronger than those in collocated teams. This means that although it is hard to foster, when you are successful, spontaneous interaction yields huge benefits.

So how do you get people to spontaneously interact across distance? Until virtual coffee becomes a reality, the short answer is that you have to work at it. Teams that wish to promote spontaneous interaction have to work – in effect – to formalise the informal. Clearly, by definition you cannot schedule something spontaneous. You can, however, schedule opportunities for such spontaneous interactions to happen.

James, a partner in Chicago, occasionally creates 'scheduled, unscheduled time' – time at the beginning of a call that is explicitly off-agenda in order to provide his team with opportunities to informally and spontaneously interact. This tactic comes with a warning, as James explained:

You can't just go ahead and put '10 minutes of free time' on the agenda. It doesn't work unless your team understands why you're doing it and what benefit it offers them. I made that mistake at first, and everyone either spent the first 10 minutes texting or showed up 12 minutes late. Once I got them to realise how important those interactions were, things started to change. It was still awkward at first, but each time we did it, it became more comfortable and now everyone agrees it is a critical part of our process.

To use this tactic effectively requires two things: understanding and perseverance. Your firm (and team) have to understand and buy in to the value of spontaneous interaction and the logic of scheduling time to promote it. At a firm level, there must be a recognition that informal interaction is not a waste of time, but rather plays a crucial role in information flow within your firm. This is not new

– as long as there have been law firms, breakthroughs have taken place in hallways, breakrooms and around water coolers – however changes in the structure of your firm are threatening this key pathway for knowledge transfer. Perseverance is required because your team has to push through the first few times when the process feels awkward and forced. The meetings will feel this way for a very good reason – they are. But that forcing is necessary and after doing it a few times you will discover that each subsequent time will feel more natural and normal.

Making all of this a tougher sell, the payoff of such interaction is not immediate, but reaped over the long term. However, in the same way that you invest in reinforcing your firm's culture to help your associates and partners better understand and work with one another, this requires investment as well. To get the benefits of spontaneous communication requires putting into place processes and structures to compensate for the things that no longer come for free.

3.4 Be predictable to increase trust

The most often cited breakdown in dispersed collaborations is a lack of trust. At its core, trust is about predictability – you know that your distant colleagues will behave in a certain way, and can therefore plan accordingly. Critically, both shared identity and shared understanding are key drivers of trust. The more you see your distant colleagues as part of 'us', the more you trust them because they are just like you. The more you share the same understanding, the more you trust them because you have the same frame of reference for understanding their behaviour.

Another source of trust is predictability itself, making it important to create as much predictability as possible within your global collaborations. A first step is regularising your meetings. When we work face to face we often rely on impromptu check-ins as the need arises, but these often fail to materialise when you are not down the hall. Pete, a tax specialist in Baltimore, explained that his new managing partner introduced a fixed schedule for conference calls and site visits with their office in Denver. At first he didn't understand why, but it was not long before he realised the regularity of the meetings helped him plan his work and interactions accordingly and what to expect in return. Obviously when the need arose they scheduled additional calls and visits but those were built on the existing foundation of the regular interactions.

Trite as it seems, one last way to build trust is to have an open and honest discussion about the challenges that you and your team face in working at a distance. Frank was struggling on a project with his colleagues in the Paris office until he decided to share his feelings:

> Finally I called Anne, who I knew a bit, and said 'look, I'm having a really hard time figuring out how to manage this distance thing'. Turned out she was wrestling with the same things but didn't think it was appropriate to mention it. We agreed to schedule a video conference with the whole team to discuss it and that meeting was a watershed – we got a better idea about what each side needed and realised we were all in the same boat.

As Frank and Anne discovered, being open and honest about the challenges serves two purposes. First, it sets expectations, gets you on the same page and helps you understand each other's behaviours. This reduces the likelihood of the surprises and expectation shortfalls that so often damage trust and also builds greater shared understanding. Secondly, the act of sharing your concerns itself builds the rapport and trust that underlies shared identity, by creating your own shared experience – the shared experience of consciously working to overcome the obstacles of global collaboration.

4. Concluding thoughts

In the end, none of these tactics will guarantee a perfectly smooth experience for global, virtual teams. The reality is that given the complexity of global collaboration the only thing we know for certain is that issues will certainly arise. However, by reinforcing your sense of a shared identity across locations, you increase the likelihood that your dispersed collaborators will give each other the benefit of the doubt when such issues arise. It helps them to take a cooperative and constructive stance when trying to address them, rather than a competitive one. At the same time, building your teams' shared understanding will help them to better interpret the actions of their distant colleagues and to ensure that their own actions predictably generate the most productive outcomes. It is important to recognise and remember that, fundamentally, the key to distributed work is not technological, but social.

Leading millennials

Henrik Bresman
INSEAD
Heidi K Gardner
Harvard Law School's Center on the Legal Profession
Samantha Sheehan
Harvard Law School

1.   Introduction

The law firms of today in many jurisdictions around the world face incredibly high rates of associate attrition,[1] suggesting that junior lawyers' job satisfaction continues to dwindle. However, firms need these young lawyers – associates put in the hard work to support partners' matters and this leverage structure helps to maximise firm profitability.[2] Further, associate classes are the breeding ground for a firm's future partners. Most of today's associates fall into the generation known as 'millennials', that is, people born between the early 1980s and the mid-1990s. Although they currently make up about 25% of the total workforce, it is estimated that in just over 10 years millennials will exceed 75% of the global workforce. Consequently, employers are not in the position of deciding whether or not to study and understand this generation; it is imperative that they do so. Strengthening associate satisfaction and providing growth opportunities are essential to attracting, retaining and preparing young lawyers to lead and are therefore vital to a firm's long-term viability.

Nevertheless, when it comes to leading associates, most firms continue to use management practices based on tradition. For example, many partners still believe that the carrot of a future partnership is a strong enough motivator for a firm to retain its most valued associates during a decade or more of grinding work, long hours and expected subservience to hierarchy. As this chapter will reveal, the relevance of some of the underlying assumptions is highly questionable when considering today's associates.

This chapter builds on an extensive research study[3] involving 16,637 millennials in 43 countries to discuss how law firms can effectively lead this generation of lawyers. Section 2 outlines some of the research findings about millennials' preferences, focusing on those areas that we believe to be most crucial for law firm leaders to understand. The aim is to provide readers with a foundation not only to

---

1   Deena Shanker, "Why are Lawyers Such Terrible Managers?", *Fortune*, January 11 2013, http://fortune.com/2013/01/11/why-are-lawyers-such-terrible-managers/ (citing a 19–20% associate turnover rate).

2   For more on leverage structure, see David H Maister, "The Anatomy of a Consulting Firm", in *The Advice Business: Essential Tools and Models for Managing Consulting* (2004), retrieved from http://davidmaister.com/wp-content/themes/davidmaister/pdf/TheAnatomyofaConsultingFirm.pdf.

3   The study was the result of a collaboration between Universum, INSEAD Emerging Markets Institute, and the HEAD Foundation, led by Henrik Bresman. For the full study, see Universum, INSEAD Emerging Markets Institute and The HEAD Foundation, *Understanding a Misunderstood Generation* (2014), retrieved from http://universumglobal.com/millennials/.

consider our proposed applications but also to find additional innovative ways of structuring their organisations to align with millennials' desires.

Section 3 then focuses on how to apply millennial research directly to law firms. We propose a handful of management practices that might best appeal to this generation of new lawyers and offer some best practices, by way of case studies, of some existing successful firms. We also delve into the roles that current firm leaders can play in addressing millennials' needs.

2.   Leading millennials

The old assumptions about millennials go something like this: millennials want the best of all worlds – rapid career advancement, but with work-life balance and without having to put in any hard work. Recent research shows that some of this may be true, but much is not. Overall trends (explored in more detail below) are that millennials crave leaders who empower them, a work-life balance, and leadership and career advancement. Importantly, these preferences seem to feed directly into the needs of associates at law firms – an empirical study of Am Law 200 mid-level associates suggests that young lawyers are willing to stay longer at firms that offer more flexible work schedules, more access to information about associates' promotion prospects and the opportunity for associates to reach partnership.[4]

2.1   How millennials want to be managed

Perhaps of highest interest to firms is how millennials want to be managed. For a start, we should note that lawyers in general are known for being difficult to manage, given their independent nature and constant need for intellectual challenge. Millennials want leaders who empower them. As figure 1 shows, empowerment is the most important attribute for millennials in North America, Western Europe and Africa. But what exactly does this mean? Although the precise definition of empowerment varies from person to person, research suggests that most millennials want to be able to make independent decisions and choose their own paths. Overall, millennials value having a general sense of autonomy more than feeling empowered in their day-to-day work.

So how does a manager offer employees a feeling of greater autonomy? In any organisation, millennials prefer that managers do not micromanage. Instead, a millennial might want a manager to assign a project, share a quick overview of the work to be done and offer their availability to help talk through any issues the millennial may encounter while working through the issues on their own. Ideally, a manager will give millennials space to take on challenging work alone, but will offer technical or functional expertise to give guidance should millennials stumble along the way. Of course, the ability to delegate pieces of work varies by matter, so we encourage partners to think through how to best divide and allocate each project's responsibilities to their team. Assigning matters is only one piece of the puzzle, however. More importantly, millennials believe that, to be effective, a manager should offer feedback. Although preferences for frequency vary, research suggests

---

4   WD Henderson and D Zaring, "Young Associates in Trouble" (2006) 105 *Michigan Law Review* 1102, 1106.

Figure 1: If you were able to choose your manager, which of the following would be most important to you? – Top 5, by region. *(From UMG, Part 4, p11)*

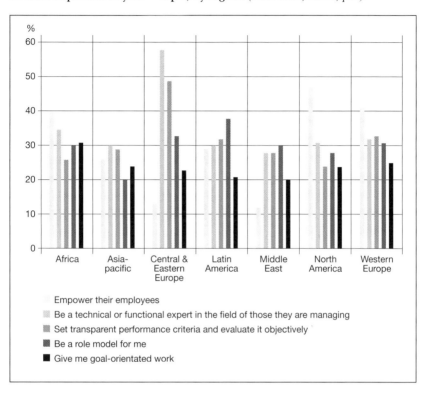

that managers should offer feedback no less than once a month, and preferably as soon as it is applicable. We will discuss below certain areas in which we believe partners have an excellent opportunity to facilitate useful feedback.

2.2 Millennials want work-life balance

Millennials also value having a work-life balance. Again, the ideal balance varies from person to person, but many millennials focus on having flexible hours and enough leisure time in their personal lives. Well over half of millennials prioritise being able to spend time with their families and nearly 50% conceded that they would be willing to sacrifice a well-paid and prestigious job in order to improve their work-life balance. Figure 2 (overleaf) shows how these preferences vary by region. This does not mean that millennials expect simple nine-to-five work days, however. Millennials want fast-tracked careers with constant promotions, and are open to working harder, for longer hours and under more stress in order to have increased chances of success. This caveat is important for firms to understand – millennials may crave more flexibility as a means of achieving a work-life balance, rather than simply working fewer hours. As one associate noted in our interviews, it is more of a decision than a balance, being able to make the personal choice about what to sacrifice in a given situation, such as

Figure 2: What does work-life balance mean to you? – Top 5, by region. *(From UMG, part 4, p20)*

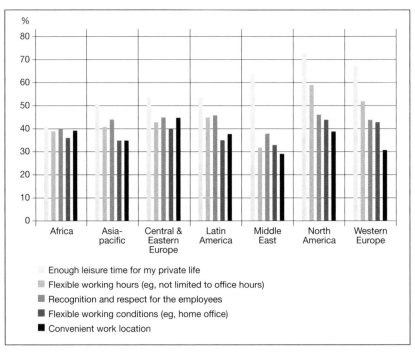

Figure 3: How important is it to you that you become a managerleader during your career? – by region. *(From UMG, part 4, p6)*

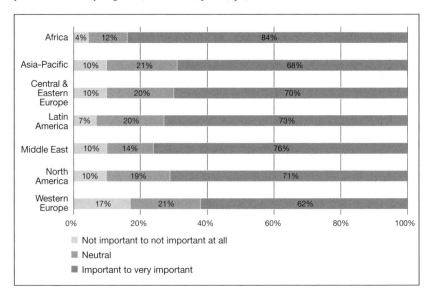

taking a professional opportunity over a planned vacation. Accordingly, firms hoping to appeal to millennials' desires for a work-life balance might consider ways in which they can offer increased scheduling flexibility, or telecommunicating options (even for evenings or weekends) rather than feeling as if they must lessen the hour requirements in order to satisfy this millennial preference.

2.3 Millennials want to achieve leadership and career advancement

Achieving a manager or leadership role is also important to a huge number of millennials. As figure 3 shows, this desire is universal. Tellingly, millennials' biggest fear is getting stuck in a dead-end career, a fact that underscores the importance of providing advancement opportunities.

Leadership appeals to millennials for a number of reasons, but high future earnings, being able to influence the company they work for and working with strategic challenges are all particularly prevalent.

Figure 4: What is it you consider most attractive in a managerial/leadership role – by region. *(From UMG, Part 7, p8)*

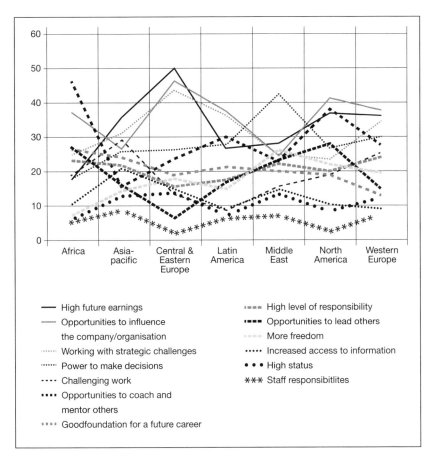

What is especially interesting is that millennials do not seem to care much about the advantages of attaining a leadership position, including:

- status;
- leadership; and
- increased access to information (see figure 4 on the previous page).

By focusing on those factors of leadership that do appeal to millennials, while placing less emphasis on those that do not, a firm can more effectively structure its partnership and alternative tracks to motivate a greater number of young lawyers to pursue this career advancement. Given the small percentage of associates that do make it to partnership level, a firm might also decide to adjust mid-level promotions to satisfy more millennial desires, thus incentivising the associates to remain at the firm for longer than they may have otherwise.

3. How millennial preferences translate to law firms

What is the most productive way to apply the above findings to law firm structures? To start with, firms should consider adapting their training and development policies to assuage millennials' concerns about being stuck without professional development opportunities. Firms also might try to adjust their structures in order to address millennial preferences for empowerment, work-life balance and opportunities for leadership roles. Notably, the importance of appealing to these millennial desires may be particularly heightened in a law firm setting. Lawyers generally crave autonomy, and this characteristic appears to be even stronger for millennials. Further, many large firm lawyers across age bands have expressed a need for a better work-life balance, saying they want to work fewer hours, have less of an emphasis on billing hours and gain more influence over their matters. Again, these desires might be especially heightened for millennials because many have peers in other industries who are experiencing more innovative workplaces. Lastly, a firm's ability to promote lawyers to partnership depends on the firm effectively training, preparing and retaining associates so that they are still around when the time comes for them to lead.

What does this mean for the firm leaders of today? Consider the two major roles that leaders of professional service firms play: architect and coach. First, the role of architect is to design formal systems and policies that affect people. A managing partner acting in the architect role might examine and reorganise firm structures to improve the attraction and retention of millennials. Secondly, a leader-coach serves as a role model, shaping firm culture and working interpersonally. This role is less structured than that of an architect – coaches act in ways that reinforce the structures put in place by architects. For instance, if the managing partner of a firm began an evaluation process to give more frequent feedback, a partner could reinforce the firm's commitment to providing feedback by enthusiastically taking part in the process, as well as going beyond it, perhaps by providing regular informal feedback and encouraging others to do the same. This is an extremely important role, specifically in regards to appealing to millennials, who place a high value on organisational culture. Figure 5 summarises the ways that both architects and coaches can influence aspects of each of these firm processes (ie, work assignment

Figure 5: Role of leaders as architects and coaches

Leader as architect: Build the system		Leader as coach: Reinforce the culture	Outcomes
Work Assignment System	• Central coordination + free-market back up • Variety of matters	• Advice on workload management • Coordinate workflow, create opportunities • Empower associates to make smart career decisions	Competitive advantage through effects on millennial talent: • Attraction • Development • Promotion • Retention
Evaluation & Promotion Process	• Formal process, regular reviews • Explicit expectations	• Invest time in giving substantive reviews • Foster a feedback culture • Provide detailed guidance on improvement opportunities	
Pro Bono Program	• Dedicated coordinator • Voluntary participation • Billable hour credit	• Encourage "giving back" • Technical & process guidance • Recognition for efforts	

Millennial associates' preferences

• Autonomy   • Empowerment
• Work-life balance   • leadership and career advancement

system, evaluation and promotion process, *pro bono* programme) in order to achieve greater competitive advantage by leading millennials more effectively.

Much of what we discuss in the following section is geared towards an architect's job, that is, setting up formal aspects of the firm. In particular, we propose three management practices that we believe can be tailored to best address these desires:

- work assignment system;
- evaluation and promotion process;
- *pro bono* programme.

In each discussion, we also offer a few highlights and examples from successful firms. Although they are by no means the only best practices, they serve as illustrations of what we believe are effective programmes. In addition, leader-coaches are essential for millennials, who typically have a strong preference for empowering management. We have noted places where coaches have major and important roles to play in effectuating firm programmes.

3.1   Work assignment system

Law firm leaders seeking to develop a more loyal and productive millennial generation of associates can design their firm's work assignment system to better address millennials' needs. Most of all, by having a work assignment system that gives associates some degree of choice in which matters they work on and who they work with, a firm will be able to grant associates a major sense of influence in their own career paths. This will aid many of the other needs of millennials because it allows for flexibility, that is, an associate might feel as if he is able to adapt which matters they take on:

- to best suit their ideal work-life balance;
- to develop skills in the practice areas of their choice;
- to challenge them at a proper level;
- to work with many different individuals throughout the firm to create an internal network to aid in furthering the associate's career; and
- to choose managers who empower, guide and give an ideal level of feedback.

A firm's work assignment system is also an important process for leader-coaches to focus on empowering associates through work delegation, effective feedback, and offering general support and guidance for associates concerned about their career development. In fact, one associate noted that what he liked about his law firm experience was:

I was treated like a professional the minute I walked in the door – I get independence and control over how I work and get my work done, and I feel like my input is valued.

(a) Coordinated work assignment system with free market back up

Although different work assignment system set-ups have different advantages and disadvantages, we propose that a work assignment system that is centrally coordinated but backed up by a free market system best addresses millennial needs. Having a coordinator who assigns matters to associates addresses millennials' fears of lacking development opportunities, which is especially important early in an associate's career when he may be nervous about building a professional network within the firm. Ropes & Gray address this issue particularly well. The firm has a system in which associates fill out weekly reports about their work – what they are currently working on, as well as how much time they have to spare for new work. Associates are able to request specific types of work, which coordinators try to find for them, and to assess how many new matters they want to take on; both aspects enhance their feeling of autonomy and being able to maintain a work-life balance. It also offers associates their desired development opportunities, by allowing them to request and pursue matters in certain practice areas of their choice.

A supplementary free market back-up system will further help to address associates' preferences for flexibility and influence. Associates need the opportunity to maintain relationships with people with whom they have previously worked. Doing this not only allows associates to find and focus on a practice area that they truly enjoy, but also strengthens associates' networks, by allowing them to opt to continue working with the same partners where they have developed good relationships. One associate noted: "When you get to choose which partners you work with and what to work on to some extent, you feel more engaged." This aspect is a hidden benefit for the firm, as engaged associates with strong internal networks show enhanced retention.

Maintaining these systems in parallel maximises associates' flexibility. If they are unhappy with the work they are getting through the coordinator, they can seek out additional work on their own; if they do not have the capacity to take on work that they are offered informally, the formal assignment process works as an oversight mechanism to ensure that a single associate is not overburdened. By working through the formal and informal systems, associates are able to continue to build a network throughout the firm by working with new partners, while reinforcing their existing relationships.

(b)   *Variety of matters for associates to choose from*
A flexible work assignment system is dependent on firm leaders ensuring that a variety of matters are available to assign associates to. It is ideal for associates to be able to request specific types of work, because that allows them to help shape what sorts of development opportunities they pursue. As one associate noted: "I want to keep developing skills and be the best attorney I can be – that's what keeps me driven." Further, having numerous options preserves associates' feelings of flexibility in deciding what work to take on in order to maintain a work-life balance. One millennial associate mentioned: "people being able to work on the things that they're more interested in keeps them really engaged." As long as there is a variety of matters to choose from, an associate can occasionally choose to forego a certain matter if he is concerned that it might take more time than he can invest in the work. On the flip side, if an associate feels that he does not have enough work, if there are a variety of matters he can choose what to take on in order to strike a more appropriate balance. It is also essential that there are other matters for associates to fall back on so that they are not stuck with only one option that they must take, even if it is undesired, for this forfeits the flexibility and development opportunities that an associate might otherwise expect.

(c)   *Coaches' role in work assignment systems*
A firm's work assignment system is an excellent opportunity for firm members to play the role of coach. Goodwin Procter's system does this particularly well. The firm has a centralised workload management system that consists of a network of attorney development managers (ADMs), who perform several important roles. First, ADMs help to integrate associates into the firm. Each office has at least one ADM responsible for assisting with an associate's initial onboarding into the firm and meeting with them one-on-one to discuss their interests. The ADMs stay abreast of associates' development through involvement in the annual review process and regular conversations with the associates and their supervising partners. Further, ADMs are all former practising attorneys who understand the demands of the firm from both the partner and associate perspective. Given their knowledge of firm structure and partner personalities, as well as individual associates' needs, goals, skills and areas to strengthen, an ADM can help empower associates to influence their career development, even very early on. Additionally, the ADMs coordinate workflow. Associates can thus rely on the ADMs to take their interests into consideration when assigning matters and suggesting team members to the supervising partners.

Moreover, ADMs can help associates to maintain a work-life balance. By regulating workflow and having regular conversations with associates, ADMs can help assess how much additional work each associate is capable of taking on. While the ADMs do more than is discussed in this section, their dual role of trusted partner and firm networker serves as an important example of how partners and staff at other firms might fill a coaching role to help guide millennial associates' success at the firm.

3.2 Evaluation and promotion process

Playing the role of architect, law firm leaders can structure their firms' evaluation and promotion process to serve millennial preferences. If set up properly, the evaluation and promotion process can set clearer expectations for what an ideal manager should be doing, helping to create empowering management. The programme can be designed so that it facilitates frequent feedback and gives associates a strong understanding of how they are being evaluated, as well as what skills they need to develop in order to progress or attain a leadership position. Providing this clarity can truly address millennials' fears of losing development opportunities, while also ensuring that the firm is focused on properly training and assessing associates for their futures at the firm. In fact, a large number of millennials want to have transparent performance criteria and effective evaluations. Additionally, the evaluation and promotion process is an excellent opportunity for coaches to take part in reinforcing a firm structure. Partners enthusiastically committing to a firm programme goes a long way to ensuring that the policy will be effective in practice.

(a) *Formal evaluation process with regular reviews and guidance*

As millennial associates want frequent feedback, firms might consider adjusting their formal review process to regularly solicit and disseminate feedback. Foley Hoag has an exemplary system – in addition to annual reviews, the firm does an additional mid-year review for anyone who has been with the firm for less than two years. The mid-year review helps to ensure that a new lawyer gets off to a good start and understands how they are doing. It serves as a check-in, during which associates can discuss their goals and how they believe they are doing with a partner in their department. Annual reviews are more substantive and provide associates with an in-depth assessment of how they are doing, based on a competency rubric that clarifies expectations and provides a career roadmap for young lawyers at each tenure level. Further, Foley Hoag augments formal review guidance with both formal and informal follow-up and check-ins. Mentors meet with their respective mentees shortly after the review has been delivered to discuss their mentee's feedback, goals and action plan. Associates are also encouraged to create a board of advisers who will provide guidance on both specific review feedback and day-to-day work and career management concerns. Additionally, department chairs and supervising partners are encouraged to provide ongoing feedback throughout the year. The professional development department is also available to provide ongoing, confidential guidance and support to attorneys with their action plans, and in their overall career development and success. This constant feedback loop review process is extremely valuable to associates, who say: "it helps you to understand your path at the firm, as well as what it takes to get there." Especially early in young lawyers' careers, this understanding is essential to their interest in remaining at the firm. In fact, sharing knowledge about associates' promotion potential over time may help to boost a firm's retention rate. Accordingly, a firm should try to provide regular feedback, ideally through a formal process to ensure that all associates receive it and are assessed using the same measures.

(b) *Explicit evaluation expectations*
Another important aspect of any firm's evaluation and promotion system is setting explicit expectations. Foley Hoag shares its competency model with associates, so that they understand what the firm expects of them at any given level of experience. During the annual review process, the firm also compiles a 'nutshell' – a summary of supervising attorneys' feedback about a particular associate, which is then given to the associate during the review. By making both general and individual expectations explicit, the firm takes much of the guesswork and fear of doing badly out of associates' self-assessments. It also allows associates to know exactly what they, in particular, should focus on. This addresses millennial associates' fears about lacking development opportunities. Clarity about what is expected of each associate allows associates to understand what they must do to progress at the firm, feeding into the millennial associate's desire for attaining leadership roles. The structure also empowers associates – it tells them exactly how, and on what, they will be evaluated, thus allowing them greater ability to focus on improving and developing competencies that the firm has identified as essential, rather than being concerned about how different partners might value different traits or what might come up in a review. Many millennials mentioned that explicit expectations were important to them; one said:
> knowing what to do each year, what opportunities to be looking for, and the preparation process for getting there early on keeps people engaged because they know what they're working towards.

(c) *Coaches' role in ensuring effective reviews*
The optimal evaluation systems require more than just regular evaluations and clear expectations. Firms should consider putting measures in place to make sure that any feedback given to associates is effective (ie, specific, clear and understandable) so that associates may apply it to their future development, understand how they are doing and where they can improve, as well as why they are given or not given a promotion. This is an area in which firm leaders must actively play the role of coach. They should create the environment for investing time in order to make evaluations an effective firm mechanism, as well as to foster a culture that values providing frequent informal feedback. This is, in fact, an extremely important part of an effective system – lawyers at a large global firm noted the difficulties of using a system when partners took an idiosyncratic approach to following it and pushed back on the responsibilities the programme asked of them. However, if coaches help to unify feedback, this will appeal to millennial lawyers' desire for more frequent feedback, as well as for empowering management. Foley Hoag's system focuses on this coaching aspect. The firm's director of professional development encourages supervising

lawyers to give very specific feedback, which is formally conveyed to associates during their annual reviews. If a lawyer offers general feedback, the director or the partner writing the review nutshell presses for a more detailed explanation, going back to them to ask for elaboration on what associates do well and what they can improve on. The professional development department runs firm training on writing strong self-assessments, providing effective feedback and responding positively to feedback. It also provides templates to guide the feedback-writing process, which include specific examples of what good and less helpful feedback look like. Associates appreciate this, describing their review experiences as very positive and saying that the feedback was concrete, with an eye towards producing a development plan for the associate's next year. They credit the firm's commitment to providing effective feedback as helping them to better understand what their future at the firm is and how to get where they want to go. This greatly addresses millennials' desire for empowering management and leadership roles, as well as their fears of lacking development opportunities. Offering associates detailed guidance on what they can improve in, as well as recommendations for how to do this, can give associates a strong sense of autonomy in their careers. They are essentially being handed detailed instructions on how to succeed, which they can choose to implement.

3.3   *Pro bono* programme

We believe that a firm's *pro bono* programme can address several millennial associates' preferences. First, it can satisfy young lawyers' desire for challenging work. By carefully filtering matters, a firm can ensure that associates receive matters that give them increased responsibility and experience in areas that they are interested in exploring. Secondly, because there is no pressure coming from a paying client, *pro bono* matters are an opportunity to give associates more independence, fostering in them a stronger sense of autonomy and flexibility to maintain a work-life balance. Thirdly, by allowing associates to explore areas beyond their practice group, it might help to lessen their fear of lacking development opportunities. Additionally, a firm could potentially use an associate's performance on a *pro bono* matter to assess the associate's managing abilities – a benefit for both the firm and the associate. We explore below some of the aspects of a firm's *pro bono* programme that leader-architects can design to help address millennials' needs and areas where leader-coaches are most likely to make a difference.

(a)   *Devoted* pro bono *coordinator*

Creating a role for a full-time staff member committed to running the firm's *pro bono* programme can greatly increase the programme's effectiveness. One firm that does this particularly well is Squire Patton Boggs, which has two full-time *pro bono* coordinators, as well as a part-time *pro bono* partner. The coordinators are an effective resource for associates seeking out particular types of work. Having staff devoted to filtering and finding *pro bono* matters ensures that a firm can offer associates a wide range of matters to choose from. The best *pro bono* programmes appeal to associates by allowing them to explore different practice areas, take on more responsibility for a matter than they would with a paying client and develop and strengthen their legal skills. In fact, associates laud firm *pro bono* programmes for allowing them to get significant experience early on in a wide range of areas. Coordinators can help to further these goals – one associate said:

> the pro bono *coordinator links up people and finds partners with special expertise for specific types of matter requests. She's been with the firm for a long time and is great at getting people in touch – she knows who works on which cases and whether there are opportunities to help out on those.*

Several aspects of a coordinator's role directly address millennial associates' needs. First, offering a diverse range of matters satisfies the millennial' desire for challenging work. By having an individual who can filter through potential *pro bono* matters and actively solicit matters in particular areas that associates may desire, a firm can ensure that it offers associates options for work that will actively challenge them beyond what they are normally given. This filtering is important not only for particular legal fields, but for allowing associates to choose between *pro bono* matters with varying levels of difficulty, so as to allow associates to assess which are the best fit for them. Secondly, a coordinator putting an associate and partner with special expertise in touch can help associates feel as if they have empowering management. Having an experienced person to consult about issues that arise during a matter gives an associate the ability to take on a challenging assignment with the assurance that he will be able to use a partner's technical expertise if necessary. The availability of a leader-coach grants associates more flexibility to develop their skills, without the worry of taking on an overwhelming project.

(b) *Voluntary participation in* pro bono *matters*

Allowing associates to choose whether or not they take part in *pro bono* matters is particularly important because of the millennial associate's focus on maintaining a work-life balance. Designing a programme where an associate may choose which *pro bono* matters to participate in is likely to foster a sense of autonomy in the associate's mind. Doing so sends the message that the associate has more influence over his day-to-day activities, giving the associate the understanding that the firm allows flexibility for how associates spend their days. A number of associates discussed their engagement with *pro bono* work, with one saying:

> I have worked on fascinating and rewarding cases with the firm's full support. They have formal programmes which they take pride in . . . [but] are also open to alternative forms of pro bono *and supported a* pro bono *matter I carried over from work in law school.*[5]

Another said:

> I don't think of pro bono *matters differently than billables – I still pull out all of the stops, work for an incredible partner, and have the same feeling of working for a corporate client . . . but I like the feeling that I'm doing good – it ends up having a positive halo effect on everything that you get to do.*

Associates also appreciate choosing which *pro bono* matters they work on because

---

5   Vault (2015), *Foley Hoag LLP: Vault's Verdict*, retrieved from www.vault.com/company-profiles/law/foley-hoag-llp/company-reviews.

they can look for projects that allow them to develop specific skills that they might not experience doing billable work. This helps to diminish typical fears about limited development opportunities. For instance, junior associates talked about handling the entire incorporation process for a company or managing an entire case, which they described as "great experience that you'd never get this early on for a paying client". In contrast, a firm requiring associates to do a minimum number of *pro bono* hours each year may diminish the positive effect of taking part in the work. One associate at such a firm mentioned one year during which she had got into trouble for not doing enough *pro bono* work. Towards the end of the year, she had to increase her *pro bono* hours and turn down other work, a difficult balance she noted: "if a partner has a deal that's going to close and you say that you're working on *pro bono*, they're not going to be happy." After this experience, she said that having to complete a certain number of hours made the *pro bono* work feel like another task to complete, rather than a valuable opportunity to develop legal skills. This change in perceptions of the work underscores the importance of associates having flexibility about which *pro bono* matters to take part in. Maintaining flexibility helps associates to frame their *pro bono* work as a positive and implies that they have more control over their work-life balance and career development opportunities.

(c) **Billable hour credit for** pro bono **work**

A system that allows associates to credit their *pro bono* hours towards their yearly billable hour minimum further strengthens their sense of autonomy. Realistically, such systems are likely to include a cap on the number of *pro bono* hours that can count towards the associate's target, although the experience of many firms suggests that a maximum might not be necessary. In fact, an associate at a firm with uncapped *pro bono* credit noted that while there was not a formal maximum, "at the end of the day, it's pretty clear what has to be done … at some point, you're impacting people's perceptions of you if you spend too much time on *pro bono*". But, by knowing she would be able to get billable credit, the associate felt that she was "encouraged to take opportunities that help make you a better lawyer". Being able to take on such matters, without a concern that they will take time away from meeting the yearly billable hour minimum, can help to mitigate associates' fears about development opportunities. Of course, *pro bono* work allows young lawyers to explore different practice areas and develop their legal skills, but by offering billable hour credit, a firm also provides associates with an incentive to take on more challenging work while also fulfilling all of their responsibilities on billable matters. Further, although it may be an unusual occurrence, one associate noted that during the transition into his firm, his department was having a somewhat slow year, which he was able to supplement by taking on *pro bono* matters that were very relevant to his practice area. Such an experience allowed the associate to focus on refining skills and legal knowledge specific to his practice area when he had the extra time, without the concern that he might do poorly in his annual review for failing to meet the billable minimum. When the practice group's work picked up, the associate was able to take on increasing responsibility; further, having a slow year had not scared him into leaving the firm for another, busier one.

Accordingly, in addition to addressing millennial preferences, associates' billable credit for *pro bono* hours helps the firm's goals. Associates feel encouraged to take on substantive opportunities to develop and strengthen their legal skills. They thus take on challenging work to refine their talents and gain a stronger familiarity with processes in matters where the firm does not have to worry about a client later disputing the billed work. One associate said: "I feel very satisfied doing *pro bono* work – I like being able to handle a matter from front to back, and taking it to a good resolution is a real confidence builder." Further, *pro bono* matters can also serve as an assessment of associate ability. One associate mentioned:

> pro bono *is a good way to gauge how an associate is doing. Partners sometimes bring in their own cases and ask associates if they're able to help on it … seeing their performance helps partners to trust those associates with more responsibility on billable matters.*

A firm's *pro bono* programme thus has the potential to serve as a great training ground that dually addresses millennial needs and firm goals, but it requires leadership in both the architect and coach roles.

(d)   *Coaches' role in supporting* pro bono *work*

A firm's *pro bono* programme is also a great area for partners to act as coaches and reinforce a culture of 'giving back'. Although many associates recognise the benefits of *pro bono* work, some individuals need encouragement. For instance, one associate said she did not find *pro bono* work very satisfying, because the cases were "logistically complicated and you have to figure out everything on your own without a lot of guidance". Associates experiencing such challenges with *pro bono* work might need some additional support – perhaps a coordinator can help to match them with better-suited matters or a supervising partner might be able to step in and offer more assistance with working through any obstacles that arise during the *pro bono* work. But beyond this, many partners can feel pressured by the economic demands of firms and thus put aside *pro bono* work to focus solely on revenue generation. Firm leaders can act as coaches here as well – leading by example to emphasise that the firm supports investing more time into public service and to help reshape firm culture to do the same, as well as to recognise the substantial opportunities *pro bono* work provides for young lawyers to develop and use their legal skills.[6]

4.   Conclusion

Today's law firm leaders have the opportunity to create a distinct sort of competitive advantage by becoming the employer of choice for high-quality associates. By better understanding millennials – especially acknowledging the difference between their motivation and those of earlier generations – law firm leaders can find ways to alter their current systems and culture in order to attract, retain, develop and promote the millennial talent that will soon help guide the firm into the future. The firm's senior

---

6   BW Heineman, Jr, WF Lee and DB Wilkins, "Lawyers as Professionals and as Citizens: Key Roles and Responsibilities in the 21st Century" (2014), retrieved from https://clp.law.harvard.edu/assets/Professionalism-Project-Essay_11.20.14.pdf.

leaders can play the role of architect by redesigning the formal systems and processes to provide experiences that millennials will find more enriching and rewarding. We should also note that leaders in the business support groups such as professional development, recruiting and other functions play a critical role in engineering better systems. The architect role should not be limited to lawyers alone.

In addition, leaders acting as coaches are essential for supporting the kinds of changes that architects design. Their willingness to support associates' *pro bono* work, guide associates' career development and provide timely, honest, constructive feedback is essential for building a culture that will help millennials to thrive. The coaching role should certainly not be limited to lawyers with formal leadership roles; indeed, every partner should feel the responsibility for playing a coaching role for the associates they work with.

While this chapter has argued for the changes based on accommodating preferences of the millennial generation, we close by noting that most of the modifications simply make good business sense. Organisations around the world – including many of your own clients – know that they get significant value by providing effective performance management including clear expectations, regular feedback and fair promotion systems. Research also clearly documents the value that firms get when their employees perform community service or *pro bono* work. It shows that employees who do so are more committed to their work, more productive in terms of revenue and business development, more willing to help their colleagues and less likely to quit.[7] In short, by considering these proposed changes and supporting them as both architects and coaches, today's law firm leaders have the opportunity to make lasting changes that will strengthen their firms for the long run. Ultimately, these changes should allow firms to win the war for talent by attracting, retaining and promoting the highest-value talent who will become tomorrow's leaders – the generation known as millennials.

---

7   Adam Grant, *Give and Take* (New York, Penguin Group, 2014). Moynihan, Donald P, Thomas DeLeire and Kohei Enami, "A Life Worth Living: Evidence on the Relationship Between Prosocial Values and Happiness", *The American Review of Public Administration*, May 2015; vol 45, 3: pp 311–326.

Leading by mentoring: lawyers' professional responsibility – and public duty – to mentor

Cory Way
Harvard University

1.   Introduction

Mentoring has become an increasingly vogue topic for managers in businesses and organisations. But the focus has been directed mostly towards industries and professions other than law, which has received comparatively little attention. This neglect is disappointing – and even dangerous – because legal mentoring is crucial for the profession and the public. In this chapter, I argue that lawyers have both a professional responsibility and civic duty to mentor their junior colleagues, and that mentoring is therefore a critical aspect of leadership for lawyers. I also raise the possibility that many attorneys are currently failing in their obligations to one another – and to society. The good news, however, is that with just modest effort the profession can change. I conclude with some practical action items for all lawyers – but especially those who lead law firms and legal organisations – to improve legal mentoring in the profession.

Before I begin, let me sketch a roadmap for the discussion in this chapter. First, I outline why all this matters. What are the potential benefits of mentoring? Why do many organisations voluntarily promote mentoring, even in the absence of any requirements to do so? Is there an even higher purpose for mentoring in the legal profession, transcending the considerable individual and institutional advantages?

Secondly, I argue (for the first time, as far as I am aware) that lawyers have an affirmative, professional responsibility to mentor. I analyse important provisions of the American Bar Association's Code of Professional Conduct, and I briefly reflect upon similar codes for solicitors and barristers in the United Kingdom.

Thirdly, I suggest that too many lawyers – in the United States and abroad – do not understand or recognise their obligations. I share some preliminary survey results that reveal lawyers' experiences with – and attitudes towards – mentoring in the legal profession. I opine that many lawyers are failing their colleagues – as well as society. Nevertheless, I optimistically conclude that – with relatively minor effort on the part of all lawyers (including, significantly, law firm leaders and their wider set of partners) – maximum gains can be realised from mentoring for attorneys, the legal system and the public.

2. Organisational incentives to mentor

Mentoring in the legal profession is important because research in other industries suggests positive results for protégés, mentors and organisations. While mentoring research can vary in quality and conclusions, several themes have emerged suggesting positive effects for most stakeholders. With respect to protégés, for example, empirical research suggests that mentoring relationships often yield "positive career outcomes"[1] including increased pay,[2] promotions,[3] mobility,[4] job satisfaction[5] and organisational socialisation,[6] as well as decreased stress[7] and turnover intentions.[8] Apart from these benefits (presumably generalisable to many professions), some lawyers have argued that "mastery of client relations, negotiation, litigation strategy and counseling [are] especially amendable to education through mentoring", which also "socializes new lawyers into the profession and develops their ethical judgment by providing opportunities for a relational 'moral dialogue' with experienced practitioners".[9]

Researchers and practitioners have also suggested significant benefits for mentors across professions and industries.[10] In addition to burnishing their managerial skills,[11] mentors receive from protégés valuable workplace information,[12] a loyal support base,[13] inspiration and energy[14] and even a sense of immortality[15] – all of which can

1   Belle Rose Ragins and John Cotton, "Mentor Functions and Outcomes: A Comparison of Men and Women in Formal and Informal Mentoring Relationships" (1999) 84 *Journal of Applied Psychology* 529.

2   See, for example, T Allen, L Eby, M Poteet, E Lentz and L Lima, "Career Benefits Associated with Mentoring for Protégés: A Meta-Analysis" (2004) 89 *Journal of Applied Psychology* 127.

3   See, for example, Allen et al, "Career Benefits Associated with Mentoring for Protégés: A Meta-Analysis" (2004) 89 *Journal of Applied Psychology* 127; Terri Scandura, "Mentorship and Career Mobility: An Empirical Investigation" (1992) 13 *Journal of Organizational Behavior* 169.

4   Terri Scandura, "Mentorship and Career Mobility: An Empirical Investigation" (1992) 13 *Journal of Organizational Behavior* 169.

5   Allen et al "Career Benefits Associated with Mentoring for Protégés: A Meta-Analysis" (2004) 89 *Journal of Applied Psychology* 127; C Koberg, R Boss, D Chappell and R Ringer, "Correlates and Consequences of Protégé Mentoring in a Large Hospital" (1994) 19 *Group and Organization Management* 219.

6   C Ostroff and S Kozlowski, "The Role of Mentoring in the Information Gathering Processes of Newcomers During Early Organizational Socialization" (1993) 42 *Journal of Vocational Behavior* 170.

7   See, for example, K Kram and D Hall, "Mentoring as an Antidote to Stress During Corporate Trauma" (1991) 28 *Human Resource Management* 493.

8   Terri Scandura and R Viator, "Mentoring in Public Accounting Firms: An Analysis of Mentor-Protege Relationships, Mentoring Functions, and Protégé Turnover Intentions" (1994) 19 *Accounting, Organization and Society* 717.

9   Veronica Ashenhurst, "Mentoring the Lawyer, Past and Present: Some Reflections" (2010–2011) 42 *Ottawa Law Review* 125, 130–131 (and sources cited therein).

10   See, generally, T Allen, "Mentoring Relationships from the Perspective of the Mentor" in Belle Rose Ragins and Kathy Kram (eds), *The Handbook of Mentoring at Work* (Thousand Oaks: Sage, 2007); see also R Burke and C McKeen, "Benefits of Mentoring Relationships Among Managerial and Professional Women: A Cautionary Tale" (1997) 51 *Journal of Vocational Behavior* 43; Belle Rose Ragins and Terri Scandura, "Gender Differences in Expected Outcomes of Mentoring Relationships" (1994) 37 *Academy of Management Journal* 957; D Hunt and C Michael, "Mentorship: A Career Training and Development Tool" (1983) 8 *Academy of Management Review* 475.

11   L Eby and A Lockwood, "Protégés' and Mentors' Reactions to Participating in Formal Mentoring Programs: A Qualitative Investigation" (2005) 67 *Journal of Vocational Behavior* 441.

12   E Mullen, "Framing the Mentoring Relationship as an Information Exchange" (1994) 4 *Human Resource Management Review* 257.

13   See K Kram, *Mentoring at Work: Development Relationships in Organizational Life* (Glenview: Scott, Foresman and Co, 1985).

14   See Thomas Dougherty, Daniel Turban and Dana Haggard, "Naturally Occurring Mentoring Relationships Involving Workplace Employees," in Tammy D Allen and Lillian T Eby (eds), *The Blackwell Handbook of Mentoring: A Multiple Perspectives Approach* (Oxford: Blackwell, 2007), at 139-140.

15   E Erikson, *Childhood and Society* 2nd edn (New York: WW Norton & Co, 1963).

also improve the mentor's work performance.[16] In the legal profession, more specifically, it has been argued that mentoring "validates senior lawyers' professional experience, but also challenges them to improve relational skills such as listening, providing criticism and generating trust", whereby "in turn, mentors gain fresh insight, a loyal support base and a chance to give back to the profession".[17]

Where an organisation shows high levels of support for mentoring, academics and practitioners have suggested important benefits for the organisation, including:

- employee acclimation (and commitment);
- increased workplace skills;
- employee diversity (and support for underrepresented groups);
- staff perceptions of fairness;[18]
- improved succession planning; and
- increased relationship building throughout the organisation.

If mentoring relationships create the potential for such significant benefits for individuals and institutions, one might expect to see mentoring warmly and widely embraced in the legal profession – in particular, by the leaders of law firms and legal organisations. But is it? There has been surprisingly little empirical research regarding mentoring in the legal profession in the United States. But Fiona Kay has examined mentoring in the Canadian legal profession in several empirical studies. In 2009 Kay and her co-authors found that when protégés had a "layering of mentors" – that is, informal mentors in addition to formally assigned mentors – this arrangement "yielded tremendous benefits to new professionals including: earnings, career progress, procedural justice, value of work and job satisfaction".[19] Kay and her co-authors also found that "the effects of mentoring begin early on in the socialization process, well before a long-term mentoring relationship is firmly established".[20] Finally, Kay and her co-authors found that "career mentor functions to be pivotal to both career success and professional happiness of new entrants to law; while psychosocial mentor functions took on growing importance as careers evolved among more experienced lawyers".[21]

---

16 See, for example, Kram, *Mentoring at Work: Development Relationships in Organizational Life* (1985) (suggesting that protégés loyalty and support can lead to improved mentor performance at an organisation).

17 Ashenhurst, "Mentoring the Lawyer, Past and Present: Some Reflections" (2010–2011) 42 *Ottawa Law Review* 132.

18 See, for example, Terri A Scandura and Ekin K Pellegrini, "Workplace Mentoring: Theoretical Approaches and Methodological Issues," in Tammy D Allen and Lillian T Eby (eds), *The Blackwell Handbook of Mentoring: A Multiple Perspectives Approach* (Oxford: Blackwell, 2007), at 80-81. J Colquitt, "On the Dimensionality of Organizational Justice: A Construct Validation of a Measure" (2001) 86(3) *Journal of Applied Psychology* 386; E Fagenson-Eland, M Marks and K Amendola, "Perceptions of Mentoring Relationships" (1997) 51 *Journal of Vocational Behavior* 29.

19 Fiona Kay, John Hagan and Patricia Parker, "Principals in Practice: The Importance of Mentorship in the Early Stages of Career Development" (2009) 31 *Law & Policy* 69, 90.

20 Kay, Hagan and Parker, "Principals in Practice: The Importance of Mentorship in the Early Stages of Career Development" (2009) 31 *Law & Policy* 91. See also Cheri Ostroff and Steve Kozlowski, "The Role of Mentoring in the Information Gathering Process of Newcomers During Early Organizational Socialization" (1993) 42 *Journal of Vocational Behavior* 170 (similarly finding that mentoring's career benefits occur early in the socialisation process); but see Kram, *Mentoring at Work: Development Relationships in Organizational Life* (1985) (assuming that mentoring's career benefits occur after initial socialisation is complete).

21 Kay, Hagan and Parker, "Principals in Practice: The Importance of Mentorship in the Early Stages of Career Development" (2009) 31 *Law & Policy* 91.

While these findings are perhaps suggestive for lawyers in the United States and other countries, it is important to emphasise that legal training in the United States (and other nations) is not identical to the Canadian experience, and further research could greatly help illuminate the unique advantages of legal mentoring in a wider range of jurisdictions.

3.   Lawyers' professional responsibility to mentor

I have argued elsewhere that there is no particularly strong tradition of robust mentoring in the Anglo-American legal profession.[22] The English Inns of Court – with splendid facilities and fanfare similar to Oxford colleges – were less impressive with respect to meaningful, long-term mentoring. One lawyer colourfully observed that the requirement to train at the Inns amounted merely to consuming "so many legs of mutton" in the dining hall, with few other substantive elements (see figure 1).[23]

Figure 1: Satisfying English bar admission requirements through consuming "so many legs of mutton" ("Middle Temple Hall – The Benchers and Members 'Taking Commons'", engraving by Thomas Hosmer and Henry Melville, 1841) (Government Art Collection, UK Department for Culture, Media and Sport).

---

22   See Cory Way, *Mentoring Lawyers: Why the Profession Fails itself and Society, and How it Can Change* [forthcoming]. While this section primarily focuses on the legal profession in England and the United States, the principles discussed arguably apply more broadly.

23   Daniel O'Connell, quoted in Gordon Bigelow, Review of *Tristam Kennedy and the Revival of Irish Legal Training* (1999/2000) 42 *Victorian Studies* 347.

One could be forgiven for assuming that a more intimate apprenticeship system in early America would have yielded more intense, long-term bonds between mentors and protégés. But much evidence suggests otherwise. Future US President John Adams complained of his apprenticeship with lawyer James Putnam, noting "I feel the Disadvantages of Putnams Insociability, and neglect of me". Adams wrote that "[h]ad [Putnam] given me now and then a few Hints concerning Practice, I should be able to judge better at this Hour than I can now".[24] Adams would later complain that Putnam simply did not adequately train him for law practice, and as a newly minted lawyer he fretted that his legal documents were "unclerklike" and unworthy of the profession.[25]

US Supreme Court Justice Joseph Story (also Harvard Law School's first Dane Professor of Law) was similarly frustrated that his apprenticeship amounted to "monasticism" because his mentor, Samuel Sewell, was also routinely absent and neglectful. "I wept bitterly," Story dramatically wrote in a letter, after he had no choice but to tackle one notoriously difficult law text without Sewell's guidance. "My tears dropped upon the book, and stained its pages."[26]

When law firms emerged to replace the apprenticeship system in the late nineteenth and early twentieth centuries, there was no strong universal tradition of legal mentoring upon which to draw. Dissatisfaction among lawyers with their training and practice therefore continued, with one attorney penning a forceful indictment of his profession in the *American Mercury* in 1936. His missive was entitled, simply, "Don't Be a Lawyer". He observed (with somewhat misplaced nostalgia) that "no longer is the average clerk taken under the wing of his preceptor", and even when such relationships do occur, "it is only the most perfunctory obeisance to an ancient rule".[27] It was argued, therefore, that the leaders and partners of these emerging law firms did not assume – let alone recognise – any formal duty to mentor their young attorneys. Most lawyers were simply left to sink or swim.

Not much appears to have materially changed over the following decades. In the early 1960s one former associate complained that law firm life continued to be "too impersonal". He left his firm to become a law professor, noting that "I wanted more social primary relationship – in my observation, very few of the thirty partners had much social contact with each other", and "there was very little close contact between the associates and the partners".[28] In fact, the "main reason" this associate left law practice was "my feeling that the practice of law should be personal and that you should have close contact with your partners".[29]

During the twentieth century the legal apprentice morphed fully into the law firm associate. Each new lawyer benefited from a more structured and sophisticated

---

24   *Diary and Autobiography of John Adams*, LH Butterfied (ed.) (1964), Vol. 1, p 63, reprinted in Steve Sheppard, "Why Study the History of Law Schools" in Steve Sheppard (ed.), *The History of Legal Education in the United States: Commentaries and Primary Sources* vol. I (Pasadena: Salem Press, 1999), pp 93–105.
25   Quoted in David McCullough, *John Adams* (New York: Simon & Schuster, 2001), p 45.
26   Joseph Story, Letter to William Story (January 23, 1831), reprinted as "Autobiography" in William Story (ed.), *Miscellaneous Writings of Joseph Story* (Boston: Charles C Little and James Brown, 1852), p 19.
27   Anonymous, "Don't be a Lawyer", *American Mercury* (January 1936), pp 33–34.
28   Quoted in Erwin O. Smigel, *The Wall Street Lawyer: Professional Organizational Man?* (London: Collier-Macmillan Ltd, 1964), p 76.
29   Quoted in *id.*

university system of legal education, and many law offices and bar associations improved training opportunities for young lawyers. Twentieth-century lawyers were therefore, on the whole, almost certainly better prepared for the practice of law than their earlier counterparts. But the prevalence of meaningful, long-term personal mentoring in the American legal profession remains largely an open question. Anecdotal evidence suggests that while education and training have almost certainly improved, meaningful individual mentoring continues to be the exception, and not the rule. And when such mentoring occurs, it is often the result of idiosyncratic individual initiative, not of organisational programming and leadership.

Concurrent with – and perhaps as a direct result of – many of these twentieth-century developments, the American Bar Association performed some soul-searching and updated its 1908 Canon of Ethics, which contained very little that could be held to apply to legal mentoring. The ABA's new Code of Professional Responsibility, which replaces the 1908 Canon of Ethics, features at least four Canons that apply (explicitly or implicitly) to legal mentoring.[30] Each of these Canons – Canon 1, 6, 8 and 9 – is briefly discussed below. Moreover, even the Code's preliminary statement highlights the duty of lawyers – and those who lead lawyers – to assume responsibility for the conduct and competence of others, noting that "a lawyer should ultimately be responsible for the conduct of his employees and associates in the course of the professional representation of the client".[31] Senior lawyers – and those who lead legal organisations – are therefore held directly "responsible for the conduct of [their] employees and associates". As analysed more fully below, effective legal mentoring is required to fulfil these ethical and professional responsibilities.

ABA Canon 1: A lawyer should assist in maintaining the integrity and competence of the legal profession

Lawyers – and those who lead lawyers – must maintain the integrity and competence of the profession. Canon 1's Ethical Consideration 1-1 (EC 1-1) explains that "a basic tenet of the professional responsibility of lawyers is that every person in our society should have ready access to the independent professional services of a lawyer of integrity and competence"). EC 1-1 affirmatively asserts that "maintaining the integrity and improving the competence of the bar to meet the highest standards is the ethical responsibility of every lawyer". Proper mentoring of younger lawyers invariably assists in improving their competence, and in the integrity of the bar more generally. EC 1-2 explores the same concept but from a different perspective, instructing that "the public should be protected from those who are ... deficien[t] in education or moral standards". While this provision seeks to protect the public from non-lawyers who attempt to practise, it also extends to include lawyers who lack

---

30   The Code contains three broad categories of ethical instructions: Canons (statements of axiomatic norms), Ethical Considerations (ECs) (objectives towards which every member of the profession should strive) and Disciplinary Rules (DCs) (mandatory rules uniformly applied to all lawyers). Notwithstanding these differences, all of the above "define the type of ethical conduct that the public has a *right to expect*" of lawyers. American Bar Association, Model Code of Professional Responsibility, Preliminary Statement (emphasis supplied).

31   *Id.*

proper training to perform their responsibilities properly. As a result, attorneys who are aware of fellow members of the profession – whether in their own organisation or in any context – who are deficient in education or character, should protect the public, and one possibility to accomplish this is through legal mentoring. Indeed, as EC 1-2 instructs, "the bar has a positive obligation to aid in the continued improvement of all phases of pre-admission and post-admission legal education". Finally, Canon 1's EC 1-5 notes the general admonition that "a lawyer should maintain high standards of professional conduct and should encourage fellow lawyers to do likewise". Again, mentoring is a crucial vehicle by which to accomplish this responsibility.

ABA Canon 6: A lawyer should represent a client competently

"Because of his vital role in the legal process, a lawyer should act with competence", according to EC 6-1, which instructs that a lawyer "should strive to become and remain proficient in his practice". Not only does an individual lawyer have a responsibility to ensure his competency to represent a client, but senior members of the profession also have a responsibility to ensure that junior members are competent. This is particularly important if the lawyers work together in the same organisation and therefore share collective responsibility to provide competent counsel to their clients. EC 6-2 further provides that "a lawyer is aided in attaining and maintaining his competence by … continuing legal education … and by utilizing other available means". Among other things, a lawyer should therefore seek to become a protégé in a mentoring relationship (or relationships) throughout his career, in order to ensure that he "remain[s] proficient in his practice". And all lawyers should assume a positive obligation to help their juniors remain proficient by serving as mentors. Significantly, EC 6-2 also provides:

> [A lawyer] has the additional ethical obligation to assist in improving the legal profession, and he may be do so by participating in bar activities intended to advance the quality and standards of members of the profession. Of particular importance is the careful training of his younger associates and the giving of sound guidance to all lawyers who consult him. In short, a lawyer should strive at all levels to aid the legal profession in advancing the highest possible standards of integrity and competence and to meet those standards himself (emphases supplied).

EC 6-2 is perhaps the strongest statement in the Code with application to legal mentoring, emphasising the "particular importance" of "careful training of … younger associates". This requires, in my view, legal mentoring involving long-term, meaningful personal relationships. Mentoring defined in this way[32] constitutes more than merely coaching for a particular assignment or client; it involves a long-term investment in the career of the junior lawyer and his role in the profession generally. The most effective legal mentoring (or any mentoring, for that matter), should therefore transcend the parochial and pecuniary interests of an organisation. The

---

32 For a more detailed argument that the entire concept of mentoring needs to be reimagined and redefined, see Way, *Mentoring Lawyers: Why the Profession Fails itself and Society, and How it Can Change* [forthcoming].

focus should remain on the younger lawyer, his long-term acquisition of skills and professional ethics, and civic duty to clients and the public. Only through this broader concept of mentoring can members of the profession truly attain the "highest possible standards of integrity and competence" required by the Code.

ABA Canon 8: A lawyer should assist in improving the legal system

Among other observations, Canon 8 notes that "the fair administration of justice requires the availability of competent lawyers" (EC 8-3) and that "judges and administrative officials having adjudicatory powers ought to be persons of integrity, competence, and suitable temperament" (EC 8-6). Lawyers must therefore assist in the creation – and selection – of competent attorneys who will, in turn, serve in important leadership roles in the legal system. As EC 8-6 notes, this is particularly important for judicial and adjudicatory positions. But it is also critical for every lawyer. Indeed, one of the unique aspects of the US legal profession is that every member serves in a public leadership capacity as an officer of the court. This public leadership role is facilitated by the state itself, and all lawyers swear an oath to faithfully execute these public responsibilities upon licensure. Ensuring that these officers of the court are competent – and continue to remain so – is of singular importance to the legal system, the profession, citizens participating in legal matters and the public generally.[33]

ABA Canon 9: A lawyer should avoid even the appearance of professional impropriety

Similarly, EC-9 observes that "every lawyer owes a solemn duty to uphold the integrity and honor of his profession". Naturally, this can – and should – be accomplished by many means, but legal mentoring is certainly a crucial method by which lawyers can directly "uphold the integrity and honor" of their profession. EC-9 also requires lawyers

> to observe the Code of Professional Responsibility; to act as a member of a learned profession, one dedicated to public service; to cooperate with his brother lawyers in supporting the organized bar ...; to conduct himself so as to reflect credit on the legal profession and to inspire the confidence, respect, and trust of his clients and the public
> ...

These requirements (cooperating with "brother lawyers" to support the organised bar, conducting oneself in a way that brings credit to the profession and inspires

---

33   EC 8-7 also explains that "[s]ince lawyers are a vital part of the legal system, they should be persons of integrity, of professional skill, and of *dedication to the improvement of the system*". This requires assisting in the selection and mentoring of "persons of integrity" and "professional skill". EC 8-7 adds that lawyers should therefore "protect the public by *insuring that those who practice law are qualified to do so*". Again, this must apply not only to the selection of new entrants to the profession, but also to licensed attorneys at every stage of their career. Because "lawyers are especially qualified to recognize deficiencies in the legal system" (EC 8-1), whether institutional or individual, they have an affirmative obligation to improve the legal system by addressing the deficiencies. Lawyers must not merely report, but also repair. That is, in order to truly *improve* the legal system, as required by Canon 8, lawyers must assist one another in *improving* their competencies as officers of the court. Non-lawyers lack the professional perspective to fully perform this task, making the role and responsibility of lawyers even greater in this regard.

confidence in clients and the public) simply cannot be fully realised without robust leadership and mentoring from senior lawyers.

While the American Code of Professional Responsibility has several areas that implicate legal mentoring, similar codes for solicitors and barristers in England appear to have fewer. But the English provisions arguably link their duties even more explicitly to those who lead law firms and similar organisations. And like their American counterparts, legal mentoring is necessary for the most effective satisfaction of the mandates.

In the *Solicitors Regulation Authority Handbook* (October 2014), for example, "Chapter 7: Management of your business", requires that solicitors who manage a practice "must achieve these outcomes":

O(7.6) you train individuals working in the firm to maintain a level of competence appropriate to their work and level of responsibility;

...

O(7.8) you have a system for supervising clients' *matters, to include the regular checking of the quality of work by suitably competent and experienced people ...* (emphases in original).

These provisions specifically reference training, competence and experience, outcomes that arguably cannot be fully achieved without effective legal mentoring.

For barristers, *The Bar Standards Board Handbook* (January 2014) similarly requires the following outcome in "Chapter 5: You and your practice":

oC24 Your practice is run competently ... Your employees, pupils and *trainees understand, and do, what is required of them in order that you meet your obligations under this Handbook* (emphases in original) (p 56).

The Bar Standards Handbook also includes the following rule in "Chapter 5.2: Administration and conduct of self-employed practice":

rC87 You must take reasonable steps to ensure that ... your practice is efficiently and properly administered having regard to the nature of your practice (p 62).

Again, in order to best satisfy this obligation, a lawyer should engage in meaningful mentoring for those in his practice. In addition to such provisions dealing with competence and efficiency, the Bar Standards Handbook specifically addresses lawyer training in the context of "duties of pupil supervisors", which includes the following rule:

rQ54 A pupil supervisor must when responsible for supervising any pupil ... take all reasonable steps to provide the pupil with adequate tuition, supervision and experience (p 149 in "Section B: Bar Training Rules" under "B5: The Professional Stage").

It is important to note that rQ54 applies only to pupil supervisors when they have assumed responsibility for training. The Bar Standards Handbook does not appear to require other barristers to "take all reasonable steps" to provide younger lawyers with "supervision and experience", unless in the context of ensuring the competency of their own employees. The same appears true for solicitors, as indicated above. Any implicit requirement to mentor in England, therefore, appears to be limited to lawyers with specific duties for training and/or for those who have managerial authority in an organisational setting.

4.   Legal mentoring: perceptions and practice

Do lawyers themselves believe that they have a special responsibility to mentor? I asked this question to lawyers worldwide in a survey published online and sponsored by Harvard Law School's Center on the Legal Profession. The exact question posed was: "Do you believe that lawyers have professional responsibility to mentor new lawyers?" Of the 604 people who answered the question, 79.1% answered affirmatively. When restricted only to US law firm partners, the percentage answering 'yes' was 81.0%. Interestingly, the number of US law firm associates answering 'yes' to this question was slightly lower at 77.2% (see table 1). This may be because many associates do not receive strong mentoring and simply assume, therefore, that mentoring is not a professional obligation. Also interesting is the fact that 82.8% of the British respondents believed that a professional obligation to mentor existed – despite the fact that their codes have weaker and narrower language with respect to mentoring.

Table 1: "Do you believe that lawyers have a professional responsibility to mentor new lawyers?"

	Yes	No	Other*
Worldwide (all) (n=604)	79.1% (n=478)	18.5% (n=112)	2.3% (n=14)
US law firm partners (n=137)	81.0 (111)	16.8 (23)	2.2 (3)
US law firm associates (n=281)	77.2 (217)	20.3 (57)	2.5 (7)
UK lawyers (all) (n=29)	82.8 (24)	17.2 (5)	0.0 (0)

Lawyers answering 'other' could input a narrative response.

The encouraging news is that roughly 80% of lawyers believe that some professional obligation exists to mentor other lawyers. This does not mean that four out of five lawyers are engaged in mentoring, however, it merely reveals that they believe an ethical obligation exists to provide it. The discouraging news is, of course, precisely the inverse: that one out of every five lawyers does not believe that any such professional responsibility exists to provide legal mentoring. In light of the discussion of the professional codes above, this result is significant. It suggests that 20% of the profession may not believe that any professional obligation exists to assist younger lawyers in their careers. The survey also asked whether lawyers believed that mentoring in the legal profession was more important than in other professions. Only half (50.3%) of all respondents believed that mentoring in the legal profession had any special importance.

One avenue to address some of these lawyer perceptions may be found in the law schools. The survey also found that respondents who were mentored in law school were more likely to believe later in their career that mentoring is a professional responsibility of all lawyers. This link was strongest when the mentoring in law school was informal (ie, organic and mutually entered into by voluntary participants) as opposed to formal (ie, a sponsored and organised programme that matched mentors and protégés – sometimes randomly, sometimes based on selected criteria). US lawyers in private firms who experienced mentoring in law school rated those relationships – on average – at 5.5 (out of 7). These law school mentoring experiences are particularly important because they signal to young lawyers – at the earliest stage of their careers – the importance of taking an interest in and supporting nascent members of the profession. Moreover, it is one of the few opportunities for lawyers to receive meaningful mentoring from someone who is not their supervisor or superior – the latter often having a greater interest in the organisation's needs than those of the full career arc of an individual.

Of course the most promising areas for change are in the legal workplace where practitioners spend the most time, and where relationships are most often the closest. The survey indicated that the most meaningful mentoring relationships were informal at work. Even though survey respondents also rated formal mentoring at work programmes positively, the informal mentoring programmes were considered the most rewarding by a healthy margin. This creates both opportunities and challenges for most practitioners. Lawyers should proactively seek out protégés – and mentors – in organic informal relationships where both lawyers are comfortable and genuinely interested in maintaining contact. These types of mentoring partnerships are generally more impactful than the (often random) pairing of individuals in sterile, formal mentoring programmes. But they require more work. Instead of relying solely on organisation administrators to set up matches in formal programmes, lawyers should preferably be constantly seeking help from – and seeking to help – others in the profession.

5. Leadership lessons for legal mentoring

In light of the above, what specifically should law firm managers and senior lawyers do?[34]

5.1 Prioritise informal mentoring

Perhaps the most important finding from our survey – reinforced by much of the general scholarship on mentoring – is that both mentors and protégés prefer informal mentoring arrangements in legal organisations. Lawyers also believed that informal mentoring is the most effective type of mentoring in the legal profession. As a result, managers and senior lawyers must do more to encourage and facilitate informal mentoring. Lawyers should receive training as to why informal mentoring is important and how they can be successful informal mentors and protégés. While this

---

34   For a more detailed treatment of these and other recommendations, see Way, *Mentoring Lawyers: Why the Profession Fails itself and Society, and How it Can Change* [forthcoming].

knowledge should be shared as early as law school, legal workplaces should routinely reinforce this message through training and incentive schemes that encourage informal mentoring relationships. As discussed below, informal mentoring should not necessarily replace formal programming, as the two can be complementary. But it should be understood that informal mentoring relationships are generally the most impactful and therefore should be prioritised as appropriate. The goal is for individual lawyers to recognise – and consistently act upon – an obligation to reach out to younger members of the profession to create meaningful, long-lasting relationships that improve competency and satisfaction. There should also be a reciprocal duty on the part of potential protégés to actively reach out to trusted and admired senior lawyers in order to reap the benefits of informal mentoring.

5.2 Continue (or create) formal mentoring programmes

Many law firms and legal organisations give lip service to the vague concept of mentoring by supporting (to varying degrees) formal programmes that match mentors to protégés. The mere existence of a formal programme, however, does not suggest effectiveness, as practices vary across organisations. Our research found that, in general, formal programmes can have a positive impact, but they are not as effective as informal mentoring (from the perspective of both mentors and protégés). As noted above, formal and informal mentoring need not be considered mutually exclusive. Indeed, if done well, these two styles of mentoring can be complementary. In order to craft successful formal mentoring programmes, research has suggested that the following elements are beneficial:

- strong organisational support – organisations must emphasise their support for mentoring programmes, and participants must perceive this support;
- tailored and clear programme objectives – programme objectives should be tailored to the organisation's needs and clearly communicated;
- care in matching process – mentors and protégé assignments should not be completely random, as mentors and protégés generally prefer to perceive some similarities;
- proactive mentor personalities – a proactive personality is a beneficial characteristic for mentors;
- clear expectations – expectations should be clear and agreed upon by all participants;
- training – training is nearly always recommended for all mentoring participants; and
- programme evaluation – some form of programme evaluation should be conducted.[35]

While the above list is not intended to be comprehensive, its content is a helpful starting point for law organisations. Senior lawyers and law firm managers should

---

35   Adapted from Lisa Finkelstein and Mark Poteet, "Best Practices in Workplace Formal Mentoring Programs" in Tammy Allen and Lillian Eby (eds), *The Blackwell Handbook of Mentoring* (Chichester: Wiley-Blackwell, 2010), pp 363–364.

strive to incorporate these and other best practices, always tailoring programme features to meet the unique needs of their employees and organisational culture.

5.3 Commit time and resources to professional development

Finally, law organisation management must be genuinely committed to providing meaningful professional training and continuing legal education to employees. As noted above, ethics codes in both the United States and England demand that organisations ensure the competency of their employees. While many firms simply (but generously) provide funding for external training, all organisations have the capacity to share knowledge internally – whether formally or informally. To best meet their professional and civic obligations, legal organisations must constantly support lawyer development, not only by underwriting participation in programming outside the workplace, but also creating important in-house opportunities. Internal programming can share local knowledge, reinforce organisational norms and create organic opportunities for informal mentoring.

The modest investments in mentoring and professional development discussed above will invariably improve the quality and competence of those practising law. This not only benefits members of the profession, but also clients, courts and ultimately all citizens.

Prior to the adoption of the American Canons of Ethics, Harlan Fiske Stone, then an Associate Justice of the US Supreme Court (later elevated to Chief Justice) asserted:

> Before the Bar can function at all as a guardian of the public interests committed to its care, there must be an appraisal and comprehension of the ... chained relationship of the lawyer ... to his professional brethren and to the public. That appraisal must pass beyond the petty details of form and manners which have been so largely the subject of our Code of Ethics, to more fundamental consideration of the way in which our professional activities affect the welfare of society as a whole.[36]

The revised American Code of Professional Conduct largely heeded Stone's advice to move consciously away from the petty details of form to broader concepts of how lawyers can best function as guardians of the public interest. The new Code emphatically recognised what Stone described as the "chained relationship of the lawyer" not only to the public, but also "to his professional brethren". The new professional responsibilities – whether explicitly or implicitly – require lawyers to better serve the public by better supporting themselves.

---

36   Harlan Fiske Stone, "The Public Influence of the Bar" (1934) 48 *Harvard Law Review* 1.

Learning to lead: perspective on bridging the lawyer leadership gap

Scott Westfahl
Harvard Law School, Harvard University

1.   Introduction

The legal profession faces many challenges in the post-great recession era. Many feel that a paradigm shift is occurring and doubt that law firms should ever expect to return to business as usual. A surprising and increasing number of new businesses are working on disrupting the legal profession, primarily through technology and management systems designed to lower legal costs through efficiency and/or to improve legal outcomes through more deliberate and careful process engineering.

In the midst of all of this change and uncertainty, law firm leaders are called upon to design strategies, implement change, communicate with clarity and even prepare for effective succession. Yet most of them have had very little – if any – formal leadership training and many insist upon continuing to maintain full legal practices of their own even while assuming enormous leadership responsibilities. Leverage is difficult for them to find with respect to those leadership responsibilities because law firms chronically underinvest in leadership development. This chronic underinvestment threatens even large, profitable law firms and is compounded by the increasing amount of leadership turnover now occurring at many large firms – a generational leadership transition seems to be happening. In the absence of effective leadership training and development, succession becomes a perilous journey and places firms at high risk.

Why do law firms invest very little in leadership development relative to any other type of professional services firm, such as accounting and consulting firms? First, there is the inertia of 'it's not broken, so don't fix it'. Many firms assume that if they choose people who are smart and have booming practices, those people will figure out how to become effective leaders. But does that not seem to be an extremely risky strategy, given the global size and scale many firms are now reaching?

Secondly, the flat structure of law firms and the need to create the illusion that all partners are equal owners of the business often stands in the way of specific leadership development initiatives. In Wall Street, accounting and consulting firms have no qualms about identifying and offering leadership training for high potentials, but law firms particularly struggle with that concept. They have not achieved the organisational maturity necessary to accept that each partner brings unique strengths and cannot be expected to excel at every aspect of being a partner, including leadership. Nor have law firms found ways to hold leaders accountable to the same degree as consulting and accounting firms. The latter use 360-degree reviews, regular rotation of leaders and advanced governance structures to monitor, develop and refresh leaders. Some observe that lawyers have a greater need for autonomy and resist rules and procedures more than other professionals. If lawyers are indeed harder to manage as a result, it is not surprising that leadership as a concept is undervalued within legal organisations.

Perhaps the biggest reason for law firms' chronic underinvestment in leadership development is the difficulty of adapting a long-term investment perspective in a business where all profits are fully distributed each year, and the effective share price of a law firm is the amount of profit each partner thereby receives. The need to retain existing talent and compete in the lateral partner hiring market seemingly justifies their short-term focus. Most firms fail to see that outlining a longer-term plan and investing in longer-term initiatives like leadership development will:

- cement loyalty;
- attract talent; and
- help hedge against total collapse due to ineffective leadership.

On an individual level, partners are in a bind. They face increasing pressure to bill hours and generate new business. There are little or no incentives or encouragement for them to build their leadership skills or volunteer for early leadership experiences. The leadership learning model is therefore high risk and almost entirely sink-or-swim. Yet, if asked, no lawyer would dispute that Michael Phelps did not become the greatest swimmer in world history by figuring it out on his own.

In the United States, at least, the leadership gap in law firms would not be so great if US law schools, like their business school counterparts, invested in teaching law students how to collaborate, work in teams, manage people and projects, and think and act like leaders. It is stunning in some ways because the evidence is clear that lawyers, including the current US President, often achieve positions of enormous leadership responsibility. Lawyers begin their professional careers at a significant disadvantage and it is hard to catch up, especially when you do not know what you do not know.

Another factor that impairs the ability of lawyers to catch up is that, early on in their careers, they need to focus most of their attention on building technical legal skills because they did not learn them in law school. The attention this requires crowds out the equally important building of professional skills such as leadership. As associates begin to delegate work and manage people and projects, their attention is not redirected. They continue to believe that technical expertise is paramount and fail to better balance their focus on learning how to lead as well as produce.

2. The origins of leadership style and behaviours

To frame a discussion of learning to lead, let us first consider the essence of leadership styles and behaviours. During the 2008 US presidential campaign, we saw two very different kinds of leaders vying for the Oval Office prize. During that election, it occurred to me that the significant contrasts between the leadership styles of Barack Obama and John McCain were similar to those I had seen first-hand somewhere before.

My father was a US Navy submarine captain during the Cold War. I grew up observing a leadership model that emphasised a quiet, calm, efficient, almost scientific, approach that also gave individual commanders a great deal of latitude to deal with uncertainty and take calculated risks. Operating at depth with nuclear weapons and a nuclear reactor, submariners think through every move with great care.

My best friend's father graduated from the US Naval Academy a few years after my father did. Presumably, they had similar leadership training in that environment. But after graduation, their career paths and the environments in which they operated quickly diverged. Like John McCain, my best friend's father became an A-4 pilot and flew off carriers during multiple deployments to Vietnam. His job was to fly over enemy territory and destroy surface-to-air missile batteries so that they could not fire at the heavy bombers following behind his attack squadron. Essentially, he made himself a target and relied upon his skills and quick reactions to destroy the batteries before they shot him down. His leadership style came out of that experience. Under pressure and enemy fire, he needed to operate independently and take quick, unexpected and often radical action to survive.

See the contrast? One leader under extreme pressure (literally under 1,000 feet of water) requires cold, calm, steady decision-making and teamwork. Another leader when under fire must be the ultimate, unpredictable maverick – doing the unexpected to survive and defeat the enemy.

Flashback to 2008: President-to-be Obama campaigned with extreme care and discipline and refused to get drawn into emotional outbursts or trapped in extreme positions. Senator-candidate McCain, by contrast, kept making radical, unexpected moves, like suspending his campaign to deal with the financial crisis and later asking unknown Alaska Governor, Sarah Palin, to serve as his running mate. Ultimately, the nation decided that in the time of financial crisis and after years of surprises and extreme reactions – including the decision to invade Iraq – a steadier, calmer hand was right for the times.

How is this relevant to learning to lead? First, any approach to learning to lead must start with the understanding that there is no one 'right' leadership style. Different leadership styles are appropriate for different contexts, and leaders adapt to face the challenges they meet. Secondly, how leaders develop their leadership style is also a matter of context. The environment in which leaders learn and grow as young professionals shapes their concepts of leadership. So do the role models they observe and the training they are given, if any. As they first ascend to leadership roles, people attempt consciously or unconsciously to develop their own leadership style out of all these kinds of factors. How they behave as leaders when faced with specific challenges will depend upon their evolving leadership styles.

3.   **Learning to lead: the process**
The purpose of this chapter is to show that learning to lead can and should be a conscious, thoughtful and deliberate process and should include a range of tools that can help people learn. Research has shown that learning for adults happens 10% by training, 20% by observation and 70% by experience and experimentation – the

hands-on component.[1] For law firm lawyers, there are significant deficiencies in the way they learn in all three of these dimensions.

4.   Executive education helps lawyers catch up

Let us start at the top of the pyramid. Unfortunately, neither law schools nor the continuing legal education world have embraced the teaching of leadership to lawyers in any meaningful way. Law schools have moved beyond the notion that their only responsibility is to teach students to think like lawyers. Yet only a few consider leadership to be a practical skill which they should teach. In the United States and around the world, training for experienced lawyers almost exclusively focuses on deepening substantive and technical legal expertise. In the United States, formal training for experienced lawyers originated principally from the desire of the bar, which is self-regulated, to protect itself from consumer complaints about lawyers. The many states that have adopted continuing legal education requirements have only in recent years begun to give credit for law practice management-focused courses. More broadly around the world, there is growing interest in teaching lawyers to be leaders, as witnessed by the increasing number of firms participating in leadership programmes at various universities and working with universities to design custom leadership programmes for their partners.

4.1   The executive education model

The good news is that a new model is emerging. Businesses around the world have long invested in executive education for corporate leaders. As executives approach new levels of responsibility, they attend intense, case-focused training programmes to accelerate their leadership readiness and capabilities. Executive education programmes for lawyers are now emerging that achieve the same effects and offer hope for a highly efficient way to help lawyers and legal organisations quickly rectify their chronic underinvestment in leadership development.

How does the model work? It started in the 1940s with partnerships between businesses and top academic institutions, which worked together to design highly immersive, relatively short-burst programmes to focus on key leadership challenges. The idea was to provide just-in-time, contextual learning to support executives across the arcs of their careers. Case studies of real leadership situations quickly became a core element of the executive education model. These cases provide the all-important context that is critical to cementing learning and ensuring its relevance.

Cases are also particularly effective because participants are more likely to remember the lessons from an executive education programme if the lessons are taught through the power of a story, which helps to embed learning in long-term memory. This happens through participants' natural inclination to pay more attention to a story than a lecture, and the deeper engagement that happens when participants grapple with the elements of the story and test them against their own and others' experiences. Research consistently shows that both attention and

---

1   Michael M Lombardo and Robert W Eichinger, *The Career Architect Development Planner*, 1st edn (Minneapolis: Lominger, 1996).

engagement correlate highly with encoding in long-term memory, and that emotion also plays a key role. When leadership cases are well written and well taught, participants debate vigorously about controversial people and situations and are thus more likely to remember and try to apply critical lessons drawn from the cases.

Another critical component of executive education is the selection of the participant group. Contextual learning requires that participants have a baseline level of shared experiences, responsibilities and perspectives. Thus, most executive education programmes try to organise courses by peer groups, with enough diversity to provide rigorous classroom dialogue but not so much as to risk disengagement among participants who feel the programme may be at the wrong level for them. In the end, these peer groups of participants learn as much from each other as from faculty. They form close bonds even in a short programme. This strengthens their professional networks and within a law firm can greatly increase trust among partners. They achieve a much stronger appreciation of each other's abilities and perspectives through class debates and exercises focused on the challenges they face in the real world.

The intense nature of executive education often surprises lawyers, who expect to be able to attend a programme, passively listen for a week and walk away with an idea or two and a couple of new contacts. When they realise on the first day that the classroom is a forum for discussion and debate and they are required fully to engage, they typically do so enthusiastically. One small trick that faculty often use on the first day is to refer and ask questions about very obscure details of a case – this signals to participants that they must do their homework and come to class very familiar with the cases assigned!

4.2   The focus: what does executive education for lawyers require?

(a)   *Taking perspective*
One of the hardest things for lawyers to do in the world of the billable hour is to step back in order to gain perspective on where they are in their careers. Indeed, one of the most tragic consequences of the task-driven, time-is-money approach to the practice of law is that lawyers sometimes lose all sense of their strengths and their goals. They lose touch with their broader networks and when suddenly faced with a career crisis (eg, a recession hits or they lose a major client), they have a difficult time thinking through what to do next. Career counsellors describe the phenomenon of lawyers writing resumes with expectations that the only thing they are qualified to do is exactly what they have been doing, even if that work is not available. Often lawyers lack perspective on their strengths and abilities, have lost focus on longer-term goals and have neglected the connections and contacts that are most likely to provide them with their next opportunities.

Through its intense, focused nature, executive education helps lawyers gain critical perspective, usually at key career transition points like moving into more senior leadership roles. Executive education programmes for lawyers often start with a case that describes the many challenges and responsibilities that participants face in their roles. The 'producer-manager dilemma' that participants all face comes to light and often provokes emotional, cathartic reactions. They have not previously taken the time to understand that their professional lives are often vastly more complicated than those of their business leader clients because, unlike business leaders, lawyers in leadership roles are required to manage and lead the business of their practices and firms while also doing real legal work and serving and developing clients. CEOs have the luxury of managing and leading without having to produce in the traditional sense. Opening lawyers' eyes to the reality of the producer-manager dilemma sets the tone and dramatically increases participants' buy-in to the executive education model. They feel understood and begin to engage.

(b)   Unpacking leadership

In some ways the word 'leadership' is a foreign concept to lawyers. It is not part of their traditional training and, unlike other professional services firms, law firms rarely use the word 'leader' to describe anyone but people in top management roles. When I first started to use the word 'leadership' in building a competency model for law firm associates, more than one sceptical partner loudly raised objections. They insisted that associates needed to focus exclusively on developing technical legal skills and any effort to build their leadership skills or their professional networks would be distracting to that purpose.

The good news is that the increasingly competitive market for legal services is generating much more interest in unpacking what leadership means in a law firm and how it can provide competitive advantage. Of most interest are the following key areas:

- Leading people and teams (eg, motivating professionals; providing feedback and having important conversations; understanding critical elements of team dynamics and effective team process; and aligning talent development systems with firm culture and strategy).
- Client leadership (eg, building client relationships; enhancing client communication to have more influence and impact with clients; innovating new models of client service; and comparing client service models from around the world).
- Practice and firm leadership (eg, understanding what strategy is and is not; understanding business unit versus corporate strategy; learning how to drive strategic planning and implementation; understanding practice segmentation and its implications; and leading change and aligning organisations to achieve strategic goals).

Interactive case discussions provide context, and faculty will facilitate this in a dynamic way that allows them to introduce leadership concepts and frameworks – and language – that participants can apply in their day-to-day jobs when they return to their firms.

For example, law firm leaders often struggle with holding their fellow partners accountable and having direct, honest conversations with them. Mid- and senior-level associates who supervise junior lawyers often neglect their responsibility to give hard feedback, both directly to the junior associates and in writing on their annual review forms.

One of the most popular cases I have seen used in executive education programmes illustrates the importance of having timely, important conversations about performance, in order to avoid the need for very difficult conversations later on. Participants are introduced to a classic model for having such conversations and role play and practise its application. Through the power of story (the case), they are much more likely to remember the key learning point. Through the power of practise (the role play), they are more likely to be effective at managing such situations in the future.

Another example relates to the need for law firm leaders to understand key principles of strategy. Many fail to see that growth in and of itself is not a strategy, and that the key to avoiding race-to-the-bottom, price-based competition is to create significant differentiation in the market. Traditional business schools strategy cases and new ones that have been developed about law firms help participants in executive education to ground their decision-making in fundamental, reliable principles.

(c) **Introducing core business skills to lawyers**

Executive education in the business world has always focused on introducing and reinforcing core business skills. Beyond leadership, such skills include, for example, finance, valuation, accounting and marketing – all skills to which many lawyers have had little or no academic exposure. Thus, a critical element of executive education for lawyers needs to be an interdisciplinary approach to such concepts, so that lawyers can learn in context how to apply core business skills. Asking law firm leaders to obtain MBAs, by contrast, is impractical and marginally not likely to be worth the effort. Learning to lead requires the building of broader business skills – but in a way that is directly applicable and relevant to the challenges faced by law firm leaders. Some US-based firms are now experimenting with mini-MBA type programmes for new associates; others are considering the example of Milbank, Tweed, the New York-based law firm that sends all of its mid- and senior-level associates to Harvard Law School for a series of week-long business and leadership skills programmes over a four-year cycle.

(d) **Applying relevant research**

Executive education for lawyers needs to be research-based. Lawyers are inherently sceptical of theories and anecdotal evidence and are the world's most skilful debunkers of hypotheses. They have earned their standing by challenging assumptions, so executive education programmes that short-cut the empirical knowledge will suffer.

As a result, it is highly advantageous to locate executive education within leading academic institutions rather than consulting firms or other independent centres. Academic-based research is rigorous, peer-reviewed and arguably much less tainted by profit motives. Within a university, executive education programmes can also introduce broader, more interdisciplinary research and learning (eg, leading academic experts on core business skills, the psychology of influence and the global economy all contribute to Harvard Law School executive education teaching).

Also, people and outside organisations much more readily share data and perspectives with academic researchers, who are not viewed as competitors. This allows for much greater development of relevant cases that touch upon current, 'hot-button' issues that participants are facing.

4.3   **Providing learning experiences that are truly differentiated**
Executive education for lawyers helps them learn to lead more effectively because of
the differentiated way the learning occurs. Lawyers typically learn through self-study,
straight lectures, 'talking head' panels, or (from law school) intimidating Socratic
dialogue. The executive education model provides an interactive, collaborative
approach that often surprises participants. The idea that you build upon others' ideas
rather than tear them down law school-style is in itself a key differentiator.

4.4   **Achieving an organisation's particular goals through custom programmes**
One form of executive education – a custom rather than open enrolment programme
– is often used to help an organisation address its own particular goals. For example,
a law firm might partner with an academic institution to create a custom programme
focused on the teaching of strategy frameworks in order to help the firm's leaders to
develop and more effectively execute the law firm's strategy. Custom programmes
can combine a mix of standard and customised cases and can be taught in a tailored
way to match a firm's specific challenges. A firm's leaders can also become involved
in designing and even co-teaching particular sessions, to provide additional context
and grounding in the firm's goals for the programme. The core elements of the
executive education model greatly enhance learning and can significantly deepen
relationships, trust and collaboration among peers within the same firm.

5.   **Thoughts on observation, experience and experimentation**
As noted above, adult learning theory suggests that, beyond training, it is critical to
provide opportunities for people to observe and also to practise the application of
what they are learning. As far behind as legal organisations are in training lawyers to
be leaders, they lag even further behind in providing most lawyers with structured
opportunities to observe, experience and experiment with leadership.

5.1   **Watch and learn**
With respect to observation, corporations routinely establish high potential
programmes through which up-and-coming people are allowed to shadow and learn
from senior executives. By contrast, law firms usually isolate leaders and very few
allow associates anywhere near discussions about, for example, firm strategy,
finances or plans to innovate. A few firms like Latham & Watkins have figured out
that including associates on key committees like the partner election committee
helps prepare them for the senior leadership positions they may someday hold.
    In an analytical study I once conducted with Indiana University Law School
Professor, William Henderson, we learned that judgement was the competency most
highly correlated with distinctive success as a senior associate at a major law firm.
That begs two questions: how do you hire for judgement and how do you accelerate
the teaching of it? Our best answer to the latter question was to provide early
opportunities for associates to shadow and observe how successful senior leaders
exercise judgement.
    London law firms anecdotally report that their tradition of having article clerks
sit at desks within senior partners' offices provides the clerks with a much better

sense of how partners make important judgement calls. Law firms would do well to consider this lesson and to deliberately structure these kinds of shadowing opportunities. Some firms, like Goodwin Procter for example, now give billable hour credit to associates for certain kinds of 'shadow time'.

5.2   Learn by doing – earlier

As a final suggestion for helping lawyers learn to lead, law firms should consider the leadership rotation principles long employed by corporations, consulting firms and even the military. At McKinsey & Co, consultants who are given leadership roles have an expectation that they will typically undertake those roles for four to six years. Leadership positions deliberately rotate and younger partners are given significant opportunities as a result. Further, because there is a culture of leadership rotation, it is much easier to convince a leader to step aside for the next person, as being replaced is not stigmatised. Also, McKinsey provides associates with direct opportunities early on to lead initiatives (eg, office hiring or running business unit retreats). Day to day, their engagement managers, who are three- to five-year associates, run client matters. The firm encourages associates to 'make their own McKinsey' and take ownership of their careers, seek leadership opportunities and find their passion. By treating them as adult professionals rather than as novices who will not be ready for leadership roles until they are partners, McKinsey has become one of the world's great leadership development organisations.

Law firms could emulate this model by providing opportunities for associates and younger partners to lead internal initiatives such as:

- office or business unit hiring;
- retreat planning;
- knowledge development efforts; or
- technology committees.

Firms spend a tremendous amount of time and money hiring terrific talent but then do not challenge them to learn to be leaders. Worse, firm governance structures do not usually include term limits and leaders are often chosen through politically charged processes rather than with a deliberate eye towards succession planning. In the United States, this has also resulted in disappointing numbers of women and minority lawyers being appointed to law firm leadership positions (as low as their numbers are in terms of equity partnerships, their leadership position numbers are much worse, as the MCCA/Vault annual reports on law firm diversity show). Since new research in the corporate world continues to prove that diverse leadership teams correlate very positively with higher returns on equity and organisational performance, law firms should take heed and re-examine how they pick and rotate their leaders.[2]

---

2   See, for example, Thomas Barta, Markus Kleiner and Tilo Neumann, "Is There a Payoff from Top-team Diversity?", *McKinsey Quarterly*, April 2012; and Anita Woolley and Thomas Malone, "What Makes A Team Smarter? More Women", *Harvard Business Review*, June 2011.

6.   **Conclusion**

The lawyer leadership gap is real and critical, particularly as the markets for clients and talent become increasingly competitive. To address this gap, law firms should:

- consider significantly increasing their commitment to formal programmes aimed at developing lawyers' leadership skills, including executive education programmes; and
- thoughtfully design and construct opportunities for younger lawyers to observe leaders in action and build leadership skills at an earlier age.

Such efforts will help current leaders to increase their leadership skills and knowledge and to develop the next generation of outstanding law firm leaders.

Leadership, power and politics in law firms

Laura Empson
Cass Business School, London

1. Introduction: the reluctant leader

Leaders, by definition, must have followers. In most studies of leadership, this statement is self-evident. Such studies assume that hierarchical relationships within organisations are relatively stable, and take for granted that the most senior people in an organisation have the formal authority to lead it.

In law firms, however, the distinction between leaders and followers is more difficult, as traditional hierarchies are replaced by more ambiguous and negotiated relationships among professional peers. As the client relationship partner in one global law firm expressed this to me:

Empson: *Does anyone have power over you?*
Partner;   *Not as far as I'm concerned, no.*
Empson: *Does anyone think they have power over you?*
Partner: *I don't think so.*

In recent years, I have undertaken two major UK government-funded research studies into governance and leadership in global professional service firms. Through these studies I have conducted more than 400 interviews in almost 20 countries with leaders and partners from many of the world's leading professional service firms. These interviews have been supplemented by archival and observational analysis. With regard to the legal sector, through my research and consulting I have worked closely with 15 of the world's leading law firms in the United Kingdom, Europe and the United States.

I have found that in law firms, which are filled with highly educated, independent thinkers, who do not like being told what to do, it is not easy to find lawyers who are happy to identify themselves as followers. Furthermore, finding lawyers who are happy to put themselves forward as leaders is even harder.

We tend to assume that the most ambitious people in an organisation will aspire to leadership roles because they crave the opportunity to influence decisions and exercise power. In a law firm, however, taking on a leadership position can potentially entail losing power. In any organisation, as in most areas of life, power comes from controlling access to valuable resources. In a law firm, or indeed in any professional service firm, the most valuable resources are specialist professional expertise and lucrative client relationships. Lawyers who take on major leadership roles necessarily reduce their fee-earning work and may find their hard-won client relationships migrating to their colleagues, or to other firms. By taking time away from frontline client work, they will struggle to ensure that their professional expertise remains at the cutting edge.

Of course the idiosyncrasies of each law firm's governance structure will determine the leaders' formal authority and the personal credibility of each individual will determine their informal authority, but the same basic conundrum applies. Individuals who take on leadership roles in law firms risk exchanging their most valuable assets (ie, their client relationships and professional expertise) for a title which brings with it relatively little formal authority but a great deal of responsibility.

2. Extensive autonomy and contingent authority

Leadership in law firms presents a complex and fascinating set of challenges. These challenges are encapsulated in two interrelated concepts: 'extensive autonomy' and 'contingent authority'.

Experienced lawyers require, or at least expect, extensive autonomy. This autonomy is justified by the requirement for professionals to preserve the right to make choices about how best to apply their specialist technical expertise to the delivery of customised professional services. It is perpetuated by the fact that the core value-creating resources of a law firm – technical knowledge and client relationships – are often proprietary to specific individuals. In the very largest so-called 'corporate' firms, a partner's autonomy may be less than it was in the past, but it is still nevertheless considerable. As long as the delivery of a legal service requires considerable customisation, the senior lawyer delivering that service must be free to exercise discretion. So, while in the largest firms partners may increasingly be required to submit to formal performance evaluations and feel increasingly removed from the leadership of the firms, they nevertheless retain a high degree of operational autonomy.

Extensive autonomy is associated with contingent authority. In a law firm, senior executives are typically elected by their peers to formal positions of leadership and can be deposed at any time if they fail to retain the support of their fellow partners. While formal votes of no confidence are unusual in the largest partnerships, more discrete 'palace coups' are commonplace. As a result, senior executives can only lead by consensus and need to be acutely aware of the implicit power structures and shifting networks of influence among their colleagues.

As the chairman in a partnership I studied explained:

My experience of authority is that it lasts about an hour if you stop refreshing it ... We've seen people get killed very quickly if their teams stop following them.

In my book, *Managing the Modern Law Firm* (Empson, 2007), I described partnerships as the best means of reconciling, or at least attempting to reconcile, the tension inherent within any professional service firm between the needs of the individual and the needs of the collective. At the heart of this tension sit the leaders of the firm who must absorb, embody and resolve that tension. It is no wonder so many lawyers refuse to take on these roles.

3. Leadership constellation: a plural model of law firm leadership

This combination of extensive autonomy and contingent authority means that leadership in law firms needs to be conceptualised differently from the way we typically understand leadership. To date, very little leadership research has been conducted in the context of law firms and most conventional approaches to leadership simply do not apply. Most studies of leadership focus on the individual leader (eg, their personality traits and behaviours) but this conventional approach is not particularly useful when it comes to understanding law firm leadership.

Fortunately, a developing area of leadership research provides useful insights into law firm leadership. In recent years there has been growing interest among leadership scholars in what has variously been termed 'collective', 'distributed' or 'shared' leadership. In this plural conceptualisation of leadership, leadership roles are shared among multiple actors, and authority relationships are ambiguous and potentially contested. Unlike most conventional leadership research, a plural model of leadership views leadership as a collective process, unfolding over time and arising from the actions and interactions of a group of individuals. Leadership, in this sense, is not something that is done by people but something that happens between people seeking to influence each other. As a result, it can be more temporary, more insecure and more subject to negotiation than traditional individualised notions of leadership.

Figure 1: Leadership constellation

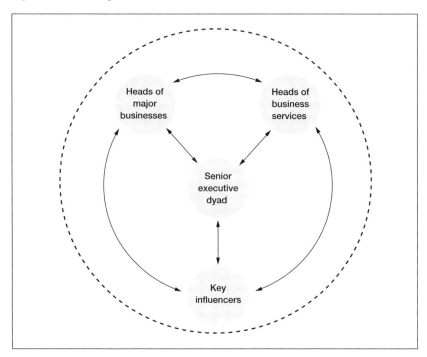

As part of my research on leadership in law firms, I developed the concept of the 'leadership constellation' as a means of expressing this plural model of leadership (see figure 1). Rather than view leadership as a quality that an individual has, or something that an individual does, the concept of the leadership constellation emphasises that leadership happens in the interactions between the key actors in a firm's leadership dynamics. In some firms this may be a very small group and in other firms it may appear more like a series of concentric circles. Whatever form it takes, the power structure which the leadership constellation represents is implicit and often highly opaque to those outside of it.

Leadership is represented by the arrows that connect the members of the leadership constellation (ie, the processes of influencing), as much as by the circles representing the leaders themselves. As a senior partner in a law firm I studied summed it up:

> The interesting thing in this role [of senior partner] is that you find that you can't achieve anything except through other people ... You can only make things happen by essentially working with this group [of powerful individuals] who in turn influence the wider group.

So who are these powerful individuals? In the context of a law firm the potential members of the leadership constellation are:

- Senior executive dyad – typically a managing partner and senior partner, or chairman and chief executive.
- Heads of businesses – leaders of major fee-earning areas such as specific practices, offices and market-sector groupings; many fee-earning areas may be excluded from the inner circle of power.
- Heads of business services – in some firms the chief operating officer, the chief financial officer or the head of human resources may have considerably more influence than most law firm partners; the partners may not realise this.
- Key influencers – these people have power derived from control of key client relationships, valuable expertise or a strong internal and external reputation; they might not appear on an organisation's chart if they have no formal role.

It is important to remember that members of the leadership constellation do not form a leadership team in any explicit sense because the constellation as a whole has no formally defined boundaries or overt identity within the firm – it can overlap with and coexist alongside formal bodies such as the executive committee or the board. The organising hierarchy within the constellation is opaque, and roles and relationships are negotiated between members as required. They recognise each other as powerful, but others may not fully recognise their power. Individuals within the firm may see themselves as leaders because they have important-sounding titles but may not be part of the leadership constellation because they are not recognised or accepted as leaders by their colleagues.

The leadership constellation therefore expresses the informal power structure of the law firm. An effective leader is one who is able to navigate this complex set of dynamics to achieve a particular purpose.

4. Identifying the leadership constellation

In my most recent research study I asked interviewees to identify where they were placed within their firm's formal governance structure and informal power structure relative to other members of the leadership constellation. I asked them to identify specific critical incidents and then recall who had been involved in the process of addressing and resolving them, at what stage they had been involved and what had been the nature of their involvement. I sought to verify their recollections by comparing them with others' recollections. I then cross-referenced interviewees' statements with formal documentation such as minutes of board meetings and transcripts of conference calls.

I was seeking to verify individuals' perceptions of their position within the power structure, to identify who recognised each other as a peer, who they deferred to and who they felt was marginalised. I used this data to map each of the firm's leadership constellations. Figure 2 is an example of the leadership constellation in a major global law firm I studied.

Figure 2: Mapping the leadership constellation in a law firm

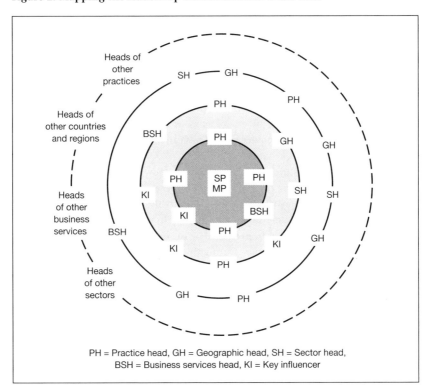

PH = Practice head, GH = Geographic head, SH = Sector head,
BSH = Business services head, KI = Key influencer

As the senior partner in this particular law firm saw it:

There's probably an inner core of leaders which is about fifteen, yes something like that, and then there's an outer core which is probably around ten or twelve people, something like that.

In fact, my research revealed that there was a hidden inner circle of around eight people in this law firm. Interviewees identified these people by observing who was invited by the senior and managing partners to key meetings (and who was excluded) and whose opinion the senior and managing partners sought at the earliest stage about the most sensitive issues (and whom they consulted at a later stage). As one practice head in this law firm described it:

> I would say there's sort of the inner group. There's one or two from [A] practice, me from [B] practice, one from [C] practice. This is quite sensitive; I wouldn't pass this on to anybody. I don't know whether this is accidental or on purpose but I think it's on purpose. There's [the senior partner], there's [the managing partner], then probably two from [D] practice. The other head of [B] practice is not included ... The group doesn't include the other head of [A] practice, and didn't include my predecessor in [B] practice.

So some practice heads considered themselves to be peers of their fellow practice heads and were unaware that they were in fact excluded from the inner circle. And there were some heads of business services (who were neither lawyers nor partners) who were closer to the inner circle than board members (who were both lawyers and partners).

5. Negotiating leadership relationships

Even for those supposedly at the centre of power in this particular law firm, the power dynamics are complex and opaque. For example, all major practices have multiple leaders who negotiate shared roles as required. How then are the members of the leadership constellation able to work together so effectively? The answer lies in the concept known by sociologists as 'social embeddedness', which helps to explain the way in which deep social ties can influence supposedly transactional and rational economic exchanges.

Many partners in a law firm may have known each other for many years. They may have studied for their law degree together or trained together when they first joined the firm. They will have been thoroughly socialised into the firm so that they share many of the same values and the way in which they understand the reality of their business world has been shaped by the organisation which has been their home for the past 25 or more years. During this time they will have built up close working relationships which enable them to negotiate their shared role space through intuitive mutual adjustment. Or as two joint practice heads explain:

> The reason it works for me and [joint practice head] is that we've worked with each other for years and years and years. We like each other. We share the same values and we find the same things amusing by and large.

> It's a very easy relationship. We're on a very similar wavelength. We seem to be able to anticipate what each other will think on things. I don't know whether that is healthy or unhealthy, but it feels quite easy.

In many global law firms that have grown by a series of smaller acquisitions this social embeddedness exists for the partners of the legacy office (eg, the London office in the case of the magic circle firms) but not for the partners in other offices. This may enhance the effective functioning of the leadership constellation but may cause difficulties for those from outside the legacy office who seek to exercise power within the firm they have joined. Where a firm has grown suddenly as a result of a mega-merger between firms of similar size, the issue of social embeddedness may present a different kind of problem. The challenge then is how to bring together two potentially highly functional leadership constellations, where there are no long-established relationships, in order to create a new power structure which functions effectively.

But before members of the leadership constellation have the opportunity to engage in intuitive mutual adjustment, how can these individuals come to be considered as leaders or potential leaders? More generally, how does a lawyer become a leader? The following section deals with these questions.

6.   Gaining and retaining legitimacy to lead through market success

To be perceived as a potential leader in a law firm, a lawyer needs to gain the respect of colleagues through professional work. Few lawyers are happy with the idea of being led by someone who has not already done their job at least as well as, if not better than, them. As one practice head in my study explained it to me:

I've dealt with some of our most difficult clients. So I've been the partner on [major client] having won that. I'm also still currently the partner on [major client] and that's not the easiest one either. And, even now I've become head of the practice, I'm just going onto [major client]. ... So if I put my little ego hat on for a moment I was sort of, you know, seen to be a good partner. You know, one of the top partners, I suppose, and one that can get out there and win work.

However, it is a specific aspect of professional work that counts. While providing high-quality advice and delivering exemplary service are important ways of gaining respect, it is market success that matters most. According to another interviewee:

I think a lot of the leadership in a firm is linked to your practice and the position in the market because those people have the credibility, those people are in the market, they actually know the client and so on and in the end all that we do is ultimately directed towards clients.

Why should lawyers assume that, just because a colleague is particularly effective at rainmaking, they are in any way fit to lead their firm? My study suggests three important reasons why market success is taken to be an indicator of fitness to lead.

First, the ambiguous nature of professional work means that it can be difficult for lawyers to judge the absolute quality of a colleague's work. Market success thus comes to symbolise professional proficiency – a tangible measure of the intangible. By succeeding in selling work, aspiring leaders demonstrate to their colleagues that they are more than just highly skilled technicians; they have a broader understanding of their clients' needs and, by implication, possess the commercial acumen to lead their fellow partners to commercial success.

Secondly, the partners value an individual partner's commercial success because it will ultimately generate income for themselves. This is clearly most marked in lockstep firms but also applies in law firms where remuneration is more directly linked to individual performance. A successful business generator creates a halo effect for his or her colleagues, whether indirectly in terms of the reputational benefits for the firm, or directly in terms of passing on additional work to their colleagues. Those who prove they can feed their partners are also deemed to be qualified to lead their partners.

Thirdly, being successful in the market has strong symbolic qualities. It demonstrates to colleagues that you know what it means to work hard. You have already made the personal sacrifices that you will be asking of your colleagues. Demonstrating that you can bear the pain is the ultimate demonstration of authenticity as a leader – you have pushed yourself to your limit as a professional and you have earned the right to ask your fellow partners to do the same. Or as one interviewee explained:

> I think that professional service practitioners ... will accept almost unlimited decision making and authority from someone that they think understands the things they are going through.

The leader has been through it all before. But it is not enough just to have done so in the past. Claiming or being granted the right to be seen as a leader is not a one-off event, you have to keep proving your leadership eligibility by continuing to be involved in winning business and working with clients.

One practice head in a law firm I studied contrasted his own experience with that of a less politically astute colleague:

> I did more billable hours than any other practice group head ... I always find if you ask people to do something, you get a lot more respect if they think 'well he's doing it', so therefore they follow that. The banking guy who's very, very good, made a classic mistake of cutting right back on his practice and becoming full-time management. And that doesn't work in a firm like ours. You do lose credibility doing that. You have to be able to show you can still cut it.

As a lawyer in a management role, showing that you can still cut it and demonstrating your continuing commitment to the firm is vital if your colleagues are to entrust you with formal authority to lead them. But that is not all. If you have been accepted as a leader in a law firm, you must be capable of leadership – but only as far as your fellow partners will allow you.

7.   Enabling autonomy while retaining control

When partners delegate formal authority to one or more of their number, it is with the understanding that they will use it to achieve the partnership's collective objectives for the firm and further its commercial success. They are by no means promising unquestioning obedience or unlimited respect. Indeed, their tacit expectation is that their individual autonomy will remain unchanged. As one law firm leader acknowledged:

> You can't really tell people what to do. You can say what you're going to do and then hope people will agree with it ... and the people you can least tell what to do are those who are most important for the success of the business. Because they are the ones who control the client relationships.

Yet these firms are not haphazard anarchies, they are highly successful global professional service firms. The leaders do in fact exercise a degree of control but within certain constraints. Control focuses on ensuring that the activities of individual partners are aligned with the strategic goals and performance targets that have been agreed by the partnership as a whole, even while encouraging colleagues to believe they are exercising autonomy. As one chairman described it, leadership in this context is like:

walking a tightrope of helping my partners feel like owners, helping them feel involved, helping them be engaged, not dominating them, not getting out in front, not having a huge ego which makes them feel like the chairman's kind of off on his own trip. At the same time, being strong and providing them with a sense of confidence that we're going somewhere.

Constraints on individual autonomy (ie, managerial discipline) occur within the informal hierarchy, with partners accepting a degree of control in the interests of the partnership as a whole. This balance between enabling autonomy and maintaining control can be clumsy and hard to sustain. As one senior partner explained:

Partners say 'you're too tight' and they say 'get looser'. So you get looser and they say 'it's chaotic, get tighter'. If the money is going up, you can do what you like. If the money is going down, you can't do anything. But the money going up or down isn't within control of the senior partner.

Sometimes there are formal constraints, but the most powerful and effective controls are the desire to win and retain the respect of senior colleagues you respect by conforming to the norms of professional behaviour that they advocate and exemplify. In other words, professionals look to their chosen role models and attempt to act accordingly. As a senior law firm partner explained:

I think the younger partners want you to spend more time (than them) thinking about what the firm as a whole is doing and ... to provide thought leadership which they will either follow or not, because it's not telling them what to do; it's actually just coming up with the prompts and ideas to maximise the business and get the best out of people. I think that's what they expect some of the more senior partners to do. So it sort of happens.

It seems that leadership in a law firm can be something that 'sort of happens'. Partners will be likely to cooperate as long as the prompts and ideas are not positioned as bureaucratic incursions or excessive management. This is the essence of the contingent nature of authority in such organisations. Leaders have, in effect, a temporary mandate from their partners to interpret and implement partners' objectives for the firm.

It is important that leaders should not try to work alone in maintaining this balance. They are acting on behalf of the partnership and should not allow themselves to become portrayed as acting in opposition to it. As my previous research has shown (Empson, 2012), it is easy for leaders in this situation to become isolated. Instead, they need to enlist the support of their colleagues within the leadership constellation and beyond to help maintain the balance between individual autonomy and managerial control. They also need to recognise when it is time to act in order to exercise firmer leadership. As one interviewee explained:

Lots of people here are crying out for leadership, you know, they just don't realise it. But they are. They do what they do but if somebody could inspire them and show them there was a better way of doing it, they'd follow that.

But such overt leadership activity runs the risk of being perceived by partners as interfering with their autonomy and is likely to be met with resistance or disdain. Control of a partnership is maintained in more nuanced and less obtrusive ways and, accordingly, requires subtle political skills.

8. Interacting politically while appearing apolitical

In order to be accepted as leaders by their peers, professionals must appear to be apolitical. But in reality politics is simply a fact of life in law firms, it is the oil which lubricates the wheels of everyday organisational interactions.

Many interviewees in my study said, unprompted, that they abhorred politics and insisted that their firms were not political. Admittedly, this is according to their somewhat naive notions of political behaviour. Interviewees seem to understand organisational politics in rather simplistic terms as self-serving, duplicitous and unscrupulous. According to one interviewee:

> To me politics smacks of alliance-building in the corridors, in offices behind the scenes. It smacks of people engineering agendas, which creep up on the firm and deliver a fait accompli in a way that becomes disruptive. Or politics could manifest as someone undermining another person. I would like to think we don't have those behaviours.

So lawyers who display these behaviours may be deemed by their peers as unsuitable for a leadership role. As another interviewee in the same firm explained:

> There are people who are clearly very ambitious in the firm who will say from quite an early age to you, particularly over a beer or over a meal or over a chat [slams hand on table], 'Do you think I'm in the frame to be managing partner or senior partner? What is it I need to do along the way?'... And they're regarded as quite pushy, will be more political in their views in terms of what they think people will want to hear and what they think people will want to vote for.

But how can someone become senior partner at a large law firm without learning how to negotiate between opposing partners, influence on a one-on-one basis and in large groups, take soundings among powerful individuals and build consensus across the partnership? These actions require social astuteness, interpersonal influence, networking ability and apparent sincerity – all key political skills.

This suspicion of political behaviour has a certain irony when you consider that the partners of the firms have explicitly and deliberately constructed political environments. They use political language, hold formal elections to senior roles and have candidates who issue manifestos and speak at candidates' debates. Senior leaders of law firms refer to their partners as 'constituents', and tell stories of rival candidates briefing against them and failed or successful leadership coups. Or as one interviewee described it:

> The previous election for senior partner was a bit of a power struggle between two individuals who were dominant characters within the organisation and [Fred] held sway on the basis of support from a number of the more senior partners including the outgoing senior partner who had quite a lot of influence... It was all closed doors – smoke filled rooms – lots of politicking etc. etc. etc. – a variety of promises being made to various senior people to get them to support [Fred].

Interviewees describe political behaviours as rife, but curiously do not interpret them as such. As one interviewee explained it:

> There was a time at a partner conference when I thought somebody was getting lynched. We were having a formal vote and discussion about electing someone to partner ... There were two or three people with a personal agenda, a particular dislike for an individual

and they were trying to scuttle this person ... It was fighting in public. I mean the way this firm operates it should all be resolved before you ever go in the room.

In other words, the conflict resolution, trade-offs and compromises that inevitably must occur within a partnership were supposed to be made in private, allowing for a public show of harmony and consensus. This is of course a much more political approach than open disagreement during partner conferences, but it allows the partners to preserve the illusion that they are not operating in a political environment.

This apparent paradox (of denigrating political behaviour while creating structures which favour skilful politicians) can be reconciled by recognising that the more adroit leaders persuade their peers that they are not personally ambitious, even while they are climbing to the top of their organisations. These individuals appear to be ambitious for the partnership as a whole rather than for themselves (though, of course, the two are not mutually exclusive). Their peers are willing to cast themselves in the role of followers because they trust these individuals sufficiently to allow them a degree of formal authority over them. As one interviewee described it:

The partnership as a whole trusts our leader, that he's going to resolve it for the best – for the good of the partnership. As long as they believe that and trust that, then there's no reason to put any other kind of hold on him.

In fact, interviewees sometimes described successful leaders as above politics entirely:

Sometimes my sense would be [senior partner] doesn't necessarily always understand how influential he is. He's very modest about it, quite self-effacing, and he himself doesn't attach such great importance to some of those things that might be under the heading of creeping as in slightly sinister. He is not himself a player in that way at all ... it's simply because his own motivations in this world are so, I think, very genuine and clean.

How can someone rise to be senior partner of a global law firm without being a 'player'? Is it perhaps that some of the reluctance to take on leadership roles in law firms, referred to at the start of this chapter, may be professed rather than genuine? After all, most senior leaders need to put themselves forward for election in the first place and in some cases fight a very tough campaign to be elected. But to win the trust of their peers, leaders must be seen as 'genuine and clean' rather than 'creeping' and 'slightly sinister'. That is, they should be looking out for the good of the firm rather than for their own self-interests. As one interviewee saw it:

We have people in leadership positions who don't appear to be having to work politically to keep their position ... The one who does [leadership] more naturally, partners will recognise that, and [he] is more likely to sustain the role. And the others are more likely to crash and burn.

Yet individuals operating in a highly politicised environment who do not appear to have to work politically to keep their position are almost certainly deploying highly sophisticated political skills – whether utilising them consciously or not, and whether using them to fulfil their personal ambitions or their ambitions for the firm.

One interviewee, the global head of human resources in a law firm, who is not herself a partner, reconciles the apparent paradox of denigrating political behaviour while rewarding political skill within these firms as follows:

It is important to distinguish between the sort of political ego, which doesn't work, and political savviness, which is absolutely essential. And that savviness is born out of empathy and the ability to see and absorb and understand what is spoken and unspoken, and what goes on sort of implicitly. I think it is critical in this organisation ... Without it you are in real trouble because if you don't have it you can't have influence.

It is worth recognising that this political savviness, and the political skills that underlie it (ie, social astuteness, interpersonal influence, networking ability and apparent sincerity), are precisely the abilities lawyers need in order to handle their clients. In the client context they are not thought of as political skills, but just as being good with clients. This is another – albeit probably unconscious – reason why professionals infer leadership ability from market success. The client relationship management skills that make you good at winning business and retaining prestigious clients are the same skills that can make an effective law firm leader.

What makes an effective law firm leader?

It seems that leading a law firm can be reduced to three tactics:

- gaining and retaining legitimacy to lead through market success,
- enabling autonomy whilst retaining control, and
- interacting politically while appearing apolitical.

This suggests that perhaps it is quite simple after all. I would say, emphatically not!

To achieve market success, lawyers must have mastered their technical professional work and be highly effective at winning and developing profitable client relationships. To enable autonomy while maintaining control they must perpetually perform a delicate balancing act between being 'too tight' and 'too loose'. And to act politically whilst appearing apolitical, they must be able to demonstrate social astuteness, interpersonal influence and networking ability, while all the time appearing sincere. To achieve all this, to put in the hours required and not become discouraged by the scale and complexity of the role, requires very high levels of physical energy and emotional stamina. In a firm where your colleagues are highly driven and high-achieving, you need to remain just ahead of them to ensure they are achieving in the right direction. In a firm where your colleagues are not as highly driven and high-achieving as you believe they should be, you need to remind them continually of the goal you are supposed to be collectively striving towards. You must not lose faith in yourself or your colleagues when progress seems too slow.

So what sort of individual can effectively negotiate his way through the subtleties and complexities of a law firm's leadership? Looking across all of the firms studied, an effective leader should:

- be highly respected for his skills as a professional – especially business generation;
- not appear to be seeking power;
- inspire loyalty and commitment;
- have a strong personal vision and be able to communicate it;
- be able to build consensus and act decisively;

- transfer responsibility but intervene selectively;
- be comfortable with ambiguity and conflict;
- spend time massaging egos;
- not expect to have his own ego massaged; and above all
- be able to identify and navigate the leadership constellation.

A romantic ideal?

The plural leadership model typically found in law firms can be seen as the antithesis of the individual heroic leader, as mythologised by the business press. Lawyers do not like to see themselves as unthinkingly or even admiringly following someone who is out in front of them, winning the kudos and controlling their actions. Instead, they elect some of their peers into leadership positions, often for a fixed term, granting them the status of first among equals.

Yet, as they do this, they may be creating an alternative leadership mythology. Interviewees describe their leaders as self-effacing, modest individuals with 'clean' motivations who are above the political fray, reluctantly accepting office only because they are putting the interests of the partnership first. By perpetuating this belief in the purity of their leaders, lawyers are also reasserting their belief in themselves as autonomous individuals working within apolitical partnerships. The reality, of course, is far more grubby, complicated and compromised than that – leadership, power and politics inevitably are.

Acknowledgements

I would like to acknowledge support of the Economic and Social Research Funding Council of Great Britain for their support for my study 'Understanding Leadership Dynamics in Professional Service Firms' (RES-062-23-2269). I would also like to acknowledge the work of Johan Alvehus of the University of Lund, with whom I am developing academic papers from this empirical material, and whose insights are reflected in some of the ideas presented in this chapter. Finally, I would like to thank the members of the Cass Centre for Professional Service Firms for their contributions throughout this study.

Selected references

Empson, L (2007), *Managing the Modern Law Firm: New Challenges, New Perspectives* (Oxford University Press).

Empson, L (2012), 'Beyond Dichotomies: A Multi-Stage Model of Governance in Professional Service Firms', in M.R. Reihlen and A. Werr (eds), *Handbook of Research on Entrepreneurship in Professional Services* (Edward Elgar), pp.274–296.

For details of ongoing academic papers arising from this study and other relevant research, see: www.cas.city.ac.uk/ipsf

Leading with values: a guide to shaping your firm's culture

Jan Thornbury
Thornbury Consulting Associates Ltd

---

1. Introduction

At a conference a few years ago, I asked an audience of partners from different law firms to raise their hands if their firm had a statement of values. Almost all hands shot up. I then said, "Now, keep your hand up if you can recite your firm's values from memory." With some sheepish smiles, at least three-quarters of the hands were lowered. What does this tell us?

First, it shows how law firms have woken up to the value of values. Fifteen years ago, the managing partner of my first law firm client was one of very few who recognised that values could be a source of competitive advantage. Today the promotion of a strong culture is regarded as an essential leadership duty, and I rarely encounter a firm that does not have some sort of values statement. The IBA Best Practice guidelines even list culture as one of seven key areas of focus in law firm governance, saying, "Firms should seek to define and communicate a limited number of fundamental values which underpin and inform decisions."

Secondly, and crucially, it tells us that few law firm leaders succeed in making values stick. All too frequently, values are forgotten, or have no impact on decision making. Culture programmes often dissipate into a handful of well-meaning HR or CSR initiatives, with only remote sponsorship from leadership. Even the IBA guidelines quickly disintegrate into endorsements of *pro bono* and community service that fundamentally miss the point of what it means to lead with values.

The problem is that many law firm leaders find themselves appointed custodian of the culture without having acquired the requisite knowledge and tools for the job. This chapter seeks to remedy that. The early sections are aimed at building a robust understanding of values. The latter sections build on this understanding and provide practical guidance on what can be done to strengthen a firm's culture. Throughout, we will highlight common errors and discuss the challenges which are particular to law firms.

2. Understanding values: questions leaders need to answer

2.1 Why are values important?

Imagine you have just presented your plans for a new culture initiative to your colleagues on the leadership team. You look around the room for their response. A few are looking bemused, but are smiling encouragingly. Others are surreptitiously prodding their blackberries, waiting for you to get down to the 'real' business; and the cynical faction retreat behind folded arms until one of them says, "Why are we doing this? And why now? It's too internally focused. It would be better for the firm if we just got out and won more work." Already you are coming dangerously close to making one of the most common errors of culture change, which is to fail to provide a robust business rationale for values. If you are to win over the cynics, you need hard evidence on the benefits of having a strong culture, and clarity about why investing in values will help your firm.

Management thinkers since the 1980s have been claiming that organisations with strong cultures exhibit superior performance, and a growing body of research-based evidence supports this. A notable study by Collins and Porras[1] in the mid-1990s revealed that, over a period of 70 years, a sample of companies with an enduring sense of purpose and deeply held core values outperformed the general stock market by an astonishing factor of 12, and their peer group by a factor of six. Not only was their financial performance outstanding, they also coped better with change, enjoyed superior reputations and better withstood changes in leadership. More recent research from a wide range of sources reveals culture as a major driver of employee engagement, which in turn correlates with productivity and performance.

This evidence alone may persuade some that there is worth in values, but a sound business rationale needs to be more specific in addressing an acute need within the firm. The immense pressures and changing landscape of the legal sector provide fertile ground for culture initiatives. Typical motivations include:

- A need to improve cohesion, either post-merger, or simply in the face of entrenched barriers. Values are key to creating that holy grail of the legal sector, the 'one firm' ethos. If people are confident that their colleagues across the firm, irrespective of role or location, are operating on the same basic principles as themselves, it makes for a greater sense of belonging and more harmonious working relationships.

- Mainstream law firms are all too aware that they have little scope for differentiation in an intensely competitive market. In a people business, brand is almost entirely about behaviour. And it is internal values that drive behaviour.

- It has long been recognised that current generations seek not only adequate reward and career progression, but also meaning in their work, and a sense of belonging. In the legal sector, where remuneration packages and career paths are broadly similar, culture is often cited as the deciding factor in joining and staying with a firm. Values are a powerful weapon in the war for talent.

- Many firms have specific cultural issues. For example, they may be seeking to repair damage sustained during the global financial crisis, needing to refresh values that have lost impact over time, or attempting to preserve their identity as they grow.

---

1   James C Collins and Jerry I Porras, *Built to Last: Successful Habits of Visionary Companies* (Random House Business Books, 1994); James C Collins and Jerry I Porras, "Building Your Company's Vision" (September–October 1996) *Harvard Business Review*.

2.2   When do values make a difference?

Let us return to the imaginary leadership team meeting. The cynics have taken it on good faith that you will provide precedents and a summary of research linking corporate culture to high performance. However, now they are scoffing at values statements they have seen in other firms, and swapping anecdotes about how such values are outrageously flouted by the very people who should be role modelling them. As with Godwin's Law, it is only a matter of time until someone brings up Enron – a company whose values of respect, integrity, communication and excellence are risible in the light of its fate.

Unfortunately there are plenty of examples of empty values statements and failed culture initiatives for the cynics to draw on, and their concerns are far from unreasonable. Many organisations struggle to articulate a meaningful set of values, never mind translate them into reality. A common error is to focus on developing values that sound worthy or are all-embracing, in preference to stating the firm's true beliefs and aspirations. This is misguided, because it is the degree to which values are shared, genuinely believed in and acted upon that determines the strength of the culture,[2] and it is the strength of the culture, rather than any particular value, that has been shown to correlate with business performance. In summary, if the benefits of a strong culture are to be reaped, the goal is to develop values that:

- are shared by everyone in the firm;
- state what is authentically believed;
- guide day-to-day behaviour at work;
- are fully integrated into the firm's strategy and decisions.

A culture initiative that is designed with this end goal in mind, rather than one that focuses on creating a perfect values statement, will ensure that your values translate into real benefits.

2.3   Where do values fit in the bigger picture?

Back at your meeting, you have successfully addressed the cynics' main concerns, and while they are not exactly punching the air with enthusiasm, they seem to be reassured for now. However, you cannot help noticing that the blackberry prodders are becoming restless. In an effort to re-engage them, you ask what they think. "Well," says one, "I'm absolutely fine about the firm doing something on values. But I thought we were here to discuss the business agenda, and I think it's time we moved on to that." Hidden in this comment is another tripwire for the aspiring culture change leader – the perception that values are a thing apart from the real business.

This common misconception often has its roots in the leader's own understanding of where values fit in the bigger picture. All too often, and certainly not only in law firms, leaders talk about vision and values as if they were separate – linked perhaps, but distinct. The problem with separating the two is that as the vision is translated into strategy, the values get lost. Then, as Peter Drucker famously

---

2   Terence Deal and Allen Kennedy, *Corporate Cultures: The Rites and Rituals of Corporate Life* (Penguin, 1988).

said, "culture eats strategy for breakfast." If strategy is not aligned with the beliefs in the organisation, the culture bites back. As an organisation's vision is the starting point for developing strategy, it is vital that its values are a positive component of that vision, rather than a troublesome conscience that tags along beside it.

A good starting point for ensuring that your firm's values are correctly positioned is the model for corporate vision proposed by Collins and Porras. This has two main components:

- A core ideology, which remains constant over time and defines the enduring character of the organisation. The core ideology comprises:
  - core purpose: the organisation's deeper reason for existing, beyond making money; and
  - core values: the fundamental beliefs that form its timeless guiding principles.
- An envisioned future, consisting of:
  - big, hairy audacious goals (BHAGs): compelling, energising and dauntingly challenging goals;
  - a vivid description that paints a vibrant and engaging picture of what it will be like to achieve the BHAGs.

The core ideology defines fundamentally who you are, and will remain, while the envisioned future describes where you are going. People need to buy into both if they are to go there with you. This is one of the reasons why values initiatives that are the side show to the strategic change programme, rather than playing a key role in the main event, tend not to work.

Furthermore, most organisations find it difficult to define values without also considering core purpose and envisioned future. Without this context, people often ask, "Where does 'making money' come in – surely that is one of our values?" In fact, the envisioned future is the best place to set out financial aspirations, either in the form of goals or in the vivid description.

In summary, leaders must ensure that values are an integral part of the firm's vision, and that the other elements of vision – core purpose, goals and vivid picture of the future – are complementary and clear.

2.4   What do you mean by 'culture' and 'values'?

This is a question you want to hear, because all too often people rush into action without taking time to understand how culture works. This can have negative consequences, as every botched culture initiative undermines the credibility of future attempts. It is also essential to develop a common language around values and culture, as otherwise people apply their own definitions, causing confusion.

Now for the science part. In the paragraphs that follow we examine a model that

3   Edgar H Schein, *Organisational Culture and Leadership*, 2nd edn (San Francisco CA, Jossey-Bass, 1993).
4   Gerry Johnson (1992) "Managing Strategic Change – Strategy, Culture and Action" (1995) 25(1) *Long Range Planning*.
5   James C Collins and Jerry I Porras, *Built to Last: Successful Habits of Visionary Companies* (Random House Business Books, 1994).

will help deepen your understanding of culture and how it can be changed. It pulls together thinking from prominent academics including Schein,[3] Johnson,[4] and Collins and Porras[5] in one cohesive framework, and underpins the practical approaches presented later in this chapter.

Figure 1: A framework for understanding culture

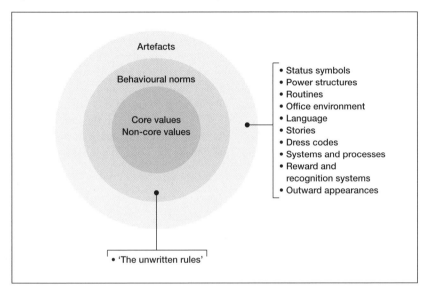

The model shown in figure 1 describes culture in terms of distinct levels. At its innermost level are values. This is also the level at which culture is mostly unconscious. The outer levels are more easily observed and constitute the more conscious processes in the organisation. In brief, the levels comprise the following.

(a)   *Artefacts*
This is culture at its most superficial. Artefacts are the visible manifestations of the culture – things we can observe and sense. They include:

*   organisational structures;
*   rules;
*   processes and routines;
*   the office layout and furnishings;
*   symbols; and
*   dress codes.

It is interesting to see how well artefacts reflect a firm's espoused values. For example, law firms often tell me they believe in listening to their clients, but some do not have robust processes for gathering, disseminating and learning from client feedback. Artefacts include what gets talked about – heroes, villains, and war stories – and the language used also hints at what is going on beneath the surface. The subtle difference between a partner referring to a peer as 'my partner' or 'a partner' can give clues to a law firm's ethos.

(b)   *Behavioural norms*

At the next deepest level we find ingrained patterns or norms of behaviour. These are the accepted 'way we do things around here' and define what it takes to 'fit in'. In a few organisations, published codes of practice reflect behavioural norms, but more often than not, it is the unwritten rules of behaviour that count.

Behavioural norms are not as obvious as artefacts to the external observer, but neither are they buried completely in the organisation's unconscious. Most new joiners pick them up within a few weeks and it is possible, with a little probing, to identify them with some precision. I sometimes conduct a light-hearted exercise where I ask clients to list examples of 'what you must do', 'what you must not do' and 'what you can get away with' if you are to fit in with the firm's culture. The last of these three lists is usually the most interesting, and it is not unusual to see comments such as "anything ... as long as you bring in lots of client work".

(c)   *Values*

At the heart of culture we find values: a system of beliefs about the organisation's work and how it should be carried out, its responsibilities, its relationships with customers and other stakeholders, its people and how they should be treated.

Not all values are equal. In the same way that an individual holds certain principles they would never compromise, while simultaneously holding a myriad of less fundamental beliefs, so it is with organisations. When working with culture, is important to understand the difference between core values and non-core values.

Core values: These are the beliefs at the deepest level of the organisation's culture. They are the small number of fundamental ideals that the organisation will not compromise. They become second nature – often acted upon without being thought about. While some companies have written-down statements of values which reflect accurately what is at the heart of their culture, in many the core values remain unconscious and can be difficult to articulate. To build a stronger culture, you must make them explicit.

Non-core values: Non-core values need to be distinguished from core values. They include:

- Values that the organisation is prepared to compromise: These are beliefs that an organisation genuinely promotes and supports, but which it will be prepared to compromise to accommodate a pressing need.
- Beliefs that follow on as natural consequences of the core values: These are not core values in themselves, but need to be given attention if core values are to be upheld. For example, a few firms I have worked with highlight 'respect for people' as a core value. They then go on to debate whether 'diversity' should also be a core value. The conclusion is generally that it is not, because if you respect people it follows that you value their differences.

However, diversity needs to be actively promoted if 'respect for people' is to ring true.
- 'Permission-to-play' values: These are often referred to as 'givens' – values that every business in the sector must adhere to if they are to participate in the market. Permission-to-play values can be difficult to distinguish from core values. For example, law firms often agonise over whether 'technical excellence' should be stated as a core value. The fact is that every firm must be able to demonstrate very high standards of technical ability in order to survive at all, leading many to conclude that this is a permission-to-play value.

2.5 What is meant by a 'strong' culture?

In a strong culture, everyone shares, believes in and adheres to the core values. Non-core values and behaviours that conflict with core values are not tolerated. Core values drive behavioural norms, and artefacts serve to reinforce that behaviour. In other words, everything seen at the outer levels of a strong culture – artefacts, behavioural norms and non-core values – is aligned with, or at least does not conflict with, core values.

A strong culture can be cult-like, and you will have to accept that not everyone will fit in. Culture can eat people for breakfast too, and most law firms have a war story about a heavy-hitting lateral hire who was ejected from the firm for breaking cultural taboos. You will need to make clear that people who undermine the values do not belong in the firm. Ideally, they should never get past recruitment, but those who do make it in should be helped to change or, failing that, managed out. This sounds harsh, but you have to remember the benefits that a strong culture brings, and that people who do embrace the values will thrive, love the firm and give their best. It is this combination of alignment and motivation that leads to superior performance.

3. Leading culture change

We now apply the knowledge gained in the previous section to developing a practical approach to culture change. Looking at the culture model, it is clear that superficial elements of culture are easy to modify while those at deeper levels are slow or nearly impossible to change. It is relatively straightforward to change artefacts, but gains from such gestures can be short-lived. It is harder, but not impossible, to change behaviour, and this has longer-lasting benefits. Core values, on the other hand, are very slow and difficult to alter. Anyone aiming to build a strong culture should therefore work with existing core values, and focus on aligning those elements of culture that can more easily be changed. Specifically, they should:
- preserve and build on existing core values when developing a statement of desired values;
- change behavioural norms to align them better with desired core values;
- adjust artefacts of the culture so that they reinforce desired behaviours and core values.

3.1   A process for culture change

The process outlined below was developed for KPMG in the late 1990s as the firm embarked on a worldwide culture change programme.[6] Since then it has formed the basis of successful culture initiatives in numerous companies and professional services firms.

The process broadly comprises four phases:

Figure 2: A process for culture change

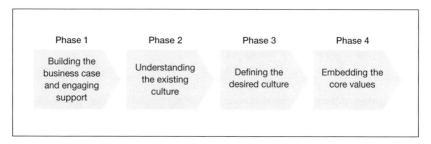

Phase 1	Phase 2	Phase 3	Phase 4
Building the business case and engaging support	Understanding the existing culture	Defining the desired culture	Embedding the core values

Phase 1: Building the business case and engaging support

The first step is to build the business rationale for values and use it to engage key stakeholders. This seems an obvious piece of advice, but it is surprising how many leadership teams overlook it, even though they would normally require pages of cost-benefit analyses for investments in other projects. Culture change requires patience and long-term dedication. Benefits are not instant and can be difficult to quantify. It also requires individuals to change their behaviour, which most find very challenging. Commitment can quickly fade, and without a robust business rationale, most culture projects fizzle out.

Let us look at the business rationale for values in three different case studies.

- The first is KPMG in the late 1990s, which – as is true for many law firms today – had an acute need to become more globally integrated. The firm was losing high profile, international clients and failing to leverage synergies across geographies. As a result, it fell from first to fourth position in the then Big Five accountancy firms. KPMG recognised that a shared set of values, practised consistently across regions, would be key in transforming its loose, federalist network into something that looked, felt and acted like a global firm.

- The second is a large financial institution, whose head of risk became the main advocate of culture change. Although the global financial crisis was still years away, he had become very concerned about the practices of overzealous salespeople. He felt that they needed to be reined in, in order to mitigate risk and better serve customers. He concluded that stronger values might be more effective than an unwieldy compliance rulebook in achieving this.

---

6   Jan Thornbury, "KPMG: Revitalising Culture Through Values" (1999) 10(4) *Business Strategy Review*; Jan Thornbury and Colin Sharman, *Living Culture: A Values-driven Approach to Revitalising Your Company Culture* (Random House Business Books, 2000).

- Finally we have a public sector organisation whose leadership team felt that changes in governance, funding and regulations were forcing them to compromise their beliefs. Feeling pulled in all directions, they recognised a need to clarify the fundamental values they must fight to preserve in a changing world.

What these three very different business rationales have in common is that they address threats and opportunities that are highly specific to each organisation, and they make clear why stronger values provide a solution.

Phase 2: Understanding the existing culture

There is a tendency to leap too quickly into defining the new culture, without paying attention to what exists already. This is a mistake – first because is not possible to bring about a radical shift from one set of values to another, and nor is it likely to be desirable. The aim should be to preserve and build on the strengths of the existing culture, rather than reinvent it. Secondly, a thorough analysis of the existing culture will expose gaps between the current and desired culture. This knowledge is essential when prioritising change activities further down the line. Finally, a thorough understanding of the existing culture will be helpful in navigating sensitivities and determining which types of intervention will work.

Understanding the existing culture in depth – that is, to the level of core values – requires rigorous research, particularly in weak cultures, where common values can be difficult to uncover. There are many 'culture audit' questionnaires on the market, but these are often of limited use and no substitute for a comprehensive programme of qualitative research. The best approach typically involves workshops with a large, representative sample of people from across the organisation. This is powerful not only in gleaning accurate feedback, but also in building the shared ownership that is essential when it comes to values.

The common themes regarding existing values that emerge from this phase will form the basis for developing a statement of desired core values. In addition, the consultation sheds light on current behavioural norms, and how well aligned – or not – these might be with desired values. It also highlights what people in the firm cherish about the culture; negative attributes that need to change; and the strength of the existing culture.

Phase 3: Defining the desired culture

The main task here is to develop a statement of desired core values, and make clear what these mean in practice.

The desired core values must stay true to the strongest beliefs that were uncovered in the previous phase. By articulating what people already believe in, authenticity is ensured. It is important to test rigorously, and narrow down the outputs of the consultation to a small number of fundamental values.

The stated values need to be credible – some degree of aspiration is acceptable, but they should not depart too far from reality. People should still be able to look at the values statement and say "yes, that's us", rather than "maybe that's how we would like to be". If there is a gap between aspiration and reality, there must be an authentic commitment to bridging it.

Values need to be simple and memorable if people are to keep them in mind as they go about their daily work. Most organisations therefore opt for concise, punchy phrases or single words to capture their desired values. This is good practice, but an effective statement of values needs more than a few headlines. Values need to be clearly understood, unambiguous and unyielding to misinterpretation. Headline statements should therefore be supported by a brief but specific explanation of what each value means.

When the core values have been articulated, it is time to turn attention to the broader culture. In particular, expectations should be set about behaviour – what will be the new norms? Setting out a few specifics about how each value translates into behaviour helps people work out 'what this means for me' and further reduces ambiguity. It also provides a useful and objective basis for recognising those who uphold the values, and challenging those who do not. The development of behaviours to support a values statement is best done through consultation. Not only does this produce examples that are relevant to people's day-to-day experience, but the process of agreeing together 'what we are going to start doing, stop doing and continue doing to ensure we live up to this core value' is a powerful means of generating commitment.

Phase 4: Embedding the core values

Now begins the process of change that will build a stronger culture. As stated earlier, the aim is to align behavioural norms with the core values, and ensure that artefacts of the culture reinforce desired behaviours and, by default, the values. There are three main strands to this implementation phase:

- Engaging: Launching the values, then maintaining awareness and commitment through ongoing communication and involvement.
- Changing behaviour: Helping individuals to align their behaviour with the values, for example through 'viral' techniques, campaigns, personal development, 360° feedback, performance management, recognition and reward.
- Re-engineering artefacts: Making changes to, for example, processes, systems, routines, policies and the work environment, so that they support and reinforce desired behaviours.

These activities complement each other, and should be coordinated to focus on priority areas where gaps between the existing and desired states are greatest. For example, in KPMG's global culture change programme, one of the biggest gaps between the existing and desired values concerned knowledge sharing. Some blamed years of underinvestment and the firm's outdated knowledge systems, but in truth these were only symptoms of a culture in which people were protective of their own knowledge, and sceptical of the 'not invented here'. While it was clear that systems needed to change, so did beliefs and behaviour. The firm made a massive investment in technology, but equal emphasis was placed on the process, structural and behavioural changes necessary to ensure that it would be used.

Culture change does not happen overnight, and this final phase of the process is the longest. However, over time, as people see new behaviours becoming the norm, their belief in core values is strengthened. As core values become woven into every aspect of organisational life, the culture initiative becomes a more subtle maintenance programme.

The issue of measurement is often raised. Quantifiable benefits, such as enhanced performance and retention, are so influenced by other factors that they cannot be attributed solely to the strength of the culture. Other benefits, such as improved morale and cohesion, are hard to quantify. Yet, like any initiative, a culture programme requires measures to keep it on track, and demonstrate its worth. A solution is to measure perceptions, asking through surveys or discussion whether things have got better, and whether the firm has got any closer to living its desired values. A good example is accountancy firm BDO,[7] which for years tracked the impact of its 2002 values programme.[8] Not only did this highlight its culture initiative's considerable success; the fact that the leadership team continued to measure progress showed how seriously they took it, and further reinforced belief in the values.

External measures such as market position and client rankings can also be useful, and the increasing number of large-scale, cross-industry surveys that assess 'best places to work' can provide helpful benchmarks.

The good news is that although the path to a strong culture can be arduous, there are clear benefits along the way.

3.2   Making it work for you

(a)   Adapting the process

While the generic approach needs to be adapted to suit the particular situation of your own firm, the same broad design principles apply. You still need to be clear about the business rationale, develop a thorough understanding of the current culture, define the desired culture in terms of core values and behaviours, and then align behavioural norms and artefacts with your stated core values. For example, if you already have stated values but they do not have much traction, you would test their authenticity as part of understanding your firm's existing culture, and adapt the rest of the approach accordingly. Or you may be trying to bring together two firms post-merger, in which case you first need to clarify whether one culture should absorb the other, or whether it is better to build something new on the common ground. Either way, you will need a thorough understanding of the two 'legacy' cultures.

(b)   Who should be involved

Since the aim is to articulate and embed a set of core values that are shared by all, it

7   Jeremy Newman and Jan Thornbury, "Values at Work in BDO Stoy Hayward" (2004) 3(5) *Strategic HR Review*.
8   Nick Tatchell, "Measuring the Impact of Values at BDO Stoy Hayward" (2006) 5(6) *Strategic HR Review*.

would clearly be a mistake to let these be developed by a small elite, or by external consultants. The approach calls for involvement from people of all levels and roles in the firm. For some of the smaller firms with whom I have worked, we have included everyone, which makes for powerful engagement.

Special attention should be given to influential stakeholders who have the power to enable or disrupt the process. In a law firm, this generally means partners and heads of support functions. As leaders in their own right, these individuals need to buy into, understand and actively support the values initiative. Of course, not all will have equal influence, and some stakeholder analysis is needed. This does not have to be over-engineered – one managing partner sat down with me and systematically went through the entire list of partners in the firm, dividing them into 'likely supporters', 'neutrals' and 'awkward so-and-sos'. On this basis, we figured out an effective approach to engaging each faction. Any good law firm leader should know his or her partners well enough to do the same.

I am often asked whether clients should provide input to the development of a law firm's values. My advice is 'no' – you should not need clients to tell you what you believe in! That is a little like the politician who asks, "What principles should I hold, so that I can get your vote?" However, client opinion is very valuable later, when assessing how well the firm is living up to its values, and feedback processes should be adapted to include questions about any values relating to the client experience.

(c)   *Style of the approach*
The approach itself should reflect the values. If you believe in integrity and you have already decided on the answer, do not pretend to consult! If you value innovation, try something new that feels a little off-the-wall. This might be stating the obvious, but it is easy to be tripped up by old habits. I have more than once heard law firm partners advocate values like 'respect' or 'inclusion', then balk at the suggestion support functions should be consulted.

At the same time, the approach should not be so alien to the existing culture that people reject it. You must be sensitive to how people might react. The cliché that you should learn to walk before you run holds true. For example, if you wish to introduce 360° feedback and your firm has a culture where people avoid difficult conversations, you might wish to make it anonymous at first.

4.   Learning and challenges for law firm leaders
In conclusion, we look at what else we can learn from others' mistakes, what you may find difficult as you lead culture change and the qualities required to lead with values.

4.1   More common errors
   •   Failure to implement: This is by far the most common error I have seen in over 20 years of consulting in this field. Values are launched with a fanfare then nothing happens. Sometimes the programme simply runs out of momentum, sometimes the tools and knowledge to embed values are

lacking, or sometimes a more pressing need takes priority. But always when this happens, there is a leader behind it who does not grasp the magnitude of the missed opportunity, and who consequently fails to get things back on track.

- Too many core values: Core values are beliefs that must never be compromised. They should be so precious that if continuing to do business meant compromising them, people would rather change the nature of the business than change the values. Core values are therefore small in number – typically between three and five. But it is so tempting to keep adding to the list. The problem is that statements that are obviously not authentic undermine the credibility of the genuine values. Absolute honesty about what you will commit to is essential. For example, the board of a start-up company with whom I worked maintained that 'people development' was on their rather long list of core values. I asked them to imagine what would happen if they could not raise much-needed capital – would they cut the training budget? "Of course!" they replied. In fact, this was one of the first costs they would cut. It was then clear that, although important, this belief was non-core. They had another core value to do with helping developing countries. I asked the same question – if things were tight financially, would they shift their business away from developing economies to more lucrative markets? The resounding answer was "No! We would rather go under than compromise that." Clearly, we had found a core value.

- Poor use of language and the wordsmithing abyss: When formulating the values statement, be alert to language that might make people cringe. Words like 'holistic' and 'empowerment' often meet with resistance even if the sentiment is bought into. Sometimes 'management speak' jars: "Can we please stop talking about 'behaviours'!" ranted one senior partner. "It's behaviour – singular!" Of course there are limits – I once had to protest when a law firm asked me not to use the words 'values', 'behaviour' or 'culture'!

The language of the values must resonate with everyone in the firm. Be cautious about 'collegiality', a word much loved by law firm partners in the English-speaking world: "I never heard that word before I started working in law firms," one senior IT manager told me, rolling his eyes. "It conjures up pictures of old boy networks and mutual back-slapping. And there's a distance to it – a bunch of individuals being 'collegiate' isn't the same as an effective team." Even simple words can be misinterpreted. A concerned partner at KPMG once cornered me and asked, "Why don't the values apply to partners?" I looked at her in utter bewilderment, then asked, "Er … what makes you think that?" "Look," she said, pointing to the values statement, "this only talks about 'our people'. There's nothing in there about partners." I had to laugh as I explained that with a few possible exceptions, the firm's partners could also be classified as people. International firms need to be careful about how messages translate. For example, KPMG used the word 'passionate' to describe their attitude to client service. This turned out to be inappropriate in Eastern Europe, where the word always has romantic connotations. The best way to ensure that values resonate is to stay true to the language used in the firm day-to-day, and test rigorously with a cross-section of people when drafting.

Agreeing a final values statement can be a painful process, particularly in law firms where individuals are often sticklers for precise language. Obviously, the values need to be approved and accepted by the leadership team, but you need to be wary of falling into the 'wordsmithing abyss' – an endless cycle of redrafting. This not only holds up progress, but with every strike of a red pen the original sentiments behind the values tend to be respun, and you can end up losing the vital authenticity and ownership that the approach set out to deliver. At some point, you may have to make the call that the wording is 'good enough'.

- Inconsistency of message: It is vital that all communication about values is consistent. In professional partnerships, where leadership tends to be more diffuse and autonomous than in a corporation, there is huge scope for conflicting messages. Often this is due to lack of engagement among partners who do not bother to get the message right, or who add their own spin. It is also not uncommon to see influential partners developing their own set of values. This is more damaging, as people in their departments wonder which of the competing values they are supposed to follow. Mixed messages make for weak cultures, and are among the few things that leaders should not tolerate.

- Misunderstanding how values help you differentiate: My local supermarket has a wall frieze proclaiming "Our values make us different". I am sometimes tempted to ask the checkout assistant what those values are, but that is purely due to my professional curiosity. The truth is, as a customer, I do not want to see their values. I just want to see the difference. Herein lie a few of the common misunderstandings around values and differentiation. First, the myth that to differentiate you need values that are radically different from those of your peers. In reality, while there may be some nuances in your values that capture your firm's personality, the real differentiation will come from how well your values are lived out. The second error is to view values as a marketing tool. Of course, if a client is interested, show them your values statement. However, the harsh reality is that your clients will probably dismiss your values as rhetoric until their experience tells them otherwise. They do not want to read in your values statement that you believe in 'approachability'; they want people in your firm to be approachable. Likewise, they are probably not interested in your grand statement about diversity; they just want to see more diverse teams.

- Delegating accountability to HR or other functions: Many leaders delegate responsibility for culture to HR or other functions, even though they would never dream of offloading any other strategic duties. Of course the design and running of the culture programme must be delegated to someone with appropriate knowledge and skills, but the leader must be the one to direct the programme, deliver the key messages, intervene to resolve issues and, most importantly, set an example for others in the firm. While the HR function holds many levers to enable culture change, they can never substitute for leadership.

4.2 Challenges for law firm leaders

- Being prepared to do difficult things: Leaders need be proactive and uncompromising in instilling values. This means removing obstacles to the desired culture, and visibly rewarding behaviour that supports the values. Everyone will be watching to gauge your commitment and whether there are negative consequences for undermining the values. This can make for difficult decisions – what to do about the partner who brings in huge revenues, but whose behaviour is unacceptable? What time-honoured partner privileges need to be removed? You will inevitably face some difficult choices, and you will need courage and conviction to follow them through.
- Knowing when to intervene: There is a fine line between leading and meddling. For example, there are likely to be some variations in culture between countries, offices or departments. Subcultures are normally not problematic as long as core values are still adhered to, but it is not always easy to tell when looking through your own lens. Awareness and open dialogue are essential to judging what to tolerate, and what to confront.
- Being a role model: This is possibly the greatest challenge to leaders of culture change – aligning their own behaviour with the values. As a leader, this is the most important contribution you will make, because more than anyone else you set the example. This may mean doing and saying things that feel uncomfortable or unnatural at first. You may be reluctant to admit your shortcomings, but if you can be open to feedback, frank about what you must change and visibly commit to doing things differently, you will inspire others to change too.

4.3 Leadership qualities

A common misconception is that only a charismatic leader can succeed in culture change. In fact, while charisma is not a hindrance, it is far less important than other qualities. To bring about culture change, a leader should have integrity: he or she should be honest about what they will commit to, and put their words into action. Openness and sensitivity to what is going on in the firm, and an ability to communicate, listen and anticipate the effects of interventions, are also vital. Determination and resilience are essential – this is a rewarding path but also a challenging one. Finally, the leader should have humility. This is not about putting his or her stamp on everything. It is about creating values for the firm, not a personal legacy. The goal is a culture that endures throughout generations of leaders, and assures the firm's long-term prosperity. Building a strong culture is an act of true stewardship.

Leadership succession in law firms: continuity or renewal?

Christopher Bockmann
Leadership Life Cycles

1. Introduction

The complexity of a leadership succession lies in the fact that it is a highly visible moment in the life of an organisation and yet it is greatly influenced by invisible factors. The combination of personal and emotional questions with firm-related issues constitutes one of the challenges of any leadership succession. Law firm partnerships amplify these challenges because of a collective approach to decision making and an individualist partner culture. For a firm, it can be a critical transition in its development, an opportunity for change or a threat to its stability. The history of the firm, its strategy and its stage of development all have an influence over the succession process. The way the succession transition is managed is also a reflection of the maturity of its governance. Attention tends to focus on identifying and nominating the heir to the incumbent leader and finding the most suitable partner to lead the firm who draws on the widest possible support in the partnership. This tends to be a rather narrow definition of succession.

There are many reasons, often informal and below the radar, for the succession process to be distracted from its main objective. These reasons find their origin in the highly personal dimension often forgotten in the formal process. One of the principal distractions is the stepping down of the incumbent leader which is an emotionally charged period and one full of questions as the absence of an exit strategy tends to be the norm. As illustrated by a Managing Partner Forum survey,[1] 86% of managing partners have no exit strategy. This effect can be amplified if the leader is also a founder or historic partner of the firm, as was the case in the widely commented on succession of Robert Dell after 20 years at the helm of Latham and Watkins. Yet, managing the process of stepping down is often left to the individual as the firm tends to put most if not all of its efforts into finding and appointing or electing a successor. This can be enhanced by a form of denial by the incumbent leader about the difficulties of stepping down.

This chapter will break down the succession process into several stages, the fourth one taking place simultaneously to the other three, as shown in figure 1 on the next page.

Firms need to focus their attention on four distinct stages when managing a succession transition:

- Growing the next generation of leaders – firms need to foster an environment

---

1   Managing Partner Forum for Northeastern Law Firms, 2010.

Figure 1: The succession process – a parallel movement for the up-coming and out-going leader(s)

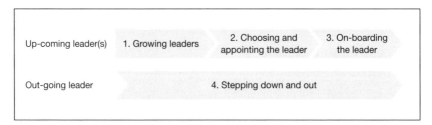

that facilitates the development and emergence of talented partners that will form a pool of successors. How a firm defines and values leadership will influence this environment. Ideally, stage 1 becomes an integral and ongoing part of how a firm is being managed rather than triggered by a succession process.

- Deciding who the next leader should be – whether formally or informally, this stage consists in narrowing down potential candidates, appointing the successor and ensuring the process strengthens the legitimacy of the successor.
- On-boarding the new leader – this stage is about supporting the successor in managing the gap between their personal expectations, their firm's expectations and the realities of adjusting to the new role (see elsewhere in this book). It will take at least a year of steep learning for the successor to start feeling comfortable in the role, well beyond the 'mythical' first 100 days. The on-boarding is also an opportunity for the successor to reveal untapped leadership talent.
- Stepping down and out for the incumbent leader – a leader will already be thinking, for some worrying, about stepping down when there will be discussion about future talent and preparing successors (stage 1); this will become more pronounced as the incumbent advances through the first three stages.

Firms typically focus on the second stage – identifying, choosing and appointing or electing a successor, yet the stages of growing young leaders, on-boarding the new leader and the stepping down of the incumbent are critical to the sustainability of the succession transition. These four stages are relevant to the partner(s) concentrating most executive powers, typically managing or senior partners. With the exception of the second stage, all stages will be equally valid for other roles such as practice heads or partners with responsibility for certain regions. In such cases, the process will tend to be less formalised and managed through a simpler decision-making process.

2. Growing the next generation of leaders

Reappointment or an uncontested election is common in law firms. This can be attributable to the qualities of the incumbent leader but also to an absence of possible successors. A succession will only be as good as the quality of talented partners who are both available and willing to put themselves forward. This willingness depends on the attractiveness of the role which can be a challenge in a partnership environment where decision making is more consensus based. Fostering leadership talent among partners requires taking the long-term view and a continuous effort by the firm (see elsewhere in this book). Leaders might even consider growing the next generation as a key part of their role, as did Jack Welch, the former CEO of General Electric, who spent more than half his time hiring, developing and firing people.[2] The more transparent and shared the understanding about what constitutes leadership, the less the chances of misunderstanding during the succession process.

2.1 Leadership in a partnership

Leadership and management are not usually the motivational drivers for lawyers to enter their profession. As with doctors, for example, mastery and self-accomplishment have traditionally been more important motivational factors.[3] Comparing the senior leadership in a corporate environment with a professional service firm reveals the limited value firms place on leadership roles as opposed to revenue-generating work which is the primary task of any partner. Leadership roles can therefore be seen as a distraction from a lawyer's professional sense of purpose.

In a partnership culture, firm leaders have narrow mandates and wield moderate positional power (see elsewhere in this book). Leadership roles become more demanding as a result. Managing partners "are expected both to set themselves apart – and above – the group, while at the same time interact as an integral part of the group, even as co-equals with other members".[4] Influence thus becomes a key factor to overcome the limits of the narrow executive mandate. As such, taking on a top role in a law firm and succeeding is a real test of leadership abilities. This influence will find its source in the ability of the leader to articulate, embody and help realise a story of possibilities[5] of those entrusting the partner with the new leadership role.

In general, this will have an impact on the perceived attractiveness of a leadership role, particularly when a partner needs to partially or completely sacrifice his own practice to focus on a leadership role. This often requires an inner calling or sense of purpose to make such risk-taking activity meaningful, even more so for partners with many years of potential practice ahead of them.

2.2 Growing leadership talent

The flat structure that represents a partnership is paradoxically conducive to growing

2   Interview by C Hymowitz and M Murray, *Wall Street Journal*, June 21 1999.
3   E Schein, *Organizational Culture and Leadership* (Jossey-Bass, 2004).
4   C Pearce and J Conger, *Shared Leadership* (Sage, 2003).
5   G Petriglieri, INSEAD leadership seminar, March 26 2013.
6   J Lorsch and P Mathias, "When Professionals Have to Manage", *Harvard Business Review*, 1987.

leadership talent. This is partly because of the producer-manager model[6] whereby managing a team and practice is done in addition to working on client matters, and shared ownership and management responsibilities are regularly distributed among partners. There is a multitude of management roles, where portfolios of functions (eg, risk management, recruitment, marketing), or practices (eg, tax or real estate) are shared among partners to the extent that nearly every partner could have some form of leadership role or lay claim to one. Partners are also often invited to express their views on various initiatives and decisions. Incumbent leaders may stimulate potential successors by involving interested and talented partners in projects dealing with clients or product development. For example, Taylor Wessing, an international law firm, regularly runs career reflection programmes to support partners in considering the next stage of their career. During the programme, a number of younger partners shared a desire to move into formal management roles. There was a range of motivations including:

- personal ambition and a sense of continued career progression;
- a desire to have more control over one's practice;
- a perception that partners were expected to contribute to the wider development of the firm by taking up such roles.

What transpired with the programme was how valuable informal experiences, even on a project basis, were to prepare for such roles, particularly if they were reinforced with mentoring or coaching to learn from these new experiences. The young partners realised that taking on responsibilities not linked to a specific role gave them exposure to leadership situations and provided a good opportunity to apply their skills. It also helped them to realise that you do not need a formal management role to be a leader and that not all who are in management roles are leaders. Confusing the two can be common. A partner has more control when managing a team for a client matter than trying to influence fellow partners on matters concerning, for example, the international development of the firm or a large client initiative. Such assignments-based learning is widely recognised to be a powerful leadership developmental activity and an opportunity to practice and make mistakes with new professional roles.[7] Taking on the management of a significant practice or a country or sitting on the executive committee can provide a rich experience in leadership. This is often considered to be part of the necessary credentials of any successor. In some cases, special roles might even be created such as, for example, deputy managing partner – but this has its downsides (see 3.2 and 4.2 below).

The collective leadership of a firm needs to take a proactive approach to growing its talent. The executive committee of a global firm reviews on a regular basis a group of young partners taking on management roles and leading initiatives. The executive committee regularly updates the list to ensure that these partners are given the

---

7   G Dalton, P Thompson and R Price, "The Four Stages of Professional Careers", *Organisational Dynamics*, 1977; H Handfield-Jones, "How Executives Grow", *McKinsey Quarterly*, 2000; and H Ibarra, S Snook and L Guillén Ramo, "Identity-based Leader Development", Harvard Business School paper, 2008.

opportunity (invited) to take on new roles and initiatives. Such attention by the senior leadership is also a way to acknowledge and value such types of contribution beyond just developing one's own practice.

Such active monitoring of end of mandates of both senior and managing partners is more sensitive because it focuses attention on a limited number of individuals who might consider that their best years are behind rather than ahead of them as would be the case for future talent. Monitoring the terms of senior or managing partners can be stigmatising. Asking questions of a managing partner about her succession could be perceived as questioning her current performance. The more succession planning stays informal, the more personalised any discussion about it becomes and therefore the more difficult it is to address. This may account for the fact that nearly a quarter of the top 200 US firms do not have a succession plan in place.[8] The absence of a mandatory retirement age in some US firms can create a grey zone in terms of succession planning. Talented partners considering taking leadership roles are also likely to watch how incumbent leaders stepping down are treated as a measure of how attractive the proposition of taking the top job is. The more transparent the process and attractive the precedent, the richer the quality and range of candidates who are likely to put themselves forward.

To grow leaders, law firms may also resort to more formal approaches such as executive development and coaching to accompany partners with leadership potential. One global law firm has developed a programme explicitly targeted at aspiring leaders. However, participation is based on self-identification or encouragement by senior leaders rather than any formal selection process. Open access to these programmes is an essential factor as any programme perceived to be for high potential would be counter to the spirit of a partnership.

3. Choosing and appointing the leader

Whether by direct appointment or an election, there is no one right approach to choosing and appointing a leader as it will vary according to a firm's history or the incumbent leader. Each approach has inherent upsides and downsides which can, however, be managed. Whatever the chosen approach, it should follow a number of core principles around legitimacy and transparency to ensure a satisfactory and sustainable outcome. The process for finding a successor should be separated and not influenced by the inherent qualities of potential or declared candidates. The succession process will rely on three elements:

- choosing the successor which is driven by the governance;
- defining the profile versus looking for a person;
- finding the candidate to match the profile.

3.1 Choosing the successor

The approach for choosing a successor can vary from the incumbent managing partner selecting and appointing an heir-successor to an open election process (see figure 2). The choice is usually influenced by the culture, history and needs of the firm.

---

8   Julie Triedman, "Meet the New Boss", *The American Lawyer*, September 2014.

Figure 2: The succession process: a range of choices – to find the most suitable candidate with the widest support

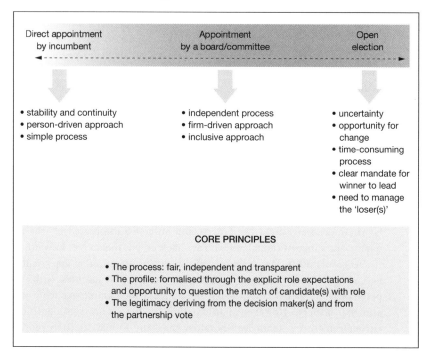

At one end of the scale there is a direct appointment by the incumbent managing partner. This can be justified when the incumbent has such legitimacy within the firm through being a founding or historic partner who has made a major contribution to the firm's development. An argument for such a direct appointment can be to ensure the continuity and stability of the firm. A direct appointment also works where the partnership is relatively homogenous (home-grown partners) and small, where all the partners know each other. The principal risk with such an approach is the dependence on the intention and personality of the incumbent leader. If there is only one candidate, a protégé of the incumbent, who has been considered for the role, this could be met with rejection by fellow partners. In worst case scenarios, the incumbent could have a more personal agenda in influencing the decision, for example appointing a successor in exchange for some form of protection when the incumbent steps down, appointing a weak successor to make the incumbent look good or creating a dependency link. Most incumbent leaders are likely to follow many of the core principles, notably some form of consultation with the partnership – if only to feel they are making the right decisions. Many conscious and unconscious biases are likely to affect the process which is why governance can have an important role to play. Direct appointment is context specific and therefore not an approach that firms should continue without careful reassessment.

The next step in the decision-making scale is for a firm to use a supervisory board with the responsibility for identifying and filtering candidates and recommending a successor. A board can either take on the main decision-making role or work alongside the incumbent leader who retains the final say. To add greater independence, a specific nomination committee can be put in place with highly regarded and representative partners. These partners might include a strong representation of younger partners as they are the ones most concerned with the future leader's decisions and actions. Such separation of decision-making powers or bodies can favour greater diversity of candidates and can be further embedded if those making the recommendations, such as a nomination committee or board, are separated from those who make the decision (eg, the incumbent leader or supervisory board). This approach fits well with the spirit of collegiality of a partnership. The more significant the perceived or actual executive powers of the leadership role, the more a governance needs to factor in checks and balances to guarantee an independent decision-making process.

The other end of the scale is an open campaign and election of a new leader. Electing a leader has the advantage of increasing transparency on the choices the firm faces and the quality of the debate as to what is expected of the new leader. An election will therefore impact positively the legitimacy of the successor, potentially providing him with a broader support base. In an election, candidates will campaign and therefore give the opportunity to the partnership to clarify and challenge the proposals of each candidate. Such campaigning replaces the consultations that might be organised when a board has responsibility for the succession process. Consultation might still have value in the early phase to validate the quality of short-listed candidates. Elections have the additional benefit of creating more space for candidates who are outsiders and therefore with a more progressive agenda than the two previous approaches. The downside is the antagonistic environment that an election campaign can create. Elections can have a polarising effect. Those involved in the succession process may have an important role in closely monitoring those partners who have lost an election. In some cases, the candidates receiving least support have the option to withdraw as a face-saving act instead of losing an election. The worst case scenario being that the partner leaves the firm. The paradox is that it may leave only one candidate left to vote for. An election is also likely to place greater emphasis on the firm leader as the principal agent of change and the election becomes the opportunity for contrasting different views on the future of the firm. Another downside of election is that it may involve a greater degree of power bargaining and patronage in exchange for support. Firms can mitigate these effects by requiring candidates to be clear and open about what they stand for (see 3.3 below) and by ensuring the governance structure can place checks on the firm leader, for example regular performance reviews by the board.

Those having a role in the succession should also be clear on the policy regarding communication as any succession process is likely to generate some form of anxiety and will have its share of rumours which might set the future new leader off to a bad start. There are also likely to be questions on how an existing balance of power will shift. Any perceived secrecy or even long periods without communication is likely to raise questions about the transparency or the fairness of the process. The objective is to ensure that corridor discussions and rumours do not completely replace a structured and maybe more qualitative open debate.

If one of the first two approaches is chosen by a firm, it is still worth considering giving the partnership the opportunity to vote on the recommended candidate for succession. Voting remains an important ritual in a partnership and an acknowledgement that each partner, ideally including non-equity in this case, has a say in major decisions. Even if it is perceived as simply rubber-stamping a decision by the board or the incumbent, as is also often the case with electing new partners, its symbolic weight is not to be underestimated. Opting for a nomination process whereby partners can put forward a number of suitable names for the succession process can also be more aligned to the culture of some firms rather than having partners put themselves forward as candidates for the succession.

3.2 Defining the profile versus looking for a person

Once the governance issues are clear, the next step in the succession process is deciding on what kind of leader the firm is looking for. There is a natural temptation to look for a particular type of person as a successor before discussing more objectively what is expected of him which is part of a wider discussion on the future direction of the firm. An incumbent managing partner may look for a partner that mirrors most his own leadership style. Leadership is very contextual; a managing partner might have made a significant contribution to his firm but when the firm reaches another stage of development, a different profile might be called for. The skills and experience of a managing partner will be different when expanding the firm through a large merger from those required for finishing the integration of a merger a few years later. There is a natural alternating movement in the development of firms between strategic change and consolidation, the former requiring a more directive style that will be less consensual and sustainable than the latter. In a similar way, the profile of a managing partner might also vary according to the current economic environment. A downturn in the economy may mean a managing partner having to make more unpopular decisions than in a period of economic growth. This might call for a different type of personality, one who is more comfortable with the tensions and conflict the context is likely to generate.

Historically, managing partners have emanated from the ranks of rainmakers or partners with the most impressive portfolio of clients. Yet credentials are often backward looking and are therefore not necessarily a good predictor of future leadership abilities. Partners are elected above all for their expertise and ability to generate revenue rather than for their ability to lead a firm. These credentials continue to legitimise accession to leadership roles today, though to a lesser extent as firms and their partners acknowledge that leadership roles become more demanding, complex and needed. Such demands also make it less attractive for rainmaker-type partners who prefer to focus on client work.

In considering the profile of the successor, three elements should be taken into account:

- Because of her experience the incumbent should make some contribution. Yet in the words of the chairman of US employment law firm, Jackson Lewis,

"it goes without saying that the former managing partner's ... input must be completely independent of her or her personal relationships and must be focused solely on the best interest of the firm".[9]
- It should be person-specific. The successor should, for example, have
- a track record as a lawyer,
- been in previous leadership roles,
- a deep knowledge of certain parts of the firm,
- an external reputation.

Agreeing and defining this can be beneficial as many people have their own understanding and definition of what leadership means.
- It should be context-specific. It should be decided what is required for the firm at this particular stage.

Those involved in the succession process need to be aware of the temptation to include criteria such as needing to alternate candidates from the largest practices or countries, or even introducing a hybrid solution with co-managing partners as a way to solve a challenge faced by the firm. This temptation might come at a cost of neglecting leadership qualities that should be sought in the successor. Such a compromise is likely only to solve the challenge superficially. One might recommend that any unfinished work or unaddressed issue should be resolved before the succession to give the new leader a sound starting basis.

Those in charge of the succession process should come up with a document outlining the profile, experience and competences expected of the new leader. An agreed description of the formal role of the new leader is also likely to facilitate discussions and minimise room for personal interpretation and other influences.

Some consultation with the partnership on the role itself could already take place at this stage. This will help legitimise the decision-making process whereby a successor is chosen because she[10] is the closest match to what is expected rather than because of a preference for a person. It is a natural bias to prefer those resembling us the most or those most likely to favour us.

3.3 Finding the candidate to match the profile
This phase of the succession process is aimed at strengthening the transparency of the process and the legitimacy of the successor.

The exact format for finding the most suitable candidate will depend on the approach a firm has adopted for the decision making along the direct appointment/election scale (see under 3.1). Depending on the number of potential candidates or consensus on the potential candidates and their quality, the board may want to filter candidates from a long to a short list to make the process more manageable. In the case of the Latham and Watkins succession,[11] there were 38

---

9   D Parnell, "Practices for Leadership Succession", Forbes, August 4 2014.
10   Please note this chapter alternates between the gender of leader.
11   Julie Triedman, "Meet the New Boss", *The American Lawyer*, September 2014.

nominees for the succession process which was narrowed down through two rounds of rankings leading to a final vote between two contenders.

From a candidate's perspective, such a consultation process is the opportunity to campaign with a manifesto or plan that becomes, if appointed or elected, the mandate to lead. It also adds a degree of fairness to the succession process in that it offers all candidates a chance to demonstrate their motivation, and express ideas on how they see the priorities for the future leader and what they propose to implement. Structuring the rules for campaigning is important to ensure a fair process.

From the partnership perspective, the objective should be to give as many partners as possible the opportunity to question and probe candidates. It is, after all, a unique opportunity to have a structured and real debate about the future direction of the firm. Besides ensuring participation in key decisions of the firm, such open discussions can also act as a way to test and gather support.

To add an element of objectivity, a firm may decide to go as far as asking candidates to go through some form of formalised assessment process, including psychometric testing, managed by an executive search firm as is done for the recruiting of CEOs in the corporate world. Externalising part of the process can be a solution when the selection of the next leader is seen to be overly influenced by some partners (eg, the founder) or specific interest groups.

The case of reappointment or re-election is a complicating factor and particular attention needs to be paid to ensure fair process. An incumbent has the clear advantage of knowing the role, communication channels and networks, and has greater access to resources. However, he is more at risk of criticism of a track record that needs to be defended. There is also a higher risk of patronage taking place in the case of an election. The strategy consulting firm, Boston Consulting Group, has introduced a 10% increased threshold for re-elections to partially address this issue. For a second re-election, a managing partner will need a 65% majority and for a third re-election, 75% of the votes.

4.   On-boarding

The new leader has just been appointed with great ceremony, spirits are up and everyone is looking forward to getting started. Yet, in the words of Marshall Goldsmith, an executive coach and author, "what got you here, won't get you there". It will be a steep learning curve, whatever the past experience. Many partners in leadership roles have shared, with hindsight, the challenges they faced upon taking on a major leadership role. After the euphoria of the appointment/election comes the swell of challenges when the new leader needs to get results and manage the gap between expectations and reality and the inevitable comparison with the previous leader. The on-boarding period can be an intense time and it can often be lonely. Admitting to having difficulties can be a challenge in an organisation full of over-achieving partners. Yet it is worth noting that the on-boarding phase is also the opportunity for a successor to actually reveal a particular leadership talent which hitherto did not have a platform or role to flourish on.

The new leader is likely to feel challenged in three areas:

- the leadership imperatives required when having the top job;
- renegotiating a range of relationships; and
- personal adjustments.

4.1   Leadership imperatives

The successor will likely need to broaden the repertoire of leadership styles to deal with the diversity of new situations he will face and not just stick to the one that he prefers. Any leadership role requires addressing critical business issues and challenging organisational inertia.

With the start-up phase passed, the new leader will want to focus on areas where she can leave a mark, ie, what she will want to be known for. This is when the partner is likely to be confronted with the challenge of change, its pace and execution. Law firm leaders are simultaneously the products and co-shapers of their own organisational culture. The ultimate challenge for a leader resides therefore in "the ability to perceive the limitation of one's own culture and to evolve the culture adaptively",[12] distinguishing values that must endure (continuity) from those that must end (renewal). This may require the new leader to consider dealing with the un-discussable or past taboos, and possibly confronting the track record or heritage of the leader that has stepped down.

4.2   Renegotiating a range of relationships

As the partner takes up the new role, she will need to negotiate a new basis for a range of relationships, starting with the leader stepping down and those close to him. An overlapping handover period is sometimes planned to facilitate the onboarding of the new leader. The advantage of such a period is to pass on the rich experience of the outgoing incumbent who can help her successor with the steep learning curve, in particular with all the formal responsibilities that will come with the top job. Such an overlap works best when there is a good relationship between the partner stepping down and her successor. Yet, it should not be too close, making it difficult to distinguish between who makes the decisions or to the extent that it becomes overwhelming and causes frustration for the successor. The relationship will also depend on how easy it is for the incumbent to let go of her responsibilities (see 5.2 below). In any event, such a period should be limited in time and scope to give the new leader the opportunity to grow into the role without being over influenced or even dominated by the one stepping down. This will also help in managing expectations within the partnership. The new managing partner of Latham declared "I cannot be another Bob Dell (former managing partner); I expect to underwhelm."[13]

Such an overlap may take place informally when a managing partner becomes senior partner. For this to work, the roles (senior and managing partner) have to be clearly defined, not by those holding those positions but by the highest governance body. Keeping too much distance from the former leader could be misinterpreted as

---

12   E Schein, *Organizational Culture and Leadership* (Jossey-Bass, 2004).
13   Bruce McEwan, "Why Are You Leading?", Adam Smith Esq. Blog, August 1 2014.

lack of sensitivity towards the style and legacy of the former leader, however being too close could weaken the authority of the new leader. It is a fine balance.

The new leader will also need to establish a new basis for influence and authority with other partners in leadership roles (eg, in an executive committee) including those appointed by the former leader.

4.3 Personal adjustments

Finally, with a new role will come a series of personal adjustments, starting with balancing time commitment between clients and the management work required by the new role. The source of satisfaction is also likely to shift from an external (clients) to an internal one (partners and professionals in the firm). Moreover, the timing cycles of strategy formulation, execution and impact which are key factors in any executive role tend to be much longer than with legal practice. So a partner in a leadership role will need more patience in order to feel a sense of professional fulfilment.

There are several sources of support and resources a partner can call upon for the on-boarding phase. Many of these will help to overcome the likely feeling of isolation that comes with a top leadership role, whether in relation to decision making, recognition of one's contribution or moments of doubt. Paradoxically, the myth and aura around a leader can prevent him from acknowledging the need for external support and asking for it. The new leader may call on support from a mentoring relationship if he has one. Mentors can bring support by sharing experience. In a mentoring relationship, conversations "can help in reframing a problem, probing and developing data, generating alternative hypotheses and designing experiments".[14] In the absence of or in addition to mentoring, the new leader may want to consider coaching for the on-boarding period. This will help him to:

- make sense of the doubt and challenges being faced;
- learn how to fine-tune behaviours; and
- improve his decision-making skills.

5. Stepping down and stepping out

No matter how genuinely dedicated to his firm and self-aware the incumbent leader is, stepping out of the limelight is a challenge. As soon as succession becomes the centre of attention in any organisation, the incumbent leader is affected and therefore cannot be a neutral actor in the whole succession process – biases and other filters are likely to cloud personal judgement and interactions. The incumbent is likely to feel a subtle change in the patterns of power which will provoke a wide range of emotions and, according to Kets de Vries, for some even basic fears of death.[15] Lord Browne, former CEO of BP, shared in his memoirs his feelings when considering his succession: "my emotional self prevailed over reason. I did not know how to leave."[16] Thus the objective from a firm's perspective is to ensure the incumbent leader has a dignified process for stepping down and, if appropriate, to provide support in transitioning out of the firm.

---

14   D Schön, *The Reflective Practitioner* (Basic Books, 1984).
15   Kets de Vries, *The Leader on the Couch* (Wiley, 2006).
16   *The Economist*, Schumpeter, February 7 2015.

5.1 Stepping down

As a firm prepares for a succession process, and until the incumbent leader has effectively moved on to a satisfactory new situation, within or beyond the firm, letting go will naturally be a challenge.

At the stage of identifying possible candidates, the incumbent leader will continually assess the abilities of any potential successors to protect and build on her legacy and continue focusing on her priorities. Any signal to the contrary might lead the incumbent leader to hamper and even obstruct the succession process. Once the new leader is in place, this can translate into hidden or even public criticism. If such is the temptation, the leader stepping down should take an extended leave and refrain, certainly during the on-boarding phase, from criticising the new leader as this damages all parties and the firm itself. As such, the words of the leader stepping down will be symbolic, certainly in the first six to 12 months, so that any form of public support, even pre-arranged, can be beneficial to the successor.

The former leader needs to acknowledge that the new leader needs to grow into the role and to develop his own style. If there is a close relationship between the two, where the successor is a protégé, there is the danger of a relationship of dependency, whereby the former leader remains the master and informally stays in control. At best, it will reduce the chances of the successor growing into the role, at worst it might eventually feed a feeling of envy towards the master. What matters in the case of such a relationship is how the one stepping down can create the space for the successor to flourish, apply his own leadership style, make independent decisions and help to contribute to the renewal that the succession is supposed to feed. It means that a protégé at some point will need to equal or surpass the master.

Letting go will also be made easier if the incumbent leader feels that he is satisfied about his own legacy and that it is secured. A firm can facilitate the process of stepping down by giving due regard to the contribution of the leader, through communications, public events and other rituals, and support the leader in moving on to the next phase in his career. David Parnell, a legal sector journalist, recommends that leaders stepping down should "compose a realistic and positive story to not only tell people about why you are stepping down, but also convey your excitement about your next adventure and laud the firm's future".[17]

Another challenge in stepping down is the leader's own narcissism: "just as trees need water and sunshine to flourish, many leaders need the admiration of their subordinates to feel truly alive."[18] Succession requires an identity adjustment on the part of the incumbent. The length of the personal transition will depend on the extent of the leader's self-esteem and awareness that its source will change. With the preparation for one's own succession comes the prospect of loss of power, status and, in some cases, financial security. This situation is further accentuated if the leader is also a founder of the firm.

All these factors apply irrespective of the next step, within or beyond the firm and even in the case of retirement.

---

17   D Parnell, "Practices for Leadership Succession", Forbes, August 4 2014.
18   M Kets de Vries, "The Retirement Syndrome", *European Management Journal*, 2003.

5.2   Stepping out and considering options

The absence of an exit strategy tends to be the norm for an incumbent leader. In a survey of US managing partners, 37% of them were "not really sure what is next on their career horizon".[19] Unless the leader is close to the age of retirement, an absence of clear and satisfactory options to move beyond the firm is likely to enhance anxieties and hamper the succession process.

If no real options are available, the incumbent leader may focus on the personal short-term at the expense of the broader long-term interest of the firm, or worse, interfere in the succession with possibly the wrong intentions, consciously or even unconsciously.

If the leader wants to remain in the firm then there are several options, depending on factors such as age of the incumbent, level of time commitment to the leadership role (full or part time) and financial security or needs. Few of these options turn out to be viable in the long term; they serve rather as a period to prepare for the next phase and recognise the contribution and achievement of the leader stepping down.

An ambassadorial role can be given such as responsibility for a specific area, or special titles can be created, in particular for founder leaders. Business drivers, for example key client relationships, can sometimes justify such decisions.

Returning to the practice and client work is another option. According to a survey of North-Eastern US law firms, only 39% of managing partners consider returning to the practice.[20] Although similar data is unavailable for other parts of the world, experience suggests that trends are comparable, especially if the managing partner is not the founder of the firm. The leader who has stepped down will have to partially rebuild a practice, client base and technical expertise, all of which might have been weakened by focusing energy and time on the leadership role. When the managing partner role is a full-time one, this becomes nearly impossible unless a specific arrangement has been agreed. Moreover, returning to full-time practice means becoming an ordinary partner again – not always an attractive proposition. The difficulty of this situation is exacerbated as partners increasingly take on leadership roles when they are younger rather than towards the end of a long career. Some firms will offer leaders returning to the practice one to two years' support to rebuild their practice, which might include reduced billing targets. However, time is not the only factor; it also requires support by fellow partners referring clients and work. An incumbent leader could take advantage of the role to secure his return to the practice but such decisions are not always in the firm's best interests.

The other alternative for a leader who is stepping down is moving out of the firm altogether, immediately or after a period of grace to give him time to prepare and consider his options. Moving out depends on how well the partner has been anticipating this phase through active involvement in the wider business community or even society at large. The partners who have reached a sufficient level of financial security may seek a portfolio of fulfilling part-time professional activities,

---

19   P McKenna, *The State of Law Firm Leadership* (McKenna Associates Inc, 2010).
20   Managing Partner Forum for Northeastern Law Firms, 2010.

involving board advisory roles in business or charities, continued legal advice for former clients or teaching.

6.   Conclusion

The health of a firm depends among other things on its ability to manage satisfactorily a leadership succession process. It also reflects its ability to transition from one generation of partners to the next. Rafael Fontana, senior partner of Cuatrecasas, Gonçalves Pereira, one of Europe's largest law firms, has a clear belief when it comes to such a transition: "our obligation is to make room for everyone coming up, they are better than us and that is what we must do." To achieve more reliable and sustainable results, firms need to move away from managing succession on a case-by-case basis because that is partly why it is so difficult to address. It is precisely because it encompasses a deep personal dimension that it requires a more systematic approach. This ability to acknowledge and integrate both individual and firm interests will facilitate the process. A succession is also an opportunity for renewal at firm level, directly with a new leader but also indirectly through the debates that it will generate. One could even argue that the renewal triggered by the succession also takes place at a more personal level for both successor and incumbent. By taking a broader and long-term approach to succession, from growing leaders to helping them step in and out, it will, in the words of Jill King (former global HR director at Linklaters), become an "organic process where the natural leaders will rise to the fore".

Leading post-merger integration processes

Gerard J Tanja
Venturis Consulting Group

1. Introduction

Post-merger integration processes in knowledge-intensive organisations are, in essence, major transformative change processes. This is no different in law firms. The legal sector is, after a period of relative stability and predictability during the financial-economic downturn, once again faced with significant change. In the next five to 10 years, questions like 'where to play?' and 'how to play?' will become decisive for all types of firms, be it national independent firms, international firms or firms with the ambition to become truly global.[1] Increased competition, new entrants and continuing pressure on revenues, margins and profitability will continue to be among the main trends. Slowly the legal market will become more mature and evolve along the lines of how other professional services markets have developed. Consolidation and growth strategies (offensive or defensive) by means of mergers among law firms are likely to dominate the legal press for the next five to 10 years.

Law firm leaders are confronted with intricate strategic questions that could be termed 'insights', 'foresight' and 'cross-sight':

- Insights – do we understand and correctly read the development of the market; what are the most important factors affecting performance, profitability, margin and growth?
- Foresight – how will the legal market most probably develop; how will this affect our (competitive) positioning (overall and/or our presence and performance in specific industries/sectors and practice areas) and perspectives for profitable growth?
- Cross-sight – how can we determine, act and capitalise on the crucial and essential elements of a truly distinctive and unique value proposition to the market and the firm's clients? This requires being able to combine and exploit elements of the positioning and truly unique strengths of the firm, thereby creating a temporary, sustainable and difficult to copy (not permanent) competitive advantage: where and how can we win?

In such a landscape, it is not surprising that many firms are discussing or at least investigating merger initiatives. According to a recent survey among the UK Top 200

---

[1] AG Lafley and Roger L Martin, *Playing to Win. How Strategy Really Works* (Harvard Business Review Press, 2013).

firms undertaken by legal communications specialists Byfield Consultancy and partnership law experts at Fox Williams, almost 50% of all non-merged UK firms would consider a tie-up over the next two years,[2] and 45% of firms that have not secured a merger in the past five years would consider a tie-up before 2017. Reports on the US legal market suggest a similar trend.

Yet, the survey also indicates that the record of success in relation to mergers is far from stellar: only some 40% of the firms involved in merger negotiations believe that the merger was a success.

Our own research and experiences at Venturis Consulting Group indicate a similar trend. More than half of the mergers we have seen and researched in the legal sector have, after three to five years, either produced neutral results or have failed to unlock the promised rewards of enhanced market position, improved competitive positioning and profit performance.[3] It seems that firms which merge are relatively weak and do not realise the full growth and profitability potential of an enhanced platform.

A merger is, without doubt, the most important and high impact strategic initiative a law firm can undertake and execute. A merger process is complex, intricate and challenging. Most merger processes are also costly in terms of leadership effort, time and money. Assuming that the firm has been able to identify and secure the right merger partner, for the majority of law firm leadership teams a merger process is high risk, unpredictable and very intensive.

The question then is how the firm's leadership needs to address and approach the critical elements in the merger process and post-merger integration or execution phase to realise the expected growth, enhanced profitability and strengthened positioning potential.

In order to succeed and to produce the required and expected results, law firm leaders must be able to create, in a complex and quite often highly fluid situation, engagement, trust and involvement among its key partners. Good leadership in a post-merger situation, therefore, is a critical part of future organisational health and an important driver of the combined firms' future performance. Yet, although a lot has been written about leadership in professional services firms and about leadership behaviour in strategic transformation processes, the relationship between leadership skills, behaviours and styles in pre- and post-merger processes of knowledge-intensive organisations and the ultimate success of combining two firms, has not been systematically researched.

2. Leadership, the five stages of post-merger integration and causes of failure

According to a recent McKinsey study, a transformative change process consists of five stages:

- goal and objective setting;

---

2   Byfield Consultancy and Fox Williams survey published in *The Lawyer*, January 28 2015.
3   Gerard J Tanja and David S Temporal, "Making Mergers Work – Realising the Positioning and Performance Potential", White Paper 2008.

- assessment of the organisational capabilities;
- designing transformation actions and initiatives;
- execution; and
- developing initiatives to sustain the changes.

Similarly, and based on our experience with developing and executing merger processes, at Venturis Consulting Group we have identified five post-merger stages that the leadership and the organisation must address:
- analysis of pre-merger organisational culture, capabilities and competences in the two (or more) firms that have the intention to merge;
- translating the overall, general goals and aspirations of the merger into concrete deliverables and strategic initiatives at practice, industry/sector and business support function level, thereby taking into account the outcomes of the analytical phase;
- designing the post-merger integration initiatives, prioritising actions and developing the required timeline and critical path;
- execution: process/project managing the execution of the merger including ensuring the alignment and coordination of the post-merger process; and
- designing programmes and initiatives to sustain the outcomes of the post-merger integration activities.

Post-merger processes consist primarily of an aligned set of execution-related initiatives and actions. As we know, law firms often struggle with achieving executional excellence and follow-through of well-crafted action plans. Nevertheless, most and definitely the more mature law firms have competent managers and experienced leadership and/or the resources to design and manage such processes.

Why is it then that a lot of mergers produce neutral results or do not achieve the expected positioning, performance and growth goals?

In our experience, post-merger processes fail for a number of reasons. The most important reasons have a direct relationship to the approach taken by the firm's leadership to the pre-merger phases:
- In the pre-merger political and/or initial analytical phase identifying the drivers of the foreseen merger, the critical conditions of the deal and any potential deal-breakers have not been sufficiently identified or researched. Leadership is cautious (and sometimes even reluctant) to address such critical issues during the preliminary negotiations.
- During the analytical phase, the strategic and business rationale for the merger, identifying the potential areas of synergy and strategic fit (a combination of the professional, cultural, practice and client fit) based on a realistic evaluation of the relative strengths and weaknesses of each firm, has not been sufficiently explored, established and explained by leaders. In other words, the modelling of the new firm in terms of resources, practice and client portfolio strengths, geographic coverage and the framework for the governance, management and partner compensation system has not been suifficiently rigorous.

- The leadership has not built sufficient commitment and support in the partnerships of the respective firms and has not prepared the partners and staff for transformative change initiatives. Communication is essential in this phase and leadership is often faced with some key dilemmas. Therefore, communication and engaging the partners throughout the process is essential in order to create sufficient support and commitment. Yet, leadership also has to ensure that confidentiality is maintained and managed. Too much consultation and information-sharing causes partners to become absorbed in details. Too little engagement runs the risk of distancing leadership from the partners causing all kinds of problems and fuelling the 'not invented by me' syndrome.
- The overall business plan for the new firm has been insufficiently developed, explained and analysed. Identification of potential synergies, cross-overs and a detailed analysis of how the two firms will be integrated is often not undertaken with sufficient rigour. Sometimes this has to do with the duration of the process. It is extremely difficult to sustain a high level of interest and energy over a long period of time and partners who are very pro-merger may become frustrated with what is perceived as slow progress, whereas those with reservations in relation to the merger (or who are neutral) want to have as much information as possible to be able to make an informed decision. In this politicised analytical phase the waverers may become vulnerable to the pressures from one or the other group. This is difficult for the leadership to manage and requires a lot of precious leadership time.

Once these hurdles have been overcome, however, the key challenge for the leadership is to realise the full value potential of the new firm by designing a realistic, effective and high-impact post-merger integration plan. This requires the use of different leadership styles, behaviours and skills than those that were critical in a successful pre-merger phase.

3. Leadership framework for post-merger success

Organisations struggle with the question of which type of leadership style and behaviour should be stimulated and developed. Business schools, magazines and academics produce a continuous stream of executive leadership programmes, 'entertainment' programmes and articles on leadership. Most of what has been written on leadership skills, traits and styles in relation to inspirational leadership has focused on the mission, the vision or the values of an organisation or on strategic leadership, linking leadership to strategy formulation and/or the strategic dialogue within an organisation. Less has been produced on leadership styles and skills that affect and create executional excellence.

For ease of reference and understanding we use the following leadership framework,[4] differentiating between four general, universal leadership styles and a subset of 15 leadership skills and behaviours.

Figure 1: Leadership styles and behaviours

Inspirational leadership	Strategic leadership
• Provide support and 'walk and talk' • Develop a mission and collective vision	• Identify, explain and engage in goal- and objective-setting • Communicate clearly, unambiguously and enthusiastically • Provide sound decision making • Offer critical and different perspectives, dare to differentiate!
Operational leadership	Performance leadership
• Focus on tasks and deliverables • Organise and project manage with strong result orientation • Solve problems fast, be informed and effective • Be able to cope with uncertainty	• Explain transformative change • Motivate, coach and mentor/bring out best in others • Show resilience • Facilitate collaboration and stimulate teaming

Pre- and post-merger leadership behaviours

These styles must be distinguished from the personal leadership attributes that authentic leaders often display, including:

- passion,
- trust,
- personal values,
- willingness to learn and develop,
- listening skills and enthusiasm,
- strong will and power.

'Inspirational leadership' is the ability to clearly formulate the values and credo of the organisation and firm; these are non-negotiable and create a feeling of unity and belonging. Leading by example is mission-critical. 'Strategic leadership' is about

---

4   See also Claudio Feser, Fernanda Mayol and Ramesh Srinivasan, "Decoding Leadership: What Really Matters", *McKinsey Insights*, January 2015. Based on extensive literature research and on the most recent version of the McKinsey Organizational Health Index, the authors identified 20 general leadership traits. According to the authors, high-quality leadership teams typically display four of the 20 possible types of behaviour. These four traits explain almost 90% of the variance between strong and weak team leadership performance (upper and lowest quartile):
- be supportive
- operate with strong results orientation;
- seek different perspectives; and
- be able to solve problems effectively.

stimulating, initiating and managing honest and rigorous dialogue. It is also about seeking and discussing critical perspectives and potentially new business models, new or blue ocean markets and (rapidly) changing client needs. Communication, engaging people and building trust are key factors. Both inspirational and strategic leadership are critical in the pre-merger phases. 'Operational leadership' and certain leadership behaviours/skills belonging to the 'performance leadership' style (sometimes referred to as 'result-oriented leadership') are more important during post-merger integration processes.

Operational leadership focuses on the skills and behaviours of leadership teams that are critical to support the unlocking of the value that were at the core of the business case for the new firm.

A merger will be a huge challenge for the leadership team. It will involve integrating and aligning processes, systems, planning and project management. It requires not only immense organisational discipline but, paradoxically, also the ability to cope with uncertainty. No GANTT or workflow chart and project management scheme has ever survived a post-merger integration process in a law firm![5] Organisational agility is critical to good execution, provided the results of creatively addressing unanticipated events remains within the overall strategic framework that has been set at the beginning.

Merger execution also means taking advantage of practice, client or market opportunities that may arise and that, ultimately, support the end game and the ultimate prize.[6] A focus on problem solving and strong result orientation during this phase is critical. Leadership must manage, facilitate and execute a 'fair process' ensuring that the three cornerstones of a fair post-merger integration process are effectively achieved:

- engagement;
- explanation; and
- managing expectations.[7]

During the post-merger integration process leaders must primarily focus their efforts on the potentially high-value-added areas of integrating the organisations through people initiatives, culture (ie, norms and values) and business-related strategic priorities, and activities at professional, client and practice level. This requires some hard choices (strategy formulation and strategic planning is about making hard

---

5   Being able, as a leader, to cope with the unexpected and to lead and implement complex strategic initiatives in times of uncertainty or transformative change. See also Jennifer Garvey Berger and Keith Johnston, *Simple Habits for Complex Times: Powerful Practices for Leaders* (Stanford University Press, 2015). In a later article, together with Zafer Achi, the authors opine that:
     "The default model of a clear-minded person, certain of his or her outlook and ideas, is not consistent with the qualities that allow possibilities to flourish. In a complex world, we're often better served by leaders with humility, a keen sense of their own limitations, an insatiable curiosity, and an orientation to learning and development."
     Zafer Achi and Jennifer Garvey Berger, "Delighting in the Possible – In an Unpredictable World, Executives Should Stretch Beyond Managing the Probable", *McKinsey Insights*, March 2015.
6   For an exhaustive discussion on strategy execution, see also Donald Sull, Rebecca Homkes and Charles Sull, "Why Strategy Execution Unravels – and What to Do About It", *Harvard Business Review*, March 2015.
7   Fair process is a leadership philosophy and decision-making method that was systematically studied and initially developed by Thibaut and Walker; see John W Thibaut and Laurens Walker, *Procedural Justice: A Psychological Analysis* (Lawrence Erlbaum, 1976).

choices and not every law firm leader feels comfortable doing so). It is convenient and comfortable to start with the less contentious and technical or administrative issues, but often this results in superficially addressing or delaying the more difficult, high-impact areas of an integration. In the most extreme situations this may result in a state of co-existence of the two legacy firms: a combination of unrealised competitive benefits with all the previous disadvantages of the two firms, complicated by the effects and consequences of an enlarged operational and geographical scale.

The required post-merger leadership skills are more about ensuring that the right environment is created to get things done. Law firm leaders must facilitate, stimulate and ensure that others engage, understand and collaborate. Result-orientation is critical and leaders must focus on coaching, motivating and mobilising those in the organisation who are best placed to execute the task. Belief in the talents of others is necessary; being able to provide effective and constructive feedback is an essential characteristic of result-oriented leadership; and staff must be empowered.[8] In a post-merger integration process, transformative change will happen as well as unpredictable and unexpected events or opportunities. This cannot necessarily be led from the top and law firm leaders must ensure that staff are empowered to deal with such issues on the ground.

As has been observed above, three leadership traits or behaviours stand out and affect the quality of executional excellence in particular: result orientation, problem solving and stimulating/empowering others.

Result orientation: this is about being able to follow through on setting objectives, agreed priorities and planning decisions. Law firm leaders with a strong result orientation are particularly focused on effectiveness and operational efficiency and must devote a lot of time to prioritising high-value initiatives (culture, people and business integration) without losing sight of the more administrative and technical, organisational integration issues that seem, at first sight, less contentious.

Problem solving: this is the process that actually precedes sound decision making. Problem solving focuses on gathering, categorising and analysing available data and information. It is the key input to making high-impact strategic decisions, including the execution of post-merger initiatives, but also guides day-to-day decision making of law firm executives.

Empowerment: leaders who facilitate the post-merger integration process by supporting, coaching and guiding others by means of empowerment understand how staff who are more remote from the main decision-making centre feel. By building trust, stimulating teaming and collaboration and motivating staff to engage, and showing that everybody can make a difference when building the new firm, they assist colleagues to overcome integration challenges, thereby contributing to organisational efficiency.

---

8   For result-oriented leadership, see also P Hersey, K Blanchard and D Johnson, *Management of Organisational Behavior* (Prentice Hall, 1996).

Building a strong foundation of trust and confidence between partners and staff (fee-earning and non-fee-earning) of the two (or sometimes more) legacy firms is an enormous task that is central to the ultimate success or failure of the new firm. Uncertainty and transformative change always go hand in hand. Engaging partners and fee-earning staff, in particular at the professional, business and client level, to create and contribute to the new firm through the planning and execution phase is, therefore, key. Again, law firm leadership must exercise a balancing act: moving too fast or becoming too confrontational runs the risk that the inevitable insecurity will force people into a more defensive mindset. Too accommodating and too consensus-driven will dilute the optimisation of the merger benefits. Communication and managing the expectations in this phase are essential.

Figure 2: Framework/elements for post-merger integration

Capabilities of respective firms	Client strength of new firm

• Resourcing and staffing
• Talent intensity of firms
• Culture/DNA
• Governance mode/financials
• Profitability
• Investment power
	• Quality of client portfolio:
	  • Client segmentation
	  • Type of engagments
	  • Type of clients
	  • Profitability of engagements

P.I.G. focus of new firm	Operational
• **P**ractice 'mix' • **I**ndustry and sector focus • **G**eographical coverage	• Human resources • ICT platforms and information technology • BD and marketing function • Knowledge management • Other organisational functions

The Integration Challenge

4. Creating trust by means of a fair process[9]

4.1 Engagement

In the knowledge-intensive professional services firm environment, and in law firms in particular, leaders must engage, explain and manage the expectations of partners and fee-earners both pre-merger and post-merger. In the post-merger phase and during the design and development of the operational plan for the integration (what has to be done, when and by whom) this means that there are at least three stages,

---

9   See also W Chan Kim and Renee Mauborgne, "Fair Process: Managing in the Knowledge Economy", *Harvard Business Review*, January 2003.

142

often taking place in parallel and on a continuing basis, to be taken into account. Together they constitute the fair process framework:

- All involved stakeholders must be fully consulted and must feel that they are being listened to. Everyone is assumed to adopt a critical and professional attitude. After all, this is the reality test for the strategy's likelihood of success. The interests of the combined and new entity take priority over individual or individual practice group interests.
- Consensus among the stakeholders is not always achieveable (and sometimes not even desirable); it is important that the 'why' of a decision is being properly and honestly explained. According to Chan and Mauborgne, fair process does not mean:

  ... a decision by consensus. Fair process does not set out to achieve harmony or to win people's support through compromises that accommodate every individual's opinions, needs, or interests. While fair process gives every idea a chance, the merit of the ideas – and not consensus – is what drives the decision making.[10]
- All partners and stakeholders have to know what is expected of them.

A fair process is crucial in a knowledge-driven organisation as it has a profound effect on behaviours, motivation and attitudes of partners and staff that drive high-performance and contribute to creating trust. Trust is required in order to achieve commitment and voluntary cooperation of partners, managers and other staff.

Developing trust is an indispensable element and an attribute of effective leadership in the post-merger phase. Without trust it is highly unlikely that the firm will see a successful post-merger integration process, despite its elegant Memorandum to the Partners setting out the anticipated benefits and advantages of the merger. Trust is vital to motivating partners, staff and stakeholders and to mobilising them to work towards a common goal. A law firm leader who communicates openly, has confidence in the ability of his staff, listens, walks the talk and keeps his promises will gain the commitment, confidence and cooperation of the partners.

4.2   Explanation

It is vital that the firm's leadership ensures that the major stakeholders in the firm understand why certain decisions, actions and initiatives have been designed and executed. Explaining the thinking that is at the basis of decisions makes people confident that the leadership and management have considered all the options, listened to ideas and opinions and have made those decisions impartially and in the best interests of the new firm. It allows partners and other stakeholders to trust the intentions of the leadership, even in situations where their own input may have been put aside or only partially taken into account.

4.3   Managing expectations

This requires that once a decision, action or initiative has been announced and is

---

10   Chan Kim and Mauborgne, *ibid.*

being executed, the rules of the game for the new entitiy are clear to everybody. To achieve fair process, it matters less what the new rules and policies are; it is more important that they are clearly understood so that everybody in the organisation knows what to expect, what the new targets and priorities are and what can be achieved.

A fair process is critical in professional services firms as it contributes to commitment, active and voluntary cooperation, sharing of knowledge and experience and, ultimately, to higher performance. Professionals in knowledge-based organisations who do not trust each other will not work together and will not share ideas, knowledge and experiences. Professionals who do not work together, will not trust each other. Lawyers are rather good at 'intelligent and intuitive sabotaging' of post-merger initiatives which, they fear, may change the status quo or where it is anticipated that new ways of working may be required.

As Chan Kim and Mauborgne observe:

Fair process reaches into a dimension of human psychology that hasn't been fully explored in conventional management practice. Yet every company can tap into the voluntary cooperation of its people by building trust through fair processes.[11]

One word of caution, however, with respect to communication by leadership at this stage. Although communication is an extremely important leadership trait in the post-merger phase, relentless communication does not necessarily and always lead to success and a better understanding of the key goals and primary objectives of the post-merger integration process. In general, it is our experience that law firm leadership overestimates the effects of its communications, messages and town hall meetings with partners and staff. The reasons are as follows:

- partners often fail to see and understand the immediate relationship between the execution of a particular post-merger initiative, its timing and the importance for the overall strategy;
- the quality and clarity of the primary communication or message is sometimes diluted because leadership qualifies too much or adds peripheral messages; and
- partners, management and other stakeholders get the feeling that the communications are insufficiently aligned and sometimes even contradictory.

Maintaining the post-merger momentum can be challenging and requires a clear focus on the end goal and ultimate prize. At the same time, leadership needs to ensure that it announces, celebrates and produces some early wins that would not otherwise have occurred and which confirm the success of the merger.

5. Conclusion

Post-merger integration means a lot of hard work, takes time (in our experience at least 18–24 months before the first, tangible and sustainable results of an integration can be identified) and requires focus and a lot of the leader's time and effort. In law

---

11   Chan Kim and Mauborgne, *ibid*.

firms, a great deal of effort is devoted to the political and analytical phases pre-merger whereas the post-merger execution phase is sometimes neglected leading to post-merger drift and reduced enthusiasm and commitment.

In our experience and when developing and facilitating post-merger integration action plans for law firms, we have found that designing and installing an integrated leadership and management framework is fundamental to achieving execution excellence. Such a framework allows law firms to deliver on time, on budget and within the formulated and anticipated strategic drivers of the merger. It also ensures the effective coordination of the respective intiatives and a fair process, creating commitment, trust and cooperation.[12] The framework includes:

- building the new leadership team, clarifying roles and responsibilities, creating a clear governance model for the new firm;
- establishing small, effective integration teams to design and oversee the execution of firm-wide business, client and people initiatives;
- establishing integration teams at practice area, industry and/or sector level and at business support level;
- designing and developing a coherent internal and external communication strategy at firm, practice, industry/sector and/or geographical level and establishing clear roles and responsibilities;
- accepting that this is a period of transformative change but leaders must ensure that it does not distract too much from the core business which should continue to offer its services, develop its business and client relationships and be able to explain to clients the benefits of the merger.

Leadership can be learned and must be earned. It can neither be copied nor will it have the required results if it is not perceived as authentic. Effective and required leadership skills and behaviours exercised and displayed during the pre-merger discussons between and within law firms are not necessarily the same as those required to undertake a successful post-merger process:

No leader is perfect. The best ones don't try to be – they concentrate on honing their strengths and find others who can make up for their limitations.[13]

Integrating two (or more) firms and creating a one-firm culture requires a lot of leadership effort, perseverance and resilience. Result orientation, problem solving and effectice communication and coordination must be at the core of a successful post-merger integration process.

---

12   See also Gerard J Tanja and David S Temporal, "Making Mergers Work – Realising the Positioning and Performance Potential", White Paper 2008.
13   Deborah Ancona, Thomas W Malone, Wanda J Orlikowski and Peter M Senge, "In Praise of the Incomplete Leader", *Harvard Business Review*, February 2007. According to the authors it is:
      "… time to end the myth of the complete leader: the flawless person at the top who's got it all figured out. In fact, the sooner leaders stop to be all things to all people, the better off their organizations will be … the executive's job is to cultivate and coordinate the actions of others at all levels of the organization. Only when leaders come to see themselves as incomplete – as having both strengths and weaknesses – will they be able to make up for their missing skills by relying on others."

Leadership in founder-led law firms

Jaime Fernández Madero
Fernández Madero Consulting

1. Introduction

This chapter explores some of the issues that affect leadership in founder-led firms. Leadership is always a complex matter among lawyers, given their desire for autonomy and independence and their resistance to external controls. But founder-led or first-generation law firms face particular challenges and solutions that warrant a specific analysis in order to understand the deepest forces involved.

One of the biggest challenges that first-generation firms face is how to achieve an effective succession process in which leadership is handed from the founders to the next generation. The complex set of economic, political and emotional issues involved results in many failures when firms need to achieve sustainable success across generations. In Latin America, the region where I have worked as a lawyer for 30 years and presently as strategy and management consultant, the difficulty becomes ostensible when one observes the leading firms in each local jurisdiction.

The 2015 rankings of *Chambers Latin America Guide* show that in top echelon firms in the biggest markets, at least half of the listed firms are first-generation, and very few of the remainder have actually remained successful and stable for periods exceeding 10 years.[1] This percentage of first-generation firms increases in smaller countries in the region. This significant proportion shows that a lot of leading firms stay successful during the best years of their founders, but thereafter suffer spin-offs or deterioration due to ineffective leadership succession.

A better understanding of how founder-led firms function will help in dealing with these recurrent problems. This chapter first explains how leadership is developed in law firms generally, and how that process may lead to a succession crisis for first-generation firms, in the context of the structural tensions faced by law firms. It concludes with some recommendations aimed at fostering a better environment that could help in a leadership succession process.

2. How is leadership created in law firms? The importance of culture

Before examining how leadership works in founder-led firms, it is important to understand how leadership is tied to culture and why it is so important. Culture works in an organisation like the personality in an individual. It is a set of basic

---

1   Top echelon firms are considered to be those in bands 1 and 2 of Corporate and M&A rankings, and the leading markets in the region are Argentina, Brazil, Chile, Colombia, Mexico and Peru. For more information on Latin American rankings, see www.chambersandpartners.com/guide/latin-america/9.

assumptions of how the firm sees and interprets the world. These were learned and incorporated while solving its adaptation challenges, and since they worked they were taught to new members as the right way to think, feel and behave.[2]

This feature is extremely relevant in a professional service firm given the great autonomy under which professionals operate. Lorsh and Tierney[3] suggest that culture is probably the dominant force that defines how members of a firm behave among themselves and with clients, since the higher the level of autonomy with which members operate, the higher the influence of culture in their behaviour.

Culture is strongly influenced by the type of leaders that a firm has. In the initial phase, culture is created by the founders, since they define the type of culture that works in the firm. For that reason, leadership and culture are like two sides of the same coin, and they have to be observed together.

Leadership in a founder-led firm has a broader scope than in more developed firms since founders define almost everything including:

- the initial vision,
- the market,
- the clients with whom the firm will work, and
- the members who will join the firm.

Leader-founders also try to influence members' way of thinking and behaving in order to achieve the firm's objectives. So great is the influence of founders in the initial stages of a firm's life that it is difficult to distinguish clearly between the firm and the founders. For all practical purposes, the founders are the firm. They produce the resources, the identity and the culture of the firm.

As other members of the firm become more influential, the firm – as a separate entity from the founders – begins to take a specific shape. Part of how a firm finds a particular identity comes from the way that leadership evolves within it. Remember, in the initial stages founders are not really leaders of the firm, they are the firm. As new members join the firm and learn its specific culture and professional characteristics, the leadership component starts to develop. Given the great importance of founders, the leadership role should give not only a sense of direction and purpose but also the true vision of the firm's existence and meaning. Initially, only founders can tell where the firm is going and provide the viewpoint of what the firm is and how it works. This essential role comes from the fact that during the initial phase – the duration of which varies from firm to firm – the distinction between founders and firm is blurred.

But this unique type of leadership that applies to founders in the initial stages of a firm's life cannot last if the firm is to grow as a consequence of its initial success. Growth means new clients and therefore new members who can service those clients, with greater or lesser levels of autonomy. Since lawyers – especially good ones – seek professional growth and independence, it is inevitable that at some point in

---

2   Edgar H Schein, *Organizational Culture and Leadership*, 3rd edn (Josey-Bass, a Wiley imprint, 2004).
3   Jay W Lorsch and Thomas J Tierney, *Aligning the Stars. How to Succeed when Professionals Drive Results* (Harvard Business School Press, 2002).

the firm's evolution founders will need to delegate power and influence to other members. This complicated process can lead to problems and even crises if not handled with vision and intelligence.

3. The Zeus and Dyonisius models

In order to analyse the leadership process in law firms, I use the typology developed by Charles Handy in his book *The Gods of Management*.[4] Handy describes four types of organisation using the names of Greek gods:

- Zeus (the club culture),
- Athenea (the task culture),
- Apollo (the role culture) and
- Dyonisius (the existentialism culture).

In the Dyonisius organisation the predominant element is the individual who has little appreciation for the organisation and its goals. Unlike all the other types of organisations described by Handy, where the individual works for the organisation's objectives, in the Dyonisius type the organisation works for the individual. Relationships between individuals and the organisation are always fragile and agreements need to be interpreted and renegotiated regularly. According to Handy, Dyonisius is the model that better fits professionals given the high autonomy, independence and limited interaction that individuals have in professional organisations. This unstable system requires a balanced understanding of the roles and objectives of their members in order to prevent fragmentation.

The Dyonisius model describes quite well what happens in law firms but, as Handy himself recognises, organisations normally have traits from more than one model. My proposition is that law firms start under the Zeus model and, at some point in their evolution, they mutate – in a more or less chaotic fashion – to the Dyonisius model. Let us look at how that happens.

Zeus is the culture of the club, and it is mainly applicable to small organisations and start-ups where the founders begin with a great idea and build a group around them who share their views and goals. These organisations develop on the basis of affinity, trust and empathy among their members. These are very informal organisations that depend on the leader's intuition and an adequate interpretation of that intuition by the rest of the group. The lack of formal rules makes a Zeus organisation work as a club based on personal contact and a set of codes and symbols which are difficult for outsiders to understand.

Although most mature law firms have to some extent a Dyonisius culture, the fact is that law firms start under the Zeus model, with a strong dependence on their founders, and the Dyonisius element grows as the firm evolves and that dependence decreases. The evolution from one model to the other is one of the key challenges that face law firms, and one of the main sources of trouble that law firms in Latin America encounter. Although my direct experience and studies are concentrated in Latin America, I would expect that the basic features of this analysis would apply to

---

4   Charles Handy, *The Gods of Management* (Oxford University Press, 1995).

first-generation law firms in all jurisdictions, but especially in less-developed markets, given the lack of powerful models that could influence the market and the founders in making their decisions and dealing with the structural tensions that will be described below. The following table summarises the Zeus and Dyonisius cultures.

Zeus and Dyonisius cultures

Culture	Dominant factor	Type of relationship	Influence pattern	Strength	Weakness
Zeus	Club culture around founders or leaders	Strong personal links based on trust	Given by the leader and the relationship with him	Strong personal relationships. Group mystique around the leader	Risk of disordered succession. Difficult in larger firms
Dyonisius	Individualistic and non-hierarchical culture	More distant professional links	Agreements that preserve professional antonomy and independence	Captures the professional's need for autonomy	Risk of individualism and fragmentation

4.   The leadership transition

The Zeus model resembles the image of a bycicle wheel (see figure 1), where the founder is the hub and all the other members are the spokes that converge at the centre. The founder – or Zeus – gives sense to the organisation and provides the interpretations of reality that are necessary to operate. Such a strong and tight network is based on trust and loyalty.

Figure 1: The Zeus model

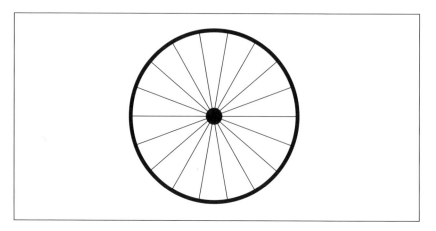

If the founder is able to create a successful firm, meaning that the organisation survives the initial internal and external challenges, then the structural tensions described below will be controlled by the founder, and he will:

- define the level of autonomy that members need to operate;
- clarify the ambiguities to interpret what is happening in the firm; and
- concentrate both the formal and real ownership of the firm.

During this stage the firm is stable and can focus on developing the basic resources to function and succeed. The founder works as the great provider and problem-solver.

However, success brings growth, both qualitative and quantitative. Professionals who functioned as helpful aids for the founders during the initial stage become autonomous and increasingly effective. As they perceive this evolution, they ask for more space and recognition, both internal and external. This is when the structural tensions described below, which were dormant in the initial phase due to the omnipresent role of the founder, start to surface and Dyonisius bursts onto the scene. In the Dyonisius model, there is no exclusive centre of influence, but rather a network with different points of influence depending on the situation (see figure 2).

Figure 2: The Dyonisius model

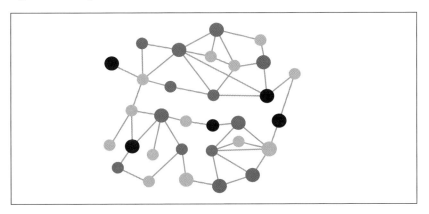

This transition can be seen a sign of success and an opportunity to face new challenges, but it is perceived by many founders as a threat to their absolute power and control. This contradiction plagues the founders, who are torn between a sense of pride in the accomplishments of their firm and the challenges this change brings to their exclusive control. It is important to understand that, more often than not, this process remains unconscious in the founders' minds and they tend to reject it. The typical strategy that many founders intuitively follow is to try to live with the best of both situations rather than resolve the structural tensions. The way to do that is to foster growth in the firm – both professional and economic – but to delay recognition and opportunities to other professionals to the maximum extent that the growing strategy allows.

5. Structural tensions in law firms: the leadership crisis

I propose an analysis of the leadership crisis in founder-led law firms through the lens of the structural tensions that law firms face. Law firms, and professional service firms in general, are subject to certain structural tensions that result from their nature as knowledge-intensive organisations. The high dependence on individual quality and the complex nature of the knowledge they produce provoke a fragile and unstable organisational environment that makes it harder for individuals to work on common objectives and reach consensus. These tensions are related primarily to the autonomy of professionals, the complex knowledge used by professionals and the intangible nature of law firms' products and services. It is important to have a basic understanding of how these tensions work since they have an impact on the leadership process.

5.1 Autonomy and collaboration

Probably the most salient feature of lawyers from a management perspective is their autonomy and their resistance to external controls. Lawyers want to do things in their own way and are reluctant to accommodate schemes or instructions with which they do not agree. It is common to hear that lawyers – particularly successful lawyers – have large egos and are too individualistic. The well-known expression that managing professionals is like herding cats appears to apply to lawyers to the fullest extent.

But law firms need to coordinate forces and capabilities to exercise their potential. In a global economy, legal issues become more complex and different types of expertise are required in order to solve problems and find solutions to clients' needs. In many instances, a lone lawyer – however capable – is simply not enough. So finding the right environment and incentives for lawyers to collaborate and work in a coordinated fashion is key to remaining competitive and efficient. But this professional and business objective finds a persistent difficulty in the exacerbated autonomy of lawyers, creating a structural tension with which law firms need to deal.

In order to permit growth in young firms, founders need to delegate work and contact with clients to other professionals. This delegation enables founders to engage with more clients, which actually ignites growth. But since many founders feel uneasy with too much delegation, they keep strategic actions and decisions for themselves. This is of course very wise while professionals are learning their job and getting acquainted with clients. The problem is when this situation is extended much further than effective service requires. When that happens, founders become a bottleneck in the firm's operation since too many decisions require their participation. Also, other professionals start to feel frustrated since their growing abilities do not match the challenges they encounter. This is particularly damaging for professionals, who are always seeking professional growth. In these circumstances, founders tend to justify their restrictive attitude by stating that the other lawyers are still immature and unprepared for certain roles and tasks, and that it is in the firm's interest that they keep tight control of the situation. This often ends up working as a self-fulfilling prophecy, since the lack of confidence that founders instil could easily produce insecure and ineffective professionals, which will then confirm the founders' strategy. In a partners' retreat workshop that I recently conducted, a founding partner expressed his frustration at his younger partners' alleged 'lack of recognition' of all his efforts in helping them and the firm. But what the younger partners were actually claiming was the need to reduce the excessive micromanagement exercised in his daily activities, by trying to participate in and influence every decision that needed to be taken.

The problem is that, in many instances, it is true that the founders can exercise many functions better than the rest of the firm. That is why they have been successful in the first place. But the growth dilemma of first-generation firms is that if founders want to consolidate the initial success they need to find an effective way to delegate power and educate future leaders. That implies taking some risks and accepting that the firm can continue without their strict control.

5.2   Ambiguity and certainty

Another relevant organisational feature of law firms is that their core business deals with complex knowledge. The complexity comes from the fact that essentially what lawyers do is apply general and codified knowledge to solve specific client's needs in a particular way. Regardless of the distinction between standarised and value-added or bespoke work, there is always some level of application or interpretation of a general rule to a specific case, which is different to some extent to other cases. This specificity makes legal knowledge complex, sometimes difficult for clients to understand and subject to various interpretations. The opaque nature of professional knowledge creates discussions as to its quality and value. This discussion not only takes place between clients and lawyers, but also within law firms in respect of roles and value that each member contributes, creating difficulties for them in reaching consensus and arranging their mutual dealings.

In order to be effective, law firms – like any organisation – need some certainty about rules, goals, values and processes. When the basic output of the organisation – legal knowledge – is opaque and subject to interpretations and ambiguity then the achievement of certainty becomes more difficult and tension occurs. The need to find common understanding in an ambiguous and highly autonomous setting means that professional service firms – as knowledge-intensive organisations – could be described as 'persuasion systems'.[5]

In young firms, as long as the founders control all external and internal resources in the firm, they can provide the required viewpoint of what is going on and what needs to be done. There is little discussion about it. But when that control begins to erode as a consequence of growth, then other viewpoints begin to emerge which are not necessarily in agreement with those of the founders. The autonomy tension described above will create in itself several viewpoints of what is happening in the firm and the role of its members. The lack of an effective system to express and discuss these various perspectives about the firm will increase tension and affect the firm's productivity. In my workshops with partners we normally try to identify what

---

5   Mats Alvesson, *Knowledge Work and Knowledge-Intensive Firms* (Oxford University Press, 2004).

each partner believes is happening in the firm, in order to reach some common view and diagnosis. It is interesting to see how partners can have such different views on the same matters, and how little they recognised these differences.

This tension does not apply only among members of different generations, but could also happen – and many times does happen – among founding partners themselves. This situation cannot be explained by the evolution model described above, but rather by the specific personalities and relationships that link founders. Successful firms typically have founders who are able to reach agreements among themselves that put the vision and interests of the firm above their personal expectations and objectives. Groups of founders do not succeed because they are friends – although that is probably helpful in the initial stages – but mostly because they agree on what the firm should be and have been able to transform their initial personal professional interests into a vision and strategy for the firm.

5.3   Real and formal ownership

Classic professional service firms, such as law firms, typically do not own substantial physical or financial assets. Also, in less-developed markets they do not even own a valuable name or trademark that is independent from the individuals who work in the firm. Firms may suffer important loss of value when professionals leave to practice elsewhere and compete with their old firm.

The main value of law firms is the professional capital that is vested on individual lawyers. That professional capital is mostly intangible since it is a complex combination of knowledge, relationships and reputational elements that are developed by individuals. Only when those individuals invest and transfer that professional capital to the firm in a consistent way, can it be become 'firm capital'.

Law firms consist of partners who through a variety of more or less formal legal structures technically own the firm. However, ownership of the real value of the firm – resulting from the amount of professional capital – rests on a group of individuals who may or may not coincide with the formal ownership structure. There are always some differences between both types of ownership and, consequently, some level of tension. But unless the differences are small and there are in place formal and informal arrangements among partners to deal with those differences, this tension could turn into a crisis, which is one of the major causes of disruption in first-generation firms.

The growing autonomy of younger professionals, as a result of professional growth and maturity, produces progressive misalignment between formal and informal ownership. As explained above, in their learning process young professionals acquire knowledge and capabilities related to work and clients. They learn to do their job in an increasingly autonomous way and clients start to get used to talking to them. Founders become less important with some clients, especially when those clients find that other professionals can solve their problems equally well and usually faster. Effective founders choose to focus on those cases where their experience and judgement is more valuable. This is the right way to do things but inevitably brings a growing importance to other professionals who become informal owners of part of the firm's capital. As in the case of autonomy, reluctant founders tend to negate this situation and therefore delay recognition of this misalignment. If this situation perisists, it is likely that tensions will turn into a crisis.

The natural autonomy of lawyers gives them transferrable skills which could tempt young professionals to seek greener pastures where they can effectively 'own' those skills. This ownership is reflected by a combination of political and economic recognition. The simple way seems to be when founders promote new partners within the firm, which normally implies political recognition (ie, the right to participate in important decisions in the firm) and economic recognition (ie, a degree of participation in the profits and losses generated by the firm). The problem is that in many cases the partner status does not entail those types of rights, either formally or in the practical world. In bigger and more institutionalised firms, political and economic rights are organised differently, but in first-generation firms with a short history professionals who are not founders also have strong feelings of ownership and participation since they may have been present from the early stages of the firm's formation. When they acquire enough autonomy and their work becomes relevant to clients, they feel they should be treated like owners, albeit with less importance than founders.

The tensions described above explain why many individuals are so powerful in law firms. Difficulties in running law firms are normally attributable to the big egos that many lawyers have. One very successful former senior partner of a leading firm used to say to his partners: 'When the egos go up, the profits go down'. This simple statement gives clear evidence of the strong paradoxes that law firms encounter as organisations. But it is important to understand that tensions do not arise only because of the particularly strong personalities that many successful lawyers have, but also from the basic organisational forces that law firms have as professional service firms.

6. The crisis stages

Founders in successful first-generation law firms tend to have strong personalities and strong views about the firm, the market and the world in which they operate. Many of those views have been correct as proved by the founders' success. In these cases, the problem is not the founders' incompetence but the blindspots they create around them as a consequence of their success. They become hostages to their own success. My professional experience as a former managing partner and as a consultant has shown that there is a process which takes place. This process has some specific stages that, although subtle, can be identified and helps to clarify its nature. Those stages are:

- *The sowing stage.* After a successful initial growth with the founders as the almost exclusive important players, the other professionals – or some of them – start to become more autonomous and relevant to clients. Founders are still essential, but others begin to play important roles. At this stage, these lawyers will begin to express – probably timidly – their individual views about the firm and about their careers. If founders remain deaf and blind to these changes, by consistently minimising demands and disregarding suggestions, then silent protests and frustrated conversations behind doors will begin affecting the climate in the firm. This increasingly negative environment – of which founders will probably remain unaware – will provide the seeds of the leadership crisis, where lawyers start to feel unhappy and question the founders' capabilities.

- *The harvest stage.* The problems that start in the sowing stage will not go away and are likely to increase as professionals grow and become more autonomous. As the distance between founders and other lawyers becomes greater, the initial timid manifestations will probably become bolder. Strong discussions and disagreements between founders and the other lawyers will begin to take place. Some founders might take these situations personally and consider them to be a lack of loyalty. This will only broaden the gap between founders and the unhappy lawyers. The difficulty in this stage is that founders are still strong and remain the principal partners. They have a sense of power and the belief that they still should run the firm as they see fit. They are the bosses and disgruntled lawyers should wait until their time comes.

   This is a critical time because founders are best placed to influence an orderly succession. Although they may have been blind during the sowing stage – and I have observed that this happens a lot in successful first-generation firms – the difficulties have now become visible and they have the power and influence to change that initial pattern. But if founders are unwilling to face this situation, then a crisis is likely to unfold through defections and spin-offs. Since the founders are still strong, these crises might not become critical during the life of the firm. Large firms have survived spin-offs and defections, and they have become even stronger by learning from previous mistakes. However, in many cases, founders are stubborn due to their big egos, and their negative attitudes create the conditions for a future decline. There are several examples of firms in Latin America – some of them leaders in their time – that disappeared due to the main partners not responding to the warning signs.

- *The decline stage.* When founders are unable to find productive solutions while they are strong and successful then they will face the declining stage of their careers in a weak condition. If any of the best professionals from previous stages are still at the firm and remain unhappy, they may create a crisis and seek to remove power from the founders, who will have lost a lot of their negotiating leverage. This might save the firm, but the founders will be unlikely to have the retirement they envisioned in their good years. If the best professionals have already left the firm, then it will decline at the same pace as the founders' own productivity. In Latin America, firms that used to be leaders in their own markets have disappeared or become irrelevant 20 years later. I started as a young lawyer in Argentina in the early 1980s, and when I look at the list of firms that were leaders in those years and compare it with the current Argentine legal market I can only find a couple of firms that are still in existence. Some no longer exist or have merged into bigger firms, some did not exist at that time and some have lost their influence in the market over this period.

The most effective leaders become aware of this situation early in the process and try to manage it in a productive way, by finding a balance between the changing needs of lawyers and clients and by putting the interests of the firm before their own, as difficult as that might be. This process involves the two main aspects that a leadership succession should contemplate: political and economic.

7. Working on the tensions: the power and governance challenge

Many of the partners in Latin America would likely choose the economic issue as the most relevant in a leadership succession. But the truth is that many successful founders have probably made substantial economic returns and, at an advanced stage of their careers, are already covered for their financial needs. What they really suffer in a succession process is the progressive loss of power and the fear of becoming less important than they used to be in their golden years. All the personal and professional factors that helped them in bringing the firm to its present situation need to be tempered to allow other forces and participants to come into play. This can be difficult and scary, since the very meaning of their role needs to change and they need to adapt to the new circumstances.

Effective leaders cope with this difficult challenge by transferring their personal sense of power and accomplishment to the firm. As the firm grows and becomes more complex and independent of the founders, power needs to be spread among more of the players. This is the transition from the Zeus model to the Dyonisius model. Depending on how founders envisage that process, the firm will pursue different paths and achieve different results. A positive transition will result in an institutional firm – the Institutional Dyonisius – where governance reflects an adequate balance of power. On the other hand, a negative transition will likely produce a decaying firm – the Decaying Dyonisius – or spin-offs that will result in new Zeus starting their own firm (see figure 3).

Figure 3: The evolution of Zeus and Dyonisius models

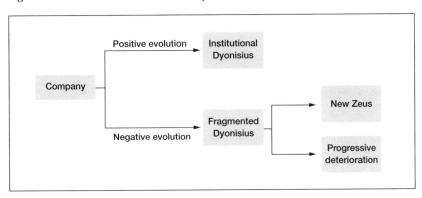

The positive transition will likely use consensus to sort out differences. This is a longer process but considerably more stable and with better results. The negative transition is based on power, in which different factions fight for control and dominance, and governance arrangements are more the results of that fight than a formula thought to be in the best interests of the firm. These two alternatives are not only seen in founder-led firms, but in first-generation firms these dynamics are defined by the leadership succession of founders and how they decide to face this challenge.

The use of consensus will likely guide the firm into the Institutional Dyonisius version. In this case, all relevant parties feel reasonably represented and their views heard and respected. In order to achieve this scenario, founders will have to create a suitable environment before formal discussions can take place. The reason is that formal government structures should be based on a set of pre-existing values and behaviours, that is, on a culture. If the culture is based on power and authority, it will be hard for the organisation to live with open and democratic structures. So founders should prepare the way for formal changes, ideally at the sowing stage, when a more democratic and less founder-dependent style can be put in place. If the sowing stage is too early – because founders were not aware of the situation – then they need to act as soon as the problem becomes clear during the harvest stage. Founders can do that by becoming more open to others' opinions and more respectful of differences. Founders need to develop a strong sense of listening and dialogue. Other relevant professionals – partners or not – should know that they can talk to the founders and that their views will be heard, regardless of the formal governance structure in the firm.

This change is normally achieved by a combination of behavioural and structural measures. A Latin American firm that was totally managed by the founding partner recently agreed to create a management committee in which certain decisions would be taken by that body. The founder agreed that this would not be enough since he might be tempted to exert total control in that committee like he used to do, so it was agreed to delegate to different partners responsibility for the proposals that need to be approved by the committee. In this way, the initiative in various matters is shared by different partners and the founder becomes another voice – and not the only voice – in the decision-making process.

The second aspect is the creation of a formal governance structure. The ideal long-term structure may not be the one to start with, since the firm has been used to living without one or with one exclusively controlled by the founders. Founders should stay actively involved in the initial phase. A sudden retirement from governance might create a sense of void and may make room for new internal disputes. So a transition period is recommended, where founders are part of the new structure. However, smart founders will find a way to become less and less important in the decision-making process and assume a role more akin to an adviser, although retaining strong leadership for those matters that are important to ensure a good transition outcome. During this transition period – which I would recommend to be a minimum of two years and no more than four or five years – the fundamental role of the founder is to ensure an orderly transition and to give support to the new partners in charge of management functions.

Once the transition is over, and depending on other professional matters, the role of the founder should rapidly decline or disappear from governance. If it is helpful, he could remain as an adviser, but this could be tricky for both the founder and the new partners as there could be a tendency to rely on the founder in difficult situations, and the whole idea of this change is to enable the firm to handle its business without the help of the founder. So if the founder remains in some role related to governance, it is important that his influence does not preclude the newly appointed partners from effectively leading the firm. It is better to face mistakes and new tensions, than come back to old formulae that will not help the firm in this new stage.

8. Working on the tensions: the financial arrangements

Probably the area where the ambiguity tension described above shows itself the most is in the discussions among partners about money. This is a huge matter that very often demands more attention than other seemingly more important aspects of the firm's life, like strategy. People from other business industries are often bewildered by how much lawyers discuss and fight about money, and the influence that has on the firm's activities and strategy. In many cases this is certainly true and is yet more evidence of how difficult it is for lawyers to build collective endeavours.

This chapter is not about partners' compensation systems but it is clear that many founders create these systems in order to maintain control over financial resources and extend their financial benefits longer than is advisable. However, only a compensation system that works for the benefit of the firm's business and strategy can help in preparing an orderly transition. For example, if the firm works with an individual compensation formula – eat what you kill – strong founders might be reluctant to delegate clients and relationship to other partners, and delay that process as much as possible. Systems that enhance collective efforts and achievements are more likely to create positive conditions for a retirement agreement, since founders have probably already delegated a lot of their functions to other partners and they are still compensated for their contributions.

A difficult topic is whether founders should be compensated at the time of retirement for creating value, that is compensation for taking the risk of starting the firm and being successful. Given the intangible value of professional service firms, it is always difficult to have pure shareholders, meaning partners who are no longer productive but still keep an ownership portion of the firm. Some founders impose these conditions on other partners in the bylaws of the firm, but those arrangements are only as strong as the willingness of other partners to accept them and not move to other firms with their own clients. It is also true that founders, by means of their unique role in the life of the firm, have probably made a type of contribution to the firm that is not comparable to any other partner, but the way to value that contribution is always a matter of discussion and agreement since there are no purely objective ways to measure it.

Being such a sensitive matter, it should always be an initiative of the founders to set or propose a financial arrangement. The ideal situation is that this arrangement is agreed well before any founder has to retire because founders are more likely to be objective if they do not need to consider their own short-term interest.

However, a greater time-span will be no guarantee that a system will be adequate and work for the firm. The fact is that we are dealing with a highly subjective and sensitive matter and there is no easy way to resolve it. Many, if not all, successful firms in this matter had leaders with one significant attribute: generosity. This has been the case in Latin America and, as far as I know, everywhere else. Steven Krill (first editor of *The American Lawyer*) said that leaders in almost all successful firms he had seen have bought their leadership role by sacrificing personal income to build the firm.[6] A founder from a very successful Brazilian firm that changed their compensation system from a purely individual formula to a lockstep structure, told me that he had to relinquish a substantial portion of his income in the initial stage of the new system to make it happen; five years later he had made up for that reduction and he was making more money than before due to the firm's success. This type of leadership is the one that produces balanced arrangements that help orderly successions.

No proven ways exist to value a founder's contributions, but one cannot value the firm as a regular company based on future income. The intangible and dynamic nature of professional service firms creates a strong link between ownership and productivity. It is difficult to claim ownership from partners who are no longer producing. So a retirement package should look more like a recognition or gratitude income, for the time and efforts given to the firm, rather than relating to any specific value created in the firm. Founders should probably receive a greater recognition than other partners, given their specific role but, at the end of the day, the generosity factor will have to come into play in order to find a scheme that is acceptable to all parties. If this is a bitter pill for founders to swallow, they might also consider the other significant benefits they derived from the firm's success, including personal reputation and status that can provide access to other professional or business opportunities, as has been the case for many successful lawyers in Latin America.

9. Working on the tensions: age and clients

Another difficult topic is the retirement age. The traditional number used in many firms is 65, but two factors often work against this.

The first is that a retirement age will affect the partnership structure and how new partners are incorporated. For a firm to grow, old partners need to make room for new partners. If partners stay on until old age with considerable stakes in the firm, then younger partners will have less stake in the firm, which could strongly disincentivise young successful partners. This is part of the financial discussion mentioned above and it needs to be resolved following the same concepts.

The other factor is that today's lawyers tend to stay productive for longer than they did decades ago. From this perspective, it may be unwise for the firm to let go partners who may be valuable and helpful in many aspects of the firm, including working with clients. The best way is to reach a reasonable balance of interests for all parties. That will probably mean that founders can step down as partners – with an established economic arrangement – while keeping a valuable role with a reasonable

---

6   Ronald J Gilson, and Robert H Mnookin, "Sharing Among the Human Capitalists: An Economic Enquiry into the Corporate Law Firm and How Partners Split Profits" (1985) 37(2) *Standford Law Review* 313–392.

compensation. All parties, especially the founders, will need to understand that roles have changed, and that others are in charge and have the primary responsibility for handling clients and the firm.

As part of the retirement process, founders need to help in handing over the prime responsibility of clients to other partners. This has to be done in a progressive and smooth way in order to avoid any inconvenience to the clients and disruption to the service. This could be a particularly difficult task since clients are the main source of power and achievement that lawyers have. So there has to be a clear vision and strategy by all parties involved, and all other matters – political and economic – need to be agreed.

10. Some final recommendations

From the issues described above, we can see how difficult leadership succession in founder-led firms can be. But a lot of this difficulty is related to how complicated lawyers make their mutual relationships and in many cases their inability to consider the firm's interest over their own.

These are some final recommendations for both founders and partners in dealing with these matters:

- Founders should make an effort to clarify what they really want from their firm. There is no moral obligation to create an institution with perpetuity; it is just a choice and a strategy. But like any other choice, it comes with pros and cons. A moral obligation does exist to be clear with both lawyers and clients since they suffer the consequences of bad leadership. Trying to live with the best of both worlds will inevitably produce crisis and frustrations.
- If the deep aspirations of the founders are in the direction of staying as leaders and owners as long as possible, with limited participation from other professionals – other than maybe relatives – then it is better to organise the firm, the strategy and the services around that concept. That will probably create limitations in growth and type of clients to seek, but the firm will be more stable and productive. More importantly, founders and professionals will be happier since strategy and incentives will be aligned for everybody.
- If, on the other hand, after deep and honest soul-searching founders reach the conclusion that they prefer their firm to succeed beyond the founders' professional life, then they need to lay the foundations for that process much earlier than the time when it becomes openly discussed within the firm.
- Those foundations are built, at the initial phase, at a cultural level. Founders should cease, as early as the firm is ready, to work under the Zeus model of the wheel explained above. They have to encourage the rest of the organisation to think on their own and make decisions. This might be difficult and, in some cases, even risky, but it is necessary to mutate progressively from the wheel to the network model of Dyonisius. This early exercise, done in an informal way, will prepare the firm for more formal changes later on and increase the chances of turning into an Institutional Dyonisius, as opposed to a Fragmented Dyonisius or even new Zeus resulting from spin-offs.

- When the time is right – but earlier if in doubt – founders and other partners should sit down to discuss how they should frame the transition, both at a political and economic level. Ask other firms who have gone through that process or seek outside help if necessary, but make sure you have an open discussion where aspirations and fears can be expressed and respected. The firm of the future – if that is what the founders want to accomplish – will develop from those conversations.
- The rest of the partners need to have a proactive and leadership approach as well. It is a mistake to think that all failures of succession are only attributable to founders. Many times the remaining partners also want the best of both worlds, meaning that they expect the founders to be more generous from an economic perspective and they resent their strong leadership but are not ready to undertake the responsibilities of leading the firm. They are just too comfortable having somebody else in the driving seat. They need to understand that a leadership succession is not just getting rid of the founders but, more importantly, how the firm is going to continue without the founders' valuable contributions.

Given the horizontal nature of law firms and the way their structural tensions work, leadership tends to be a very dynamic phenomenon, with changes that occur related to actual working factors more than formal governance arrangements. A good leadership succession process will take into account those dynamics and try to work with them for the benefit of the firm and its members.

Given their strong individual component, law firms are unstable organisations. However, they thrive when they find the right balance between their members and are able to provide superb collective service in a consistent manner. Since consistency is only achievable through stability, firms should work hard to find the arrangements that will provide internal peace and allow the focus to be on service and clients. This has always been a good recipe, but in the current global and competitive market it will become a matter of survival.

What law firm leaders need to know about big data

Peter Zeughauser
Zeughauser Group

1. Introduction

In law school, students are taught to think like lawyers. In the Western world, this indelible experience largely involves teaching people who have fared well enough academically to gain admission to law school to apply a body of law that has evolved since the middle ages to a set of facts so that they can predict the outcome of a dispute over the facts or the law with a degree of success that merits payment for it. The principle of *stare decisis* provides for the predictability of outcomes, that is, the same rules applied to the same facts result in the same outcome. The ability to do this well (ie, analyse facts, apply the law to them and predict an outcome) has been the bedrock of lawyering.[1] When this is consistently accomplished on behalf of clients in a timely manner and with a superior level of service at a price that is not out of whack with the value of knowing the answer, more business is likely to result. Over time, the growing complexity of the body of law has resulted in specialisation, and lawyers have found that collaboration among lawyers with different perspectives and areas of specialisation yields better results for clients.[2] The ability to produce better results in this fashion has brought lawyers together to form law firms, some of the best of them growing in size to thousands of lawyers practising together in firms which span the globe. Now, 'Big Law' finds itself entering an era when machines will be able to do all of this better than lawyers. Big Law is on the eve of disruption.

This chapter provides law firm leaders with the basic elements of 'Big Data' and analytics. First, you will find out how some cutting-edge companies have harnessed customer data to create billions of dollars in value and transform their markets. The chapter then outlines specific implications for law firm leaders, including those related to technology, talent management and client service. The final section delivers a clear approach that law firm leaders should take so that their firms are among the few that will thrive in a disrupting market.

2. The cutting edge of data analytics

At the beginning of the twenty-first century, in the midst of the gradual evolution in the business of law, data analytics began to disrupt the way business is done across many industries at warp speed. Pundits have posited that that the legal industry is

---

1   Randall Kiser, "Evolution to a Data Driven Legal Industry", Zeughauser Group Chair Roundtable, Meadowood, St Helena, CA, November 6 2014, Lecture.
2   Heidi K Gardner, "When Senior Managers Won't Collaborate", *Harvard Business Review*, March 2015, pp 75–82.

ripe for disruption, yet none have been able to successfully put their finger on how their predictions will come to pass. Data analytics may well be the answer. The ability to analyse Big Data is poised to challenge three key underpinnings of the way lawyers practise law:

- how lawyers predict outcomes (which is the essence of what lawyers do);
- how lawyers serve clients and build client relationships; and
- how lawyers price their services.

If the personal computer and mobile computing enabled the legal industry to leap from Law 1.0 to Law 2.0, then data analytics is about to usher in Law 3.0.

Big Law is trying adjust to what many have called the post great recession 'new normal' of pricing pressure, including further convergence of client relationships, serial laterals, consolidation, 6,000 plus lawyer global mega-law firm vereins, the re-entry of the accounting profession into the practice of law globally and what some pundits claim is falling demand for legal services. However, its destiny is more likely to be determined by whether it leads and embraces disruption empowered by data analytics itself, or complacently lays itself open to disruption by others, then by all of the other inexorable competitive pressures combined.

The best way to envision the radical changes that data analytics portend for the practice of law is to look briefly at the essential components of the business model of three of the twenty-first century's most successful start-up to large cap success stories.

Amazon introduced the twenty-first century business model as a start-up online bookstore selling books, and ultimately nearly everything else, at razor thin margins. At twenty-one years old, it is the largest online retailer in the United States. It has never made a penny, yet it is worth over $150 billion. How can this be?

As the largest US internet retailer, Amazon collects and analyses enormous amounts of data about what its customers want and what they actually buy. Amazon's ability to analyse Big Data about what customers want and what they buy enables it to predict what a visitor to its website might want to buy, because it knows what other visitors who bought what the visitor expresses an interest in buying also bought. For instance, if a visitor to 'amazon.com' places pee odour remover in her shopping cart because her cat peed on her carpet, then Amazon knows she might also want to buy special carpet shampoo to remove cat pee stains, a book on how to train your cat not to pee on your carpet and even a glow-in-the-dark pet i.d. tag. If an Amazon customer is sceptical about the value of any of those items, then Amazon links to many customer reviews indicating how other people rated those items. If the customer does not want to read the reviews, Amazon displays a simple, user-friendly dashboard summarising the customer review data. Amazon's ability to instantly analyse data to predict customer needs, therefore opening new markets for Amazon and sellers on its site, has created enormous value in Amazon.

Amazon, the first online retailer, without ever making a penny in profit, now has over $150 billion in shareholder value, all because it figured out how to analyse and create value from data.

Google was next up. It too is one of the most valuable companies in the world.

It is also one of the most profitable. Google achieved this by setting out to make all of the world's information available through its search engine for free. This has made Googling one of life's great conveniences. To access the data, Googlers happily type their inquiry into Google's search engine. With 3.5 billion searches typed in every day, Google knows what nearly everyone who has access to the internet is interested in finding out. Google analyses all of this data instantly to answer each Googler's search and sells adjacent online advertising space to those who sell products that correlate with the inquiries of Googlers. Part of the genius of Google's business model is that users do not have to buy anything. Just by searching they perform the manual labour required to create for free the data Google advertisers crave. This simple model has transformed the print media and advertising industries almost overnight. Google was an ingenious leap forward in the commercial application of data analytics in the advertising industry. In the old model, advertising relied on expensive market research to find out what people wanted and then spent even more money to tell those people what their clients were selling. In the new model, Google gives information away and, in the process, learns from the search data what Googlers want and immediately pairs them with sellers of that product or service. A process that used to take months now takes seconds. All participants in the process perceive that they get great value. Google is 15 years old and is worth more than $350 billion. It has made a lot of money using the business model for the twenty-first century.

Facebook is not a search engine, but it is built on the same business model as Amazon and Google, that is, gathering and analysing data. The difference is that when an internet user is Googling, the user is looking for something. Google is a search engine. Facebook, on the other hand, gives away a virtual place for Facebook members to share their stories with others and network. When a person joins Facebook, they are provided with a wall. Facebook members can put virtually anything and everything they want on their wall, and share it with anyone and everyone. But to do that they must share it with Facebook. Facebook instantly analyses it, correlates it with what everybody else has on their walls, predicts what someone with a wall like the one created by each member might want and connects each member with sellers who sell products and services of interest to members like them. Facebook introduced one simple yet ingenious innovation – not only does it get Facebook members to share their interests on their walls, Facebook also gets its users to tell each other (and Facebook and its customers) what they 'like'. Facebook created and is acquiring a treasure trove of a database full of what 1.5 billion Facebook members around the world 'like', all for sale to those who want to sell things to people. Facebook is 10 years old. 'Liking' has created more than $200 billion in shareholder value, and is still growing. Surely, someone at Google must have asked "Why didn't I think of that?" Many believe that Facebook will overtake Google in value. It has already made a lot of money using the business model for the twenty-first century.

In the business model of the twenty-first century, Big Data and the ability to create value by analysing it (data analytics) creates 'Big Value'. Indeed, from 2004 to 2014 the value of technology acquisitions soared, but the number of acquisitions that involved financial advisers dropped precipitously from 76% to 31%.[3] This is because Wall Street's hallmark financial valuations are no longer relevant in determining value. Instead, Silicon Valley uses what Larry Paige, one of Google's founders, calls the 'toothpaste test',[4] a quaint criterion for whether an activity creates data. If something is used once or twice a day, it has great value. In Silicon Valley, using something once or twice a day means going to a website and keying in keystrokes. The term first coined was 'eyeball'. An eyeball indicates an expression of interest in whatever was viewed. Every time an internet user looks at something, a valuable data point is created. The more eyeballs on a site, the more valuable the site is. Value has little to no relationship to revenue or profit so that is why companies like WhatsApp, Snapchat, Instagram and other internet companies with no sales are worth billions of dollars. We used to say 'cash is king', now we know 'Big Data is king'.

3. Implications for law firms and their leaders

Many lawyers have been able to send their children to the best colleges on the back of helping Amazon, Google, Facebook, LinkedIn, Yelp, Instagram, Twitter, WhatsApp and countless other twenty-first-century data-based businesses ensure the sanctity of their cash cows. Venture capital funding, initial public offerings, intellectual property litigations and off-shore tax strategies are only a few of the ways the new business model of the twenty-first century has sustained the legal industry. It is ironic that Amazon, Google, Facebook and all of the other data-based companies survive in no small part because of lawyers and the legal industry, while Big Law is still using brains instead of computers and logarithms to create value out of data. The very business model that sustains Big Law, hiring really smart lawyers, is about to be disrupted by data scientists.

The upshot of the new business model for the twenty-first century for the law industry is that machines will be able to do what lawyers do but better, faster and cheaper. Clients have already balked at paying first- to third-year associates for sifting through documents and cases in an effort to identify relevant facts and applying the law to them. Lest there be any doubt that machines can already outperform the most gifted brains in the legal profession, algorithms that can predict with a 25% greater level of accuracy the outcome of US Supreme Court cases than a distinguished group of 83 Supreme Court experts (including 38 former Supreme Court law clerks, 33 chaired professors and five current or former law school deans) have been around for a decade.[5] As the old saying goes: "There must be a pony in this pile somewhere". How to dig it out is the question before Big Law.

3.1 Technology implications

If Big Law is going to find the pony in data analytics, it will have to master new tools

---

3   David Gelles, "In Silicon Valley, Mergers Must Meet the Toothbrush Test", *New York Times*, August 17 2014, Deal Book sec.: 1.

4   *Id.*

5   Theodore W Ruger, Pauline T Kim, Andrew D Martin and Kevin M Quinn, "The Supreme Court Forecasting Project: Legal and Political Science Approaches to Predicting Supreme Court Decisionmaking", 104 *Colum L Rev* 1150 (2004).

for partner performance and new metrics for measuring it. Big firms will have to transform themselves from data sieves into data mongers and modern day data analysts. Big Law is swimming in all sorts of data with which they do little but the most rudimentary financial analyses, largely for compensation purposes. Big firms have hundreds of thousands if not millions of digital interactions with clients and prospects daily (eg, emails, voicemails, timesheets, write-downs, write-offs, collections, bills, briefs, memos, other documents, fact patterns, decisions, website visits and untold other digital interactions) and they do nothing to mine the data. They work with public data such as cases, statutes, regulations, rulings and opinions every day. Terabytes of data coursing through firms are dumped in cyberspace garbage cans called 'servers' (most of them private clouds). Not only do big firms do little with the data they have, they do even less to collect data about what their clients want, like and are interested in buying. The sooner Big Law understands how to make use of the data it has and what other data it could collect and use to create value for itself and its clients, the less likely it will continue to be disrupted by those who do.

Listed below are the four tools Big Law will need to dig out its pony.

(a)   *Data analytics*

Big Law needs to collect more data about its clients and what its lawyers do, and do a better job analysing the data it already has. Beefing up on data and data analytics will not be for the faint of heart, nor will it be cheap or easy. The financial industry has already undergone one big data transformation. Trading today is driven by data scientists, as will soon be the practice of law. As a result, there is heated competition to recruit data scientists. For instance, a quarter of Goldman Sachs' 32,000 employees are technologists.[6] Goldman competes for top data scientist graduates as hotly, if not more so, than law firms compete for top law graduates. These technologists are not backroom nerds, they are fully integrated into the business and they drive Goldman's success.

What Big Law needs are data scientists to work with the firm's clients, lawyers, marketing professionals and IT, and to mine the firm's data with the goal of sharpening its value propositions, professional and business development skills and initiatives, and the quality, efficiency, service, results, value, pricing and profitability of its work. To stay ahead of disruption, Big Law, business schools and law schools will have to collaborate with computer science and engineering schools in order to churn out graduates with joint degrees in law and data science just like business schools are churning out graduates with joint degrees in finance and data science.

(b)   *The cloud*

There is a wealth of data available on public clouds (eg, published laws, rulings, decisions, regulations and research) that must be correlated with each firm's proprietary data about cost, productivity, service and results that resides on each firm's servers (ie, private clouds). Business today is about correlating proprietary data

---

6   Nathaniel Popper, *New York Times*, November 13 2014, Business sec.: 1.

with public data to expand and create new markets. Lawyers are accustomed to accessing the public data available through, for example, Google, Lexis and Westlaw. What law firms have not done is correlate the publicly available data with the data stored on their private cloud. The experiences of their own lawyers and clients are typically kept in precedent files. There is only anecdotal information in law firms about which lawyers have been most successful in writing and arguing successful summary judgment motions in front of a particular judge, and much less is known about the attributes of those motions. Accessing this in a database may not be as important in a six-partner firm as it is in a 600-lawyer litigation department, or a 6,000-lawyer law firm, in which this information is virtually impossible to capture anecdotally. This is especially important when it is integrated with client preferences in a system of engagement, described below.

(c)   *Systems of engagement*
Big Law needs to find a way to get clients to tell them more and more often about what they want, like and need. Part of this is devising a way to attract clients to a virtual place where Big Law can get them to reveal their predilections and preferences about what they want, like and need. Some of this can be discerned from analysing visits to a firm's website and blogs. However, websites and blogs typically broadcast messages about the firm instead of inviting insights from clients. A good place for firms to start would be by building a 'honey pot' that gathers data about client satisfaction. Ideally, for ease of use, many of these honey pots will be apps available on mobile devices. Bespoke client service interviews are and will always be invaluable. But customer satisfaction scoring systems like the Net Promoter Score have been overlooked too long by lawyers, and the conclusions that can be drawn from the databases are every bit as valuable as those drawn from bespoke interviews. Indeed, Big Data reveals unvarnished truths that can go unspoken in personal interactions. The firms that get the honey pot right fastest stand to gain enormous first-mover advantages, not unlike Google, Facebook and Amazon.

Apps that gather data will also take the form of self-help Big Law versions of LegalZoom.[7] Clients will key facts into templates designed by legal data scientists. The apps will produce documents, answers to compliance questions, disclosure requirements, government filings (eg, TurboTax) without a lawyer needing to be involved. These apps will be sold or given away as added-value loss-leaders to gain insights about client needs and to create stickier client relationships. An example of this is ComplianceHR, a recently launched joint venture between NeotaLogic and Littler Mendelson.[8]

(d)   *Predictive decision making*
As noted at the outset of this chapter, the best lawyers are those most capable of correlating facts at hand coupled with experience using a system of rules embodied in case law, codified law, regulations and other information (eg, opinions and non-

---

7   See www.legalzoom.com.
8   See www.compliancehr.com, launched in May 2015.

binding private and published information) in order to provide clients with advice about likely outcomes. In the world of Big Data, computers are already more capable at correlating complex databases like this than lawyers. They just have not yet been let loose on the law. When they are, they will devour the work of lawyers like hungry bears eat salmon during the salmon run. Big Law must become adept at harnessing powerful new computing, and developing, working with and enhancing predictive decision-making models for everything they do, including:

- hiring and training lawyers;
- deciding on partnership admission;
- serving as advocates and trusted advisers;
- measuring financial performance.

3.2   Talent management implications

Mastering these four tools to collect and analyse data will enable lawyers to enhance their ability to predict outcomes, serve clients, build client relationships and price services. However, to achieve this, Big Law is going to have to turn to a new way to measure partner success, not just using the size of the business book. Instead, the most successful partners will be those who can consistently lead collaborative, diverse teams in complex matters to produce results that satisfy clients well enough to bring them back for other matters at a level of profitability high enough to attract, develop and retain more partners with those skills.

This calculus may seem relatively simple, but like all other changes in a profession steeped in *stare decisis*, the execution will be difficult. Partner and matter profitability and client satisfaction on each matter and for each client will have to be measured. Of course, entering time into a billing system is a system of engagement. However, many law firm leaders will have to give up their long-held concerns and embrace a model that measures partner and matter profitability, a metric for success at both, and a regular means for communicating it constructively and rewarding it. None of this will be easy but the model does not have to be finely tuned. Firms should not let perfect get in the way of good. David Maister sets forth a worthy methodology for analysing matter level profitability in his book *True Professionalism*.[9] While Maister notes that even in 1997 law firm software could produce engagement level P&Ls, the state of the art has made a huge leap forward since then. Today, nary a Big Law firm is without off-the-shelf software for producing reports on matter, client and partner profitability.

3.3   Client service implications

New ground will have to be broken by Big Law innovators to devise a system of engagement for clients to provide feedback on results, service, cost and value at key junctures in each engagement. The Net Promoter Score would be a good place to start.[10] Enticing clients to engage will likely require extensive effort by partners and

---

9   David H Maister, *True Professionalism: The Courage to Care about Your People, Your Clients, and Your Career* (New York: Free Press, 1997), pp 133–134.

10   Frederick F Reichheld, "One Number You Need to Grow", *Harvard Business Review*, December 2003.

client relationship managers. Once firms have this data, though, and correlate it with partner, matter and client profitability, they will be able to discern where the sweet spots are in their practices, which partners consistently perform at the highest levels of satisfying clients and delivering high levels of profitability and which client relationships and markets (broadly defined as practice areas, industry sectors and geographic locations) are optimal to grow. Measuring and performing to these metrics will make getting the best team on the field for each matter an integral attribute of a firm's culture. All of this will be accomplished through data analytics available to a firm's lawyers, staff and clients through apps at their desktop and on mobile devices.

Persuading partners to replace pipes and tweed suits with pocket protectors and algorithms to predict outcomes and the cost of delivering results for matters will also be heavy lifting. Yielding to data in the prediction of outcomes will not be easy in an industry that prides itself on its judgment, but the data indicates that there is vast room for improvement in attorney decision making and the ability of lawyers to predict outcomes.[11]

4.   Essential approach for law firm leaders

Changing behaviour in Big Law is never easy, and it is clear that the order of change that will be driven by Big Data is unprecedented. Other industries have faced the challenges of Big Data and failed. There are lessons that Big Law can take from these failures. McKinsey has identified seven traits of companies that have fared well.[12] Interpolating them for law firms yields the following approach:

- Be unreasonably aspirational. Think differently. If your targets are not making the majority of your firm feel nervous, you probably are not aiming high enough.
- Acquire capabilities. For law firms entering into data analytics at the level required to fend off disruption, this will mean creating a robust data scientist department to complement marketing, finance and IT.
- Ring fence and cultivate talent. Create incubator teams comprised of lawyers highly motivated to embrace data analytics.
- Challenge everything. Examine all aspects of the practice: client facing, talent facing and back office. Think expansively about alliances with other service providers.
- Be quick and data driven. Continuous improvement requires continuous innovation with a process for responding to bits of information.
- Follow the money. Focus on both finding new revenue sources and on reducing the cost of doing business.
- Be obsessed with the client. Push to improve the client experience at all points of contact across the platform.

---

11   Randall Kiser, *Beyond Right and Wrong: The Power of Effective Decision Making for Attorneys and Clients* (Berlin: Springer, 2010). Kiser's research also validates the proposition that diverse teams are better at predicting outcomes than individual lawyers or non-diverse teams.

12   Tunde Olanrevraju, Kate Smaje and Paul Wilmott, "The Seven Traits of Effective Digital Enterprises", available at www.mckinsey.com/insights/organization/the_seven_traits_of_effective_ digital_enterprises.

The disruption of the business model about to be foisted on Big Law by Big Data and data analytics is nothing short of apocalyptic. The prescripted change is systemic. However, the alternative could spell the end for an industry whose historically high barriers to entry are about to come down.

About the authors

Christopher Bockmann
Executive coach, Leadership Life Cycles
cbockmann@icloud.com

Christopher Bockmann is an executive coach, he advises professional service firms on leadership development and coaches partners and executives at critical moments in their career. He also has extensive experience in coaching leadership teams going through change. This has led him to work with the legal departments of large multinationals.

Mr Bockmann has a diverse professional background. He first joined the European Commission and its large scale aid and change programmes and then moved to global professional service firms structuring professional development to reinforce post-merger integration for Clifford Chance and Linklaters.

Mr Bockmann taught a leadership development programme for lawyers at Sciences-Po Business School (Paris). He has also undertaken major research Europe-wide on partners' careers in professional services firms. He speaks regularly at conferences on careers and has contributed to several books on coaching, leadership succession and law firm leadership.

Henrik Bresman
Associate professor, INSEAD
henrik.bresman@insead.edu

Henrik Bresman is an associate professor of organisational behaviour at INSEAD, where he heads the INSEAD Global Leadership Centre. He is also the academic director of the HEAD Foundation, a Singapore-based education think tank. He received his PhD from the Massachusetts Institute of Technology.

Professor Bresman is an expert on leadership and high-performance teams. His research has been published in peer-reviewed academic journals, including *Academy of Management Journal*, *Journal of International Business Studies* and *Organisation Science*. His work has been profiled in many media outlets, including *Time Magazine*, *New York Times*, *Wall Street Journal*, *Financial Times*, *Forbes* and the *Economist*. His current teaching at INSEAD focuses on developing principled and effective leaders.

Before entering academia, Professor Bresman worked in several roles as a manager, consultant and entrepreneur. He co-founded a venture capital firm focused on early-stage technology businesses.

Laura Empson
Director, Centre for Professional Service Firms
Cass Business School, London
Laura.Empson.1@city.ac.uk

Laura Empson's research into professional service firms encompasses such issues as leadership, governance, organisational change, professionalisation of management, mergers and acquisitions and partner reward systems.

She has published numerous articles in leading academic journals. Her 2007 book *Managing the Modern Law Firm* (Oxford University Press), was described by *The Times* as marking a "seminal moment in the development of management theory in this sector". She has recently edited the *Oxford Handbook of Professional Service Firms* (2015).

At Cass she teaches the MBA elective Managing Professional Service Firms. In 2013 she was selected as the *Financial Times* Professor of the Week.

Professor Empson acts as an adviser to many of the world's leading legal, accounting, investment banking, actuarial and management consulting firms and is a regular speaker at partner conferences. She is an independent non-executive and chair of the Public Interest Committee of KPMG LLP.

She was previously associate professor (reader) at the University of Oxford. Before becoming an academic, Professor Empson worked as an investment banker and strategy consultant. She has a PhD and MBA from London Business School.

Heidi K Gardner

Distinguished fellow, Harvard Law School's Center on the Legal Profession

hgardner@law.harvard.edu

Heidi K Gardner PhD is a distinguished fellow at Harvard Law School's Center on the Legal Profession, a Harvard lecturer on law and faculty chair for some of Harvard Law School's executive education programmes. She previously served on the Organisational Behaviour Faculty of Harvard Business School.

Professor Gardner's research focuses on leadership and collaboration in professional service firms. She is currently writing a book on the topic to be published in 2016 by Harvard Business Press. She has also published extensively in peer-reviewed academic journals and practitioner-focused print and digital media. Her research was awarded the Academy of Management's Prize for Outstanding Practical Implications for Management.

Professor Gardner has lived and worked on four continents, including positions with McKinsey & Co and Procter & Gamble. She holds

a BA in Japanese studies from the University of Pennsylvania (*summa cum laude, Phi Beta Kappa*), a masters from the London School of Economics (with honours) and a PhD from London Business School.

Jaime Fernández Madero

Founder, Fernández Madero Consulting

jfm@fmaderoconsulting.com

Jaime Fernández Madero is founder of Fernández Madero Consulting, a strategy and management consultancy for law firms in Latin America, associated with Hildebrandt Consulting. He specialises in leadership and cultural change and assists firms across the region in their institutionalisation processes.

Mr Madero is also a founder of Bruchou, Fernández Madero & Lombardi Abogados, a leading law firm in Argentina, and was a managing partner for 10 years until he left the firm to start his consultancy practice. He practised corporate law and mergers and acquisitions in Argentina for 30 years.

Mr Madero has a masters in organisational studies from *Universidad de San Andrés* in Buenos Aires (2011), and has written a book about managing law firms in Latin America (*Organizando Firmas de Servicios Profesionales, El caso de los Abogados*, Ed La Ley, 2012).

Mark Mortensen

Associate professor, INSEAD

mark.mortensen@insead.edu

Mark Mortensen is an associate professor of organisational behaviour, based in Fontainebleau, France.

He holds a PhD and MS from Stanford University, as well as a BA from Colby College. His research focuses on the changing nature of collaboration, with a particular emphasis on global and virtual work and dynamic teams. He publishes his work in a range of academic, professional and popular press outlets and his contributions are recognised through academic awards, as well as leadership and editorial board positions. At INSEAD he teaches in many custom and open-enrolment executive programmes, the MBA core and the doctoral programme. He also consults and speaks widely on team dynamics, global work, power and networks and related topics.

Before joining INSEAD, Professor Mortensen was on the faculty at the MIT-Sloan School of Management and McGill University School of Management.

Rebecca Normand-Hochman

Partner, Venturis Consulting Group
Founder and director, Institute of Mentoring
rebecca.normand-
hochman@venturisconsulting.com

Rebecca Normand-Hochman is a partner in Venturis Consulting Group, a strategy and management consultancy based in several European countries – she heads the Paris office. She is also the founder and a director of the Institute of Mentoring which provides insight, research and advice to advance mentoring best practices in the legal profession.

Ms Normand-Hochman practised international finance law in London and Paris for a number of years. Her experience with Allen & Overy in Paris laid the foundation for her present work on talent and leadership for lawyers. She has carried out extensive research on law firm talent management, which draws on best practices and collaboration with leading experts in leadership, change management, coaching and mentoring.

Through her work with Venturis Consulting Group and the Institute of Mentoring, Ms Normand-Hochman researches, speaks, writes and consults on talent and leadership challenges and strategies that relate to the practice of law.

Since 2012 she has been leading the main talent management initiatives of the International Bar Association Law Firm Management Committee, including coordinating the books

Managing Talent for Success and Mentoring and *Coaching for Lawyers* and leading the IBA Law Firm Mentoring Programme between 2012 and 2014. Ms Normand-Hochman is an officer and advisory board member of the Law Firm Management Committee, where she chairs the Talent and Leadership Working Group.

Stuart Sadick

Partner, Heidrick & Struggles
ssadick@heidrick.com

Stuart Sadick is a partner in the business services sector at Heidrick & Struggles, located in the firm's Boston office. He holds undergraduate degrees in French and economics from Connecticut College and an MS in management from the Sloan School at MIT.

Mr Sadick has led teams on a variety of engagements related to the recruitment, assessment and development of talent in law firms, management consulting, IT services and business-to-business services. These have included partner, chief executive officer, chief marketing officer, chief human resources officer and chief financial officer level engagements.

Samantha Sheehan

Law student, Harvard Law School
ssheehan@jd16.law.harvard.edu

Samantha Sheehan is a student at Harvard Law School. She has a bachelor's degree in psychology and a background in marketing and business development.

Ms Sheehan has researched how to maximise associate satisfaction in a law firm context. She is interested in exploring how to structure firms to best align the organisation's incentives with young lawyers' needs.

Gerard J Tanja
Venturis Consulting Group
gerard.tanja@venturisconsulting.com

Dr Gerard Tanja is a partner at Venturis. He holds an LLM and PhD in law and has an MBA from the University of California. Before establishing Venturis, Dr Tanja worked at the University of Leyden, was legal adviser of the Minister of Foreign Affairs and, before moving to Clifford Chance (world firm management committee), he was general director of the TMC Asser Institute for International Law.

Dr Tanja specialises in strategy formulation, including merger consultancy, post-merger integration projects and strategic human resource management. In particular, he has been involved in a number of leading law firm mergers, he has assisted several Anglo-America firms to establish their European offices and has undertaken a series of strategic reviews of European offices for Anglo-America firms. In addition, he has been heavily involved in a number of law firm restructuring and governance initiatives in the Benelux and Germany.

Jan Thornbury
Director, Thornbury Consulting Associates Ltd
jan@thornburyconsulting.com

Jan Thornbury is an expert in organisational culture and strategic change and an experienced facilitator of groups from boardroom to conference hall. She set up her own consultancy in 2000 and advises blue chip organisations and professional services firms. Alongside consulting, Ms Thornbury speaks and writes on culture change. She is author of a book and several journal articles on the subject.

She had a brief career as a physicist and academic before joining KPMG as a management consultant in 1989. In her final years at KPMG she was director of the office of the international chairman, where she was responsible for developing and rolling out the firm's globalisation strategy and leading its worldwide culture change programme.

She holds an MBA and a masters degree in atomic physics. She has broad international experience and deep insight into the challenges of operating a global business.

Cory Way
Assistant dean, Harvard College, Affiliated Faculty, Harvard Law School Centre on the Legal Profession
coryway@gmail.com

Cory Way is assistant dean of Harvard College, lecturer on sociology at Harvard University and affiliated faculty at Harvard Law School's Centre on the Legal Profession.

Dr Way holds a doctorate from Oxford and is a licensed attorney who has practised litigation and corporate law at Sullivan & Cromwell in New York and Zuckerman Spaeder in Washington DC. He has been active in *pro bono* matters, most recently winning political asylum for a Rwanda genocide survivor whose entire family had been murdered; his work on this novel case earned a *pro bono* award from the Washington Lawyers' Committee for Civil Rights.

Dr Way holds degrees from Princeton, Harvard, Virginia and the University of Oxford, where he also served in dean positions at Merton and Corpus Christi Colleges. While in England he was also appointed as course director for a masters degree programme at the University of Cambridge. Dr Way's public service includes four years at the US Department of Justice and one year as a law clerk for the US Court of Appeals for the District of Columbia Circuit.

Scott Westfahl
Professor of practice, Harvard Law School
swestfahl@law.harvard.edu

Scott Westfahl is the faculty director of executive education and a professor of practice at Harvard Law School. As the faculty director of HLS

Executive Education, he leads the law school's effort to support and develop lawyers across the arc of their careers, particularly as they advance to new levels of leadership and responsibility. He also teaches in Executive Education's global leadership programmes, focusing on leadership, motivation and development of professional, organisational alignment, diversity and inclusion. Within the law school's JD curriculum, he teaches courses on problem solving, teams, networks and innovation. Before joining the Harvard faculty, Professor Westfahl served for nine years as the director of professional development at Goodwin Procter LLP, spent six years leading professional development for the Washington DC office of McKinsey & Company and practiced law with Foley & Lardner for 10 years. He is a graduate of Dartmouth College and Harvard Law School.

Peter Zeughauser
Chair, Zeughauser Group
zeughauser@consultzg.com

Peter Zeughauser is the chair of Zeughauser Group, a leading international law firm consultancy. He has served as a trusted adviser to the leadership of Am Law 100 and 200 and Global 100 law firms for 20 years.

Mr Zeughauser's consulting practice focuses on strategic growth planning and law firm mergers and acquisitions, as well as enhancing leadership, teamwork, financial performance, governance, succession planning, partnership structure and compensation systems.

Mr Zeughauser has been a contributing editor to *The American Lawyer* magazine since 1996.

Before consulting, he served as senior vice president and general counsel of The Irvine Company for over a decade. He served as chair of the Corporate Counsel Association in 1991.

Other titles in this series

Globe Law
and Business

For further details, including free sample chapters,
please go to: **www.GlobeLawandBusiness.com**